MW00447975

The Book of
Saints and Heroes

Andrew Lang and Lenora Lang

The Book of
Saints and Heroes

SOPHIA INSTITUTE PRESS®
Manchester, New Hampshire

The Book of Saints and Heroes was originally published by Longmans, Green, and Company, New York, in 1912. This 2006 edition by Sophia Institute Press® contains minor editorial revisions and an abridged preface. The text in this book was provided by the Baldwin Online Children's Literature Project (www.mainlesson.com).

Copyright © 2006 Sophia Institute Press®

Printed in the United States of America

All rights reserved

Cover illustration and design by Ted Schluenderfritz

No part of this book may be reproduced, stored in a retrieval system, or transmitted in any form, or by any means, electronic, mechanical, photocopying, or otherwise, without the prior written permission of the publisher, except by a reviewer, who may quote brief passages in a review.

Sophia Institute Press®
Box 5284, Manchester, NH 03108
1-800-888-9344
www.sophiainstitute.com

Library of Congress Cataloging-in-Publication Data

Lang, Mrs.
    The book of saints and heroes / Andrew Lang and Lenora Lang.
        p. cm.
    Originally published: The book of saints and heroes / by Mrs. Lang ; edited by Andrew Lang. New York : Longmans, Green, and Co., 1912. With abridged pref.
    ISBN-10 1-933184-13-2; ISBN-13: 978-1-933184-13-5 (hdbk. : alk. paper)
    1. Christian saints — Biography.   I. Lang, Andrew, 1844-1912. II. Title.
    BR1710.L3 2006
    282.092'2 — dc22
    [B]
                                                                2006000173

07 08 09 10 9 8 7 6 5 4 3 2

Contents

Preface

When Christianity came first to be known to the Greeks and Romans, and Germans and Highlanders, they, believing in fairies and in all manner of birds and beasts that could talk, and in everything wonderful, told about their Christian teachers a number of fairytales. This pleasing custom lasted very long. You see in this book what wonderful stories of beasts and birds that made friends with saints were told in Egypt about St. Anthony, and St. Jerome with his amiable lion, and St. Dorothea, for it was an angel very like a fairy who brought to her the fruits and flowers of Paradise.

These saints were the best of men and women, but the pretty stories are, perhaps, rather fanciful. Look at the wild fancies of the Irish in the stories of St. Brendan; and of St. Columba, who first brought Christianity from Ireland to the Highlands. I think St. Columba's story is the best of all; and it was written down in Latin by one of the people in his monastery not long after his death.

Yet many of the anecdotes are not religious, but are just such tales as the Highlanders where he lived still tell and believe. Some of them are true, I daresay, and others, like the story of the magical stake given by the saint to the poor man, are not very probable. The tales of St. Cuthbert are much less wonderful, for he did not live in the Highlands, but among people of English race on the Border, near the Tweed. The English have never taken quite so much pleasure in fairyland as other people, and the stories of St. Cuthbert are far more homely than the wild adventures of Irish saints like St. Brendan. The story that somehow came to be told about the patron of England, St. George, is a mere romance of chivalry, and the part about the dragon was told in the earliest age of Greece concerning Perseus and Hercules, Andromeda and Hesione. About that English saint, Margaret, queen of Scotland, there are no marvelous tales at all; but a volume would be needed for all the miracles wrought by the intercession of Thomas à Becket after his death. In his life, however, he had nothing fairy-like.

No saint has more beautiful and innocent fairy-like tales told about him than St. Francis, the friend of the wolf, whom he converted, and the preacher to the birds; St. Anthony of Padua was even more miraculous when he managed to make the fishes of the sea attend to his sermon. Fishes, we believe, are deaf to the human voice; you may talk as much as you like when you are fishing, as long as the trout do not see you. It is not easy to sympathize with the saint who stood so long on the top of a pillar. Perhaps he thought that by this feat he would make people hear about him and come to hear his holy words, and, so far, he seems to have succeeded.

Perhaps St. Colette had a similar reason for shutting herself up in such an exclusive way for a while, after which she went out and did good in the world. Like many saints, she was said to float in the air occasionally; but not so often as St. Joseph of Cupertino, who, in the time of King Charles II, once flew a distance of eighty-seven yards, and was habitually on the wing. In other respects, the life of this holy man was not interesting or useful like the noble lives of St. Francis Xavier, St. Vincent de Paul, St. Louis of France, and St. Elizabeth of Hungary, and the good lover of books, Richard de Bury. In their histories there is scarcely a wave of the fairy wand, but there are immortal examples of courage, patience, kindness, courtesy, and piety toward God and man.

Andrew Lang

The Book of
Saints and Heroes

St. Paul and St. Anthony

The First of the Hermits

Travelers in Egypt during the third and fourth centuries after Christ must have been surprised at the large number of monasteries scattered about in desert places, and the quantities of little cells or caves cut in the rock, which formed the dwellings of hermits. In those times, each lonely anchorite lived as pleased him best, or rather, as he thought best for his soul; but, of course, when many of them dwelt in the same house, this was not possible, and certain rules had to be made. In almost the very earliest of the monasteries, built a long way up the Nile, the monks were allowed to do as they liked about fasting, but were forced to work at some trade that would be of use to the brethren, or else, by the sale of the goods made, would enable them to support themselves.

So in the house at Tabenna we find that among the thirteen hundred monks there were basket-makers, gardeners, carpenters, and even confectioners, although probably these last were obliged to seek a market among the inhabitants of the various towns scattered up and down the Nile. In spite, however, of the numerous dwellers in the group of buildings that formed the monastery, Pachomius, the founder, had no intention of allowing his brethren to waste time in idle gossip. Whether working in the carpenter's shop, or hammering at the anvil, or shaping sandals, each man was bound to repeat the Psalms or some passages from the Gospels. He might eat when he was hungry, and could choose if he would give up bread, and live on vegetables and fruit and wild honey, or if he would have them all; but he was strictly forbidden to speak at his meals to other monks who happened to be present, and was enjoined to pull his cowl or hood over his face. And lest the monks should become fat and lazy, they were given no beds, but slept as well as they could in chairs with backs to them.

∞

Paul, who is generally thought to be the first man to spend his life alone in the Egyptian desert, was the son of rich parents, who died when Paul was about sixteen. They were educated people and had the boy taught much of the learning of the Egyptians, as well as all that was best in Greek literature and philosophy, but as soon as they were dead, the husband of Paul's sister, hoping to get all the family money for himself, made plans to betray his young brother-in-law, who was a Christian; for at this time the Roman emperor had commanded a persecution of all who would not sacrifice to the gods of Rome. Vainly did his wife implore him to spare her brother; the love of money had taken deep root in his soul, and he was deaf to her prayers and blind to her tears. Fortunately she was able to warn Paul of his danger, and one night he crept out of the house in northern Egypt and fled away to the desert hills on the south. When the sun rose over the river, he explored the mountains in search of a hiding-place and discovered at length a cave with a large stone across its mouth.

"If I could only roll that stone away!" he thought, and with a great effort he managed to move it and clamber inside.

"No one will ever think of looking for me here," he murmured. "And how clean it is!" he added, for he had been used to a house tended by slaves, and did not consider dirt a sign of holiness, as did the later hermits.

So Paul took possession of his cave, and although he lived to be very old, he nevermore quitted the mountainside, but went every day to fetch water from a tumbling stream, and to gather dates from the palms, while he made himself clothes out of their leaves. But we are not told that he saw or spoke with anyone until a few days before he died and was taken up to Heaven.

∞

Paul had spent so many years in his mountain cell that he had almost lost count of them and could scarcely have told you his age if you had asked him. Several miles away dwelt another old man called Anthony, who, when he settled in his cave beyond the great monastery, thought he had gone further into the desert than anyone living, until in his dreams he heard a voice that said, "Beyond you and across the hills dwells a man holier than you. Lose no time, but set out at once to seek him, and you will gain great joy."

Then Anthony awoke, and after eating a handful of dates and drinking a little water, he took up his staff made out of a palm branch, and set forth on his journey.

The sun was hot, and the sharp grit of the burning sand hurt his feet. Indeed, it was so long since he had walked at all, that it was wonderful his legs were not too stiff and too weak to support him. But he kept on steadily, resting now and then under the shade of a tree — when he happened to pass one — and kept his eyes fixed on the distant mountains that seemed to give him strength.

In this manner he was pressing forward when a being came up to him, so strange to look upon that he doubted if the like had ever been seen. The head and the front of it resembled a man, and its body and legs were those of a horse. As he gazed, Anthony remembered the verses of the poets he had read in his youth, describing such a creature, which they called a centaur; but at the time he had held these to be vain imaginings. The fearful beast planted itself in front of him and gave utterance to horrible words. As he listened, Anthony grew persuaded that it was Satan himself come to vex him, and he shut his ears and went on his way.

He had not traveled far before he beheld, standing on a rock nearby, another beast, smaller than the first, with horns growing out of its forehead. "And who are you?" asked Anthony, trembling as he spoke, and the beast said, "I am that creature whom men know as a satyr, and worship in their foolishness," and at its answer, Anthony left it also behind him and passed on, marveling how it happened that he understood what the two beasts had said; for their language was unknown to him.

Night was now beginning to fall, and Anthony feared lest his steps might stray in the darkness, and that the morning sun might find him far away from his goal. But even as the doubt beset him, his gaze lighted upon the footprints of an animal leading straight to the mountain, and he felt it was a sign that he would not be suffered to wander from the right path, so he walked on with a joyful heart. And when the sun rose he saw before him a huge hyena, and it was galloping with all its speed in the direction of the mountain, but swiftly though it moved, Anthony's feet kept pace with it. Up the sides of the hill after it went the holy man to his own great wonder, and when they had both crossed the top, they ran down a steep slope where a cave with a very little opening was hidden among the rocks. Big though it was, the hyena's sides were very flat and it passed easily through the opening. Then Anthony knew in his heart that in the cave dwelt Paul the Hermit.

∞

Although the walls of rock almost met overhead, the cave was not dark but full of a great light, and he beheld Paul sitting in the midst of it. He did not dare to enter without permission, so he took a small pebble and knocked with it on the wall. Immediately the rock was rolled across the opening, with only so much room left as a man might speak through.

"Oh, let me in, I pray you!" cried Anthony, falling on his knees. "Small need is there to shut me out, for I am alone."

"But wherefore have you come?"' asked Paul, and Anthony answered, "I am not worthy to stand in your presence, full well I know it; but since you receive wild beasts, will you not receive me likewise? For I have sought you from afar, and at last I have found you. And if, for some reason that I know not, this may not be, here shall I die, so give my body burial, I pray you."

Paul bowed his head as he listened to the words of Anthony, and rolled away the stone, and they sat together and talked, and the hermit asked many questions of his guest about the world he had left.

"Tell me, I beseech you," he said, "something of the children of men, for much must have happened since I took up my abode here, well-nigh a hundred years ago. Are the walls of the ancient cities still growing bigger because of the houses that are being built within them? Do kings yet reign over the earth, and are they still in bondage to the Devil?" These and many more questions did he ask, and Anthony answered them.

Now, while they were speaking, they both looked up at the moment, and on a tree that hung over the cave they beheld a raven sitting, holding in its beak a whole loaf of bread and waiting until they had ceased speaking. When the two old men paused in their conversation, the raven fluttered to the ground and, laying the loaf down between them, spread its wings and flew away.

"Behold," said Paul, "what mercies have been given me! For sixty years and more, this bird has brought me half a loaf daily, from whence I know not, but now has a double portion been bestowed on us. Take, then, the loaf and break it."

"No," answered Anthony. "That is not for me to do."

But Paul would not hearken to him, and darkness came on while they were yet disputing over the matter, until at the last each took hold of one end of the loaf, and pulled it until it broke in two. And after they had eaten, they stood up and prayed until the dawn.

They beheld a raven holding in its beak a whole loaf of bread.

∞

"The time of my rest has come, brother Anthony," said Paul in the morning, "and you have been sent hither by the Lord to bury my body." At his words Anthony broke forth into weeping and entreated that Paul would not leave him behind, but would take him into the heavenly country.

But Paul answered, "It is not fitting that you should seek your own good, but that of your neighbors; therefore, if it is not too much for your strength, return to the monastery, I entreat you, and bring me the cloak that was given you by the holy Athanasius, that I may lie in it when I am dead."

This he said, not because he took any heed what might befall his body more in death than in life, but because Anthony might not have the pain of watching him depart.

∞

Anthony wondered greatly that Paul should set so much store by the cloak or, indeed, that one who had been for so long set apart from the world should ever have heard of the gift; but he arose at Paul's bidding and said farewell, kissing him on his eyes and on his hands.

Heavy of heart was Anthony, and weary of foot, when his long journey was done, and he entered the monastery.

"Where have you been, O Father?" asked his disciples, who gathered eagerly around him. "High and low have we sought you, and we feared greatly that illness had come upon you, or that some evil beast had devoured you."

But he would tell them nothing of his pilgrimage. He only went into his cell and took the cloak of Athanasius from the place where it hung, and having done this, he set forth again on his road to the mountains, making all the speed he could, lest he might be too late to see Paul alive.

That day and all through the night Anthony went on without resting or eating food; but on the second day, at the ninth hour, he had a heavenly vision. In the air before him was a multitude of angels and prophets and martyrs, with Paul in their midst, his face shining like the sun. The vision lasted but a moment, yet clearly he beheld the faces of them all; and when it had vanished, he cast himself on the ground and wept, crying, "O fearer of God, why have you left me thus without a word, when I was hastening to you with the swiftness of a bird?"

Then he rose up and climbed the mountain, and soon the cell of Paul was before him. The stone that kept it fast had been rolled away, and in the entrance knelt Paul himself, his face raised to Heaven.

"He is alive, and I am in time," thought Anthony, and he stood and prayed, and the body of Paul stood by him and prayed also. But no sound came from his mouth, and a certainty crept over Anthony that the vision had been true, and that the soul of Paul had ascended to Heaven. So he spread the cloak of Athanasius on the earth, and laid the body of Paul upon it and wrapped the cloak about him as the holy hermit had desired. Yet another task lay before him, and in what manner to accomplish it he knew not.

"How shall I bury him?" he said to himself. "For I have neither axe nor spade with which to dig a grave, and it will take me four days to go and come from the monastery. What can I do?"

Now, as he pondered, he lifted his head and beheld two great lions running toward him, and his knees knocked together for fear. But as he looked again, his fear passed from him, and they seemed to him as doves for gentleness, monstrous of size though they were. While he gazed, the lions drew near, and by the body of Paul they stopped; then they lifted their heads and fixed their eyes on Anthony and wagged their tails at him, laying themselves down at his feet and purring. By this Anthony understood that they desired his blessing, and he blessed them. When they had received his blessing, they began to dig a grave with their claws, and the hole that they made was deep enough and wide enough and long enough for the body of Paul. And as soon as it was finished, they knelt down a second time before Anthony, their ears and tails drooping, and licked his hands and his feet. So he thanked them for their good service, and blessed them once more, and they departed into the desert. Then Anthony took the body of Paul and laid it in the grave the lions had dug, sorely grieving.

Roses from Paradise

Early in the fourth century, a group of girls were living in the city of Caesarea on the coast of Palestine. They were all Christians, and most of them came of noble families and had played together on the shores of the Mediterranean since their childhood. Now they had little heart for games, as Fabricius, the Roman governor, was seeking out the Christians in his province and offering them the choice between death and sacrifice to the gods of Rome. Many had failed to stand the test — a test that the girls were aware might be put to them at any moment. Would they be stronger than these others when the trial came? Would they fail also?

It was not long before they knew, for two of them, Agnes and Lucy by name, were betrayed to the governor, dragged from their homes, and thrown into prison. In a few days, they were brought before Fabricius and called upon to deny their Faith or die for it. Now that the dreaded instant was actually before them, they were no longer afraid. Christ Himself seemed to be standing by them, and their eyes were steady and their voices calm as they answered the governor.

"Take them away," he said after he had asked a few questions. "Take them away, and do with them even as unto the others," and he left the court to be present at a banquet.

The evil tidings soon reached the ears of Dorothea, who was born of noble parents and held to be the most beautiful maiden in all Caesarea; and while she rejoiced that they had stood fast and gone gladly to their deaths, she trembled greatly for herself lest, when her turn came, as come it surely would, she might prove too weak to face the sword, and be herself a castaway. It was horrible to think of, yet all her life she had shrunk from pain, and how was she to bear what certainly lay before her? Then she knelt and prayed for strength, and waited.

∞

"Dorothea, Fabricius the governor has sent for thee." The summons soon came, and Dorothea was almost thankful, for the strain of expecting something day after day is very hard to endure. She rose at once and accompanied the officer, who was in such haste that he hardly allowed her to say farewell to her parents, and in a few minutes, she was in the governor's house and in the presence of Fabricius.

The Roman was a hard man, not wantonly cruel perhaps, but not permitting anything to interfere with his duty, and he prided himself on the manner with which he carried out his orders from Rome. Yet when Dorothea stood before him in the beauty whose fame had spread far and wide, his heart suddenly melted, and a strange feeling came over him that was quite new. He tried to shake it off; to recall to his mind all the lovely women he had seen in Rome and in Greece, lovelier surely than this Christian girl. But it was the Christian girl and not they who made his pulses throb, and he kept his eyes fixed on the floor, as he put the customary questions.

"Remove her to the prison," he said at last, "and, Marcellus, bid the keeper treat her well, or he shall answer for it to me." So, with her hands unchained and her head held high, Dorothea walked between her guards to her cell, while Fabricius watched her from the window. She sank down with relief as the door was locked behind her. The first part, perhaps the worst, of the trial was over, and out of her weakness she had been made strong. Now there remained only the scaffold; for she never dreamed that she would see Fabricius again, still less of what he would say to her.

The jailer brought her some food and wine, which she ate gladly, for she was much exhausted; then she fell asleep and was awakened by the noise of the key grating in the door. Had the moment come?

But there entered only two women, strangers to her. Tired though she was, Dorothea noticed something odd in their manner, for they appeared shy and troubled, yet to be making an effort to be bold and at ease. Dorothea spoke to them gently and inquired if they had any message for her and who had sent them.

Their reply did not help her much. They stammered and hesitated, and interrupted each other, but at last Dorothea understood with horror who they were and what they wanted: they were apostates, who had denied Christ, and they were offering her money to deny Him also!

Dorothea gasped, and for a while the words seemed to die in her throat. The women saw the depths of the shame that possessed her, and knew it was for them, that they should have sunk so low. Suddenly they beheld themselves with Dorothea's eyes and covered their faces with their hands.

"I did not mean to pain you," she said when at last she spoke. "I dread my own weakness too much. Who knows if I shall be any stronger than you?" And she told them how her friends had died and how fervently she prayed to follow in their footsteps, until the faith the apostates had forsworn was born in them again, and with it a courage that never had been theirs.

"Enough. We will go to Fabricius," they said at length, "and will tell him that you have given our souls back to us. Farewell, for never shall we meet in this world again."

Yet meet they did, as Fabricius, burning with love for Dorothea and with rage at the failure of his plan, ordered them to be burned

They had denied Christ, and they were
offering Dorothea money to deny Him also!

in the public square and bade the jailer take care that Dorothea was present, so that she might learn what fate awaited her. It was a sore trial, but when the maiden beheld the faces of the two poor women brighten as they caught sight of her, she rejoiced at the cruelty that had brought her there and encouraged them with her prayers and brave words until their sufferings were ended.

⸎

"Dorothea, Fabricius the governor has sent for thee." A second time the summons came, and she was led into the governor's house.

Long and earnestly he pleaded with her; she would be his wife, he said, and a great Roman lady, and have servants and slaves and all that she could desire, if only she would sacrifice to the gods. It was such a little thing he asked of her, merely to throw some incense on the altar of the emperor, and that only once. Was it reasonable that she should throw her life away for nothing? She had, he knew, spent many hours visiting the poor of her own people. Well, the Romans had their poor too; and she might help them if she wished, and would she not listen to him, who loved her and would fain save her?

"I am the bride of Christ," answered Dorothea, "and am content with roses from the heavenly garden, which fade not away."

When Fabricius saw that nothing he could say would move her, his love turned to fierce wrath, and he called a centurion and bade him tell the headsman to be ready at sunset, as there was work for him to do. After that he shut himself up in his own room and would see nobody.

⸎

The streets of Caesarea were crowded with people as Dorothea walked through them on the way to the scaffold. The story of the sudden love Fabricius had felt for her, and her answer to his offer of marriage, had gotten abroad, and all were eager to see the girl who had preferred death to marriage with a Roman governor.

In the chief street, where the throng was thickest, a young man, Theophilus by name, stepped in front of her, and mockingly cried, loud enough for all to hear, "Goest thou to join thy Bridegroom, fair maiden? Do not forget me, I pray thee, but send me some of the fruit and flowers.

"Thy prayer is granted, O Theophilus," replied Dorothea, and the young man and his friends laughed again and lost themselves in the crowd.

The scaffold was set up in the square, where Dorothea had stood only yesterday watching the death of the two poor women. She went quickly up the steps of the little platform surrounded by soldiers, where the headsman awaited her and, kneeling, covered her face with her hands for a short prayer. Then she looked up at the headsman, in token that she was ready, and she saw between him and her a boy holding out to her a basket full of apples and roses, sweeter and more beautiful than any she had ever seen before.

"Take them to Theophilus," she said, "and tell him Dorothea has sent them, and that they come from the heavenly garden, whither she is going, and where he will one day find her."

Theophilus and his friends were feasting and making merry when the boy appeared at his side.

"Whence comes he?" asked one of the young men. "His face is not of this country, nor yet is he Roman. And as for his apples and roses, tell me where they grow that I may get some, for never have I seen the like.'"

Then the boy spoke and delivered his message, and the tongues of all were silent.

For a time, Theophilus was seen no more in Caesarea; but one day he came back and confessed himself a Christian and was sent by the governor to pluck the roses of the heavenly garden.

St. Jerome

The Saint with the Lion

Have you ever seen a picture of a thin old man sitting at a desk, writing, with a great big lion crouching at his feet as composedly as if it were a dog or a cat? Well, that is St. Jerome, and now you are going to hear his story, and how the lion came to be there.

Jerome was born at Stridon, near the town of Aquileia at the head of the Adriatic, in the year 346, but although his father and mother were Christians, they did not have him baptized until he was twenty years old. Eusebius and his wife had quite enough money to make them comfortable, although they were not considered very rich, and Jerome had plenty of slaves to do his bidding. He had besides, what was much more important to him, a playfellow called Bonosus, with whom he was brought up, and who went with him to Rome, when the two boys were about seventeen. All through his life Jerome showed strong affections and gained many friends, and it was a bitter grief to him when he lost any of them, especially as it was often his own fault. Unluckily he had a hot temper and a quick tongue, which led to his saying things he did not mean, and thus making enemies; but a word of regret from anyone who, he thought, had done him an injury softened his heart at once, and he never bore malice. And in spite of his being rather easily offended, he was so lively and amusing, so prompt to notice anything that was odd, and so clever in telling it, that his company was always welcome wherever he went.

Such he was as a boy, and such he was to a great extent as an old man.

∞

From his earliest childhood, Jerome was very fond of reading, although he liked to choose his own books and frequently neglected the lessons assigned him by his tutors to talk with the slaves or to play with Bonosus. But perhaps this did not do him as much harm as his teachers thought, for all kinds of learned men used to meet at the house of his father, Eusebius, and Jerome picked up a great deal from them without knowing it; so that when he and Bonosus entered the grammar school at Rome at the age of seventeen, Jerome was declared, much to the surprise of himself and Bonosus, to be quite as advanced as the rest.

For three years he stayed in Rome, living in the same house as his friend, but although he began well, very soon the reports of his conduct, sent home by the man who had charge of the foreign students and was bound to watch over their behavior, were not so good as they had been at first. "He went too much to theaters," said the inspector, "and was too often seen at the chariot races." In fact, he was carried away by the excitements and pleasures of a great city and of being, to a certain degree, his own master. "But idle though he certainly was," continued the inspector, "he was invariably to be seen at the law courts, listening to any celebrated case that was going on, following the pleaders eagerly with his eyes, and trying to make out for himself which were the weak points."

After a while, matters improved, and the inspector's letters became more cheerful. Jerome had seemingly grown accustomed to the amusements of Rome, and went less and less to the theaters. Besides, he was older now and had discovered that the companions he had thought so clever in the beginning were really only silly and vulgar, and their jokes tired and annoyed him. He was in this frame of mind when chance threw him into the society of a very different set of young men, who considered the pleasures of this world to be snares of the Evil One; and his mother rejoiced, when he wrote home to Stridon that most of his Sundays were spent in exploring with his newly found companions the hidden passages and tombs cut out of the solid rock underneath Rome, where the Christian martyrs were buried.

After this he received Baptism, while Liberius was Pope.

By the Roman law, no foreigner was allowed to remain as a student in Rome after his twentieth birthday, and Jerome and Bonosus wended their way back to Aquileia, Jerome carrying with him the precious library he had already begun to collect, and from which he never parted. Of course, the "books" were very different from ours and did not take up so much room. They were copies in ink from other manuscripts, which took a long time to make, and were sometimes very costly to buy, and in those days, and for eleven hundred years after, men earned their living by copying, as they now do by printing.

But the two young men were too restless to settle down quietly in Stridon. At least Jerome was too restless, and Bonosus seems usually to have followed his lead. Therefore together they set out for Gaul, where they became acquainted with Rufinus, the man whom Jerome loved with devotion and whose after-treatment caused him such deep sorrow. It was the influence of Rufinus that fixed his mind on the study of the Scriptures, which henceforward was the work of his life.

When after their journey through Gaul, which lasted several months, the two travelers returned to Stridon, they found that many changes had taken place during their absence. In Aquileia a society had been formed especially to study the Scriptures, the members giving up all kinds of pleasures and seeking only the good of their souls. Very soon their fame became noised abroad, and others arrived to join them, and among these were the noble

Roman lady Melania, and, to the intense joy of Jerome, his friend Rufinus. As the members of the society cared about the same things and most of them had been carefully educated, their constant meetings were a great pleasure to them; and with the arrival of Evagrius from Antioch shortly after, and his lectures on the holy places in Palestine, a fresh interest was awakened.

Unhappily something happened — what we do not know — to put an end to these pleasant gatherings, and the friends parted and went different ways. Bonosus sailed across the Adriatic to a little island, where he became a hermit; Melania, Rufinus, and some of the others went to the East; and Jerome determined to follow Evagrius to Antioch, traveling through Greece and Asia Minor. He left behind him his parents and a small brother and sister, but he carried with him his beloved books.

At Antioch he was ordained a priest — although it seems doubtful whether he ever performed even a single service — and after resting for a few months in the groves on the banks of the Orontes, he went alone into the desert that stretches between the mountains of Lebanon and the river Euphrates. This was a very foolish step for him to take, for his health was always bad, and the fatigues of his journey from Italy had brought on a severe illness from which he had hardly recovered. However, he remained in the desert for nearly five years, seeing none that were not hermits like himself, for the country was dotted over with their cells, and "scorpions and wild beasts" were, as he says himself, his daily companions.

Still it was fortunately not in Jerome's nature to sit idle and spend his time trying to think about his religion, which often ends in really thinking of nothing at all. From morning until night, he was working at something: either tending a little garden, where with great trouble he had managed to grow a few vegetables in the dry soil; or weaving baskets from the rushes that grew on the banks of a small stream some distance off, to sell to traveling merchants;

or writing letters to his friends; or learning Hebrew from a converted Jew who came over from a monastery to teach him.

It was probably with the help of this man that he was able to get the manuscript of St. Paul's letter to the Hebrews, which he first copied for himself and then translated into Greek and into Latin, which was, of course, his own language.

∽

Quarrels with the hermits about the doctrines and discipline of the Church drove Jerome from the desert, first to Antioch, next to Constantinople, and then to Rome. Here he found himself much sought after, for his fame for learning had gone before him, and some even expected him to be chosen pope on the death of Damasus. But ambition was not one of Jerome's faults. The magnificence of Rome, which, when he was a boy, had proved so attractive to him, now filled him with disgust, and he longed to get away into solitude and give himself up to his books.

In spite of all the business thrust on him by the pope, and the disputes in which he eagerly took part, he contrived to find some time for his own special work and devoted himself to making a Latin version of the translation of the Old Testament from Hebrew into Greek, known as the *Septuagint*. This name, meaning "seventy," was derived from the fact that seventy men were engaged in it, and it had been done by some Jews about five hundred years before, for the benefit of their fellow countrymen who were living in Egypt, under the rule of the Greek kings. Jerome's translation was thought so good that it was universally used in the churches for twelve hundred years.

Among the friends made by Jerome in Rome at this time were a number of noble ladies who, like him, were interested in the study of the Bible, and listened eagerly to all he could tell them about it. Greek they had long ago been taught, and now they learned Hebrew, the better to understand the history of their religion. Jerome always thought highly of women, for the few he knew well were clever as well as good; and on one occasion, when he was reproached by his enemies with dedicating to ladies some of his books, he remarked in scorn, "As if women were not better judges than most men."

Of all the little group of ladies who met in the house on the Aventine hill, perhaps the most remarkable was the widowed Paula, who sprang from the family of the Scipios, one of the noblest in Rome. She had three daughters and a large number of friends, all of whom had withdrawn themselves from the world, and who passed their time in study and in looking after the poor.

Fired with the wish to see the places of which the Bible had told her so much, Paula took her second daughter with her and followed Jerome to Antioch when, in 385, he quitted Rome, leaving the youngest girl and a little boy behind her. It was winter when they arrived, and Paula at once began to make plans for her journey through Palestine. It was in vain that Jerome urged on her the difficulties and dangers that would beset her and entreated her to wait for the spring. Paula would listen to nothing, and all Jerome could do was to persuade her to take the easier road by the coast, instead of the one over the mountains of Lebanon.

By this time, some of the other ladies had landed from Rome, and were ready to join the travelers. Most of them were carried in litters, but Paula preferred riding one of the beautiful tall donkeys of which we read so often in the Bible, and insisted on stopping at every place that had been the scene of some great event in the days of long ago — every place, that is, which was Christian, for no heathen legends had any charms for her whatever they may have had for Jerome, with his thirst for knowledge of all sorts.

All along this route, which had already been trodden by so many pilgrims, Jerome was constantly at hand, to tell them everything that had happened there. At Mount Carmel, Zarepta, and Joppa, the caravan halted in turn; and at last arrived at the goal, Jerusalem itself, hardly to be recognized under its Roman name of Aelia Capitolina. Here the governor or pro-consul received the noble Paula with a guard of honor, and wished her and the rest of the ladies to take up their abode in his palace. But it seemed to Paula unfitting to live in splendor in the city where her Lord had been scourged and crucified, and she begged the pro-consul to find a humble lodging for her and her friends.

After visiting the holy places in Jerusalem itself, and those near it, whose story they knew so well — Bethhoron, where Joshua had fought his great battle and the sun had stood still; Bethel, where Jacob had slept and dreamed of the angels going up and down the ladder; Mamre, the burial-place of Abraham and Sarah; Bethany, the home of Lazarus; and above all, Bethlehem — they set out for Egypt, happy to think that they were treading in the steps of the two Josephs who had gone that road in the space of seventeen hundred years. Crossing the Nile by the numerous branches into which the river spreads out toward its mouth, they paused for three days at Alexandria, where Jerome was able to see the famous library and to talk with some of the celebrated teachers and orators who lived in Alexander the Great's city. From Alexandria they journeyed to the district known as Nitria, at that date filled with monasteries and also with scattered hermits.

Now the ladies could indulge themselves in mortifying their bodies to their hearts' content. They lay upon hard beds in a long room and ate — as seldom as possible — the coarse food that was the monks' fare. Indeed, so much did they admire this mode of living that they seriously thought of remaining in Nitria forever.

It was during this visit to Nitria that the lady Melania had a very unpleasant adventure. Tired of being carried in a litter or of riding on a camel, she wandered away one evening from the encampment toward a small lake covered with the blossoms of the lotus. She was fond of flowers, and here was one quite new to her. Hastening downhill to the edge of the sunken lake, she was just about to stoop and pick the nearest bud, when a loud cry made her stop and look around. To her surprise, she beheld a man climbing down a rock, waving his arms wildly. She hesitated and instinctively drew back; then her eyes fell upon a great scaly creature with a soft yellow throat and long teeth, which had stolen toward her from its lair in the reeds. Fascinated with terror, she watched it approach, and it would certainly have seized her leg in its jaws and drawn her into the water, had it not been for Macarius. Even his shouts did not make the crocodile give up its prey, but it continued to move over the ground with astonishing swiftness, until its advance was checked by a stunning blow from an iron bar held by the hermit, who by this time had reached the frightened woman.

But the desert of Nitria held other dangers besides the prospect of being eaten by crocodiles, or of being taken captive by a tribe of Bedouins. The ground was in many parts covered with sharp stones that pierced the hoofs of the horses and the sandals of the guides, while there was always the risk of sticking in the marshes of half-dried lakes or of falling victim to low fever from the poisonous vapors. However, all these perils were braved successfully, and in the end, the pilgrims bade farewell to their Egyptian friends and sailed from Alexandria to the old Philistine port of Gaza, forever bound up with the memory of Samson.

For the company of pilgrims had at last made up their minds to settle at Bethlehem and, on their arrival, lost no time in building a monastery there for the men and a convent for the women, Jerome being the head of one and Paula of the other. They erected besides, at Paula's expense, a church that served for both men and women to worship in, and a house to lodge passing pilgrims who formed an incessant stream from all parts of the Roman world. The cost of all this fell almost entirely upon Paula, who gave away all she had, and when she no longer possessed anything more to bestow, Jerome sold the estates he had inherited from his father and employed the money for the common good. At Bethlehem he spent the last thirty-four years of his life, writing letters on various subjects that were agitating the Christian world, studying the Hebrew and Chaldee languages, making translations of various sacred writings, and publishing the great version of the Old Testament still in use in the Roman Catholic Church, known as the Vulgate.

He was sitting — so runs the story — with some of his monks in the cell of Bethlehem, when a lion entered the open door. The brethren all jumped up in a fright and tumbled as fast as they could through the window, while Jerome stayed quietly in his chair and waited. The lion looked at him doubtfully for a moment, then limped toward him, holding up a paw. This Jerome took, and examined carefully. At first he could see nothing, the soft pad was so badly swollen; but at length he detected a thorn, near one of the nails, and managed to pull it out with a pair of pinchers. He next boiled some water, in which he soaked some dried herbs, and bathed the sore place until the swelling began to go down, when he tied a linen rag around it, so that the dirt might not get in and inflame the wound afresh.

As soon as he had finished, and the look of pain had disappeared from the lion's eyes, Jerome expected him to depart, but instead the huge beast stretched himself out comfortably on the floor. Jerome pointed to the door; the lion wagged his tail happily and took no notice. This happened several times, until at last Jerome gave up the struggle and went to bed, the lion on the floor sleeping beside him.

Next morning Jerome said to this visitor, "You seem to intend to live forever in my cell" — the lion wagged his tail again — "but learn that no one here spends his time in idleness. If you stay here, you must be ready to work" — the tail wagged a second time — "and you will therefore accompany my donkey daily to the forest

"You seem to intend to live forever in my cell."

to defend her from robbers and savage wolves, when she brings back the firewood needful for the monastery."

So, for many months, the lion and the donkey could be seen setting off side by side every morning to the forest, and the lion lay down and watched while an old man heaped up the donkey's panniers from the stack of wood he had gathered in readiness. The work took some time, but when the panniers could hold no more, the donkey gave itself a shake, and the lion jumped up, waiting until she began to move. The journey back to the monastery was much slower than the one to the forest, as the donkey had to be very careful not to make a false step. If she had stumbled and fallen, she would have found it very difficult, with her loaded panniers, to get on her feet again, and even the lion could not have helped her.

But one morning, a terrible thing happened. The sun was very hot, and when the lion lay down as usual, he fell sound asleep and never heard two men creep up behind the old man and the donkey and tie a cloth over the mouths of both man and beast, so that they could not utter a sound. Then the robbers drove them away, wood and all, to the caravan that was waiting a little distance away.

At last the lion awoke and gave a great yawn and stretched himself. He lay still for a few minutes, until suddenly he noticed that the shafts of light that fell through the trees struck the ground in a different way from usual.

"It must be later than I thought," he said to himself. "They never look like that until the sun is going to set. Has the donkey been waiting for me all this time? Poor thing, how tired she must be! But why didn't she wake me?" And he rose to his feet and turned toward the old man's hut, but no donkey was there.

"She must have gone home," he said to himself again. "But then — where is the old man?" and bending his head, he examined the soil carefully.

"These are human footprints; I am sure they are," he exclaimed in his own language. "More than one man has been here. And here are the donkey's. She was stolen while I was asleep, and I, who was set to guard her, have been unfaithful to my trust! How shall I face the holy father who cured my wound?"

However, there was no use waiting or trying to track the lost donkey; the thieves had got too long a start. And with bent head and heavy heart, the lion followed the road home and entered, as he had done once before, the cell of his master.

"Wherefore are you here, and where is the donkey?" asked Jerome sternly. In answer, the lion bowed himself to the earth, with his tail between his legs, awaiting his sentence.

"I had faith in you, and you have put me to shame," continued Jerome, "and as it is quite plain that you have eaten the donkey, you must take her place, and for the future the panniers will be put upon *your* back, and it is *you* who will fetch the wood from the forest."

And the lion, when he heard, wagged his tail in relief, for he had been very much afraid that his master would send him away altogether.

Now, it was at the end of the summer that the donkey had been stolen, and as soon as the spring came round, the caravan went past again, the camels laden with swords and silks from Damascus for the cities of Egypt. The lion was standing behind a group of trees, while another old man was piling up the panniers with wood, when the crackling of twigs caused him to turn round, and a little way off he beheld the long train of ugly, swaying creatures, with the donkey walking at their head. At the sight of his friend, he gave a bound forward, which knocked over the old man, and sent the wood flying in all directions, and he so frightened the camel-drivers that they ran away to hide themselves. As to the rest of the caravan, he drove them before him into the monastery, keeping his eye carefully on the riders; and if anyone's hand so much as moved toward his side where his short sword was buckled, the lion had only to growl and to show his teeth for the hand quickly to move away again.

In this manner they proceeded until they reached the monastery, and Jerome, who was seated in his cell, unfolding the copy of a new book, beheld their arrival with astonishment. What were all these people doing here, and why was the lion with them? And surely that was — yes, he was certain of it — his old donkey, which he had imagined was dead months ago.

So he hastened out of his cell to the courtyard, where the merchants, who by this time had dismounted from their camels, fell on their knees before him.

"O holy father, if you are the lord of this lion, bid him spare our lives, and we will confess our sin," they cried. "It was we who stole the donkey, while her guardian, the lion, was sleeping; and behold, gladly will we restore her to you, if we may go our way."

"It is well. Go in peace," said Jerome, and the merchants needed no second bidding.

Joyful indeed was the donkey to be at home again; and the next day she got up early and trotted off to the forest by the side of the lion, throwing up her head and sniffing the air as she went, from very delight at being freed from captivity. And the heart of Jerome rejoiced likewise that, after all, his trust in the lion had not been in vain.

That is the story of the lion of St. Jerome.

∞

The last part of Jerome's life in Bethlehem was full of trouble. From all parts of the Roman Empire news came of the invasion of the barbarians, and in 410 the Goths, under Alaric, sacked Rome itself. Like other countries, the north of Palestine was laid waste, and the monks had to share their scanty food with the crowd that poured into the monasteries for refuge. Then, too, some of the little band of friends who had followed Jerome from Rome fell ill and died, among them Paula and Marcella. In spite of his sorrows, he still worked hard at his studies and translations on the various books of the Bible; but his eyesight was now failing fast, and he must have been thankful indeed for the companionship of Paula the younger, and of the younger Melania who, with her husband, came to live with him.

These two ladies attended him in his last illness, and were present at his funeral, which took place in September 420.

Travelers to Bethlehem are still led through a passage cut in the rock to the cell where Jerome wrote the commentaries and epistles and translations, which have given him the foremost place among students of the Bible. In this cell — his paradise, he called it — he would talk over passages that puzzled him with the elder Paula and her daughter Eustochium, who knew Hebrew and Greek as well as he, and dictate to his young monks his letters to Augustine or Rufinus. Next to this cell, we shall find another, consecrated not to the living but to the dead, for here are two graves, in one of which Jerome was first buried, while the other is the tomb of Paula and her daughter.

The Reluctant Bishop

If you have ever read a novel called *Hypatia,* written by Charles Kingsley, you will hear a great deal about a young man called Synesius, who came to Alexandria, in Egypt, about the year 393 A.D., to listen to Hypatia's lectures and to study in the library that was one of the wonders of the world.

Alexandria had been founded more than six hundred years before by Alexander the Great, and its lighthouse, or pharos, threw its beams far out into the Mediterranean. The city had a magnificent harbor that was always crowded with ships of different build, and its streets were filled with men in the costumes of all nations speaking all tongues. At the time it was built, the North African coast was full of flourishing cities, of which the two most famous were Carthage and Cyrene. Carthage was, of course, built by the great traders of the old world, the Phoenicians, but the people of Cyrene were very proud of themselves as the descendants of a body of Spartans, who had come over — so the tale ran — from Greece, nobody quite knew when, and settled along the part of the coast that lay west of Egypt. Certainly the Spartans had chosen a beautiful place for their new home, for Cyrene stood on a ridge of high ground overlooking the Mediterranean, and below it was a green plain where corn grew as if by magic. There were harbors, too, in plenty, close at hand, for at that date, the ships were small to our ideas, and worked by oars as well as sails, so that they could come quite near the shore and take off the cargoes the merchants had ready for them. Very soon other towns sprang up, but none was so large or so famous as Cyrene, where a quantity of Jews speedily arrived, eager to share in the trading advantages.

When Synesius was born, about 375 A.D., the glory of Cyrene was a thing of the past. It no longer took the lead in the study of medicine, and its school of philosophy had died out. Although the sea had as yet kept it safe from the flood of barbarians of all sorts, which had for some time been pressing on the boundaries of the empire in Europe, the fierce tribes of Libya were constantly pouring in from the south, taking prisoners and holding them for ransom. Besides this, locusts — formerly almost unknown — appeared to have discovered the country, and eaten up the crops, while the houses tumbled down in frequent earthquakes, and sailors from distant lands brought horrible plagues into the once-healthy province of Cyrenaica.

Such was the state of matters at the birth of Synesius.

∞

He seems to have been the eldest of three children, his brother Euoptius coming next, while his beautiful sister, Stratonice, was the youngest. The parents of the children were rich, and had a country place near Cyrene, and as that is all we know of them, it is probable that they died early and left their sons and daughter to the care of a guardian. The children were well-mannered, affectionate little creatures and made many friends in their native city, but Synesius tells us nothing about their education, and most likely their guardians were too busy to take much trouble about it. However, Synesius, who was very proud of his Greek ancestors, had his father's good library open to him, and the study of books is the very best of all educations. The men and women who are most interesting to talk to, and who know most about things, are nearly always those who have lived *with* a library and *in* a library, and have read books because they loved them and not because they were forced to do it.

Thus it was with Synesius. When he was a very small child, he could have told you stories of the Spartan boy and the fox (he might have secretly hoped that the valiant young person was one of his own forefathers), and of Perseus and Andromeda and of the Seven Labors of Heracles — from whom he really *did* think he was descended — and of Bellerophon, the winged horse, and many more. But as he grew older, he felt that there were some books even outside the library that he wanted to read, and where could he find them as well as at Alexandria? So the guardian's consent was obtained, and when Synesius was almost eighteen and Euoptius a year younger, they took ship at the port of Apollonia and sailed eastward to the famous city.

For several hundreds of years, a colony of Jews had been settled in Alexandria. Some were engaged in trade; others, students of the Hebrew writings, collected in the immense library, destroyed later by the Mohammedans; others, again, came to learn mathematics and medicine in the schools. By the time Synesius took up his abode there, the school of medicine was no longer as famous as formerly; but the books were still in the library, and lectures on Greek philosophy were given by the celebrated Hypatia to a large audience.

In this year, 393 A.D., Hypatia, although always beautiful, was not nearly so young as she is represented in the novel, but that did not matter to Synesius. They made great friends, although he sometime afterward became a Christian and she remained a pagan, and he wrote to her about everything in which he was interested. He attended her lectures on philosophy, she gave him lessons in mathematics, and before he published his books, she always read them and criticized them. Of course, in those days publishing was not quite the same as in these. An author sent his book straight to a bookseller, who added its name to a list outside the door, with the price to be paid for it. And no doubt it was he who arranged with the author as to the number of copies to be made, and settled the cost of each with the scribes who earned their living in this way.

Synesius stayed in Alexandria two or three years, and during that time mixed freely with both pagans and Christians, most of them well-educated people. Now and then, some order of the emperor reigning in Constantinople, or some action on the part of the bishop or his monks, would cause an outbreak on the part of the populace — it was in one of these that Hypatia later met with a horrible death — but in general each party was content to be at peace with its neighbors and obey its own laws. So Synesius went happily about among his friends, seeing everything, enjoying everything, and watched, with a lump in his throat, the tall lighthouse fading from his sight on the day he sailed back to Cyrene.

Things had changed for the worse in the province of Cyrenaica since Synesius had left it. We do not know very much of what had happened, but we gather that some of the officials whose business it was to collect the taxes and carry out the laws either kept back part of the money due to the government, or took bribes from the rich in order to wink at their offenses. Cyrene, like old Rome, had a senate, but the senators were powerless to fight against the governor of the five cities of Cyrenaica, who was responsible only to the imperial prefect itself. But one thing it could do was to send an ambassador to the emperor stating the cause of complaint, and, in 397, the young Synesius was chosen for this purpose.

∞

With what feelings of excitement Synesius must have sailed up the Aegean and gazed on the country he always considered his native land. Almost every name recalled something to him, some story, or some event in the great past of Greece, and how his heart burned to think that only a year earlier, the Gothic invaders had dared to tread that sacred soil and destroy the ancient landmarks.

With thoughts such as these crowding upon him, Synesius entered Constantinople. It did not take him long to understand that only a miracle could save the city from ruin. The reigning emperor, Arcadius, was a poor, weak creature, governed entirely by his wife or by his minister and slave, Eutropius. This Eutropius was a person entirely without shame, who put up to auction all public posts. The richest man, therefore, could always obtain the highest office, and the money went into the pocket of Eutropius. Everybody knew this and bore him a bitter hatred, but there was only one man who did not fear him: the bishop John, surnamed Chrysostom, or the "golden-mouthed."

The insurrection of a colony of Goths, established in Asia Minor, brought about the downfall of Eutropius, for one of the conditions of peace made by the rebels was the head of the minister. For a moment, the emperor wavered; even to him there seemed something base in giving up his servant, but his wife had no such hesitations.

"If they demand Eutropius's head, they can have it," said she; and as ill-news flies fast, her words shortly reached the ears of the doomed man. Without losing an instant, he fled for sanctuary to the altar of the great church of St. Sophia, forgetting in his terror that he himself had declared that there was no refuge for man even in the Holy of Holies.

Next day a vast crowd filled the church, but the excited murmurs died down into silence as the bishop went up the pulpit stairs and turned to gaze at his enemy, clinging to the altar. After a stern rebuke of the wickedness of his deed, he begged the multitude who listened to him to spare Eutropius's life. The appeal was unexpected, and for some time no one could tell what counsels would prevail. Still, in the end, Chrysostom gained the day; Eutropius was sent into exile and allowed to live a little longer.

It must have been a wonderful scene if Synesius was there to witness it, but it was by no means the last or the worst that he was destined to see. The Goths demanded more victims, and the emperor was ready to yield them. The barbarians likewise required to be allowed to enter Constantinople, and soon there was fierce fighting in the streets. At last they were gotten rid of, and for a while Arcadius breathed freely.

Now that these enemies were disposed of, Synesius felt that his long waiting was over, and that there was a chance of obtaining an audience with the emperor. According to custom, he appeared before Arcadius with a golden circlet for an offering, and began his speech. It was very long and very eloquent, and clearly pointed out to the emperor where his duty lay, but only a man as young as Synesius would have expected any good to result from it. Most likely Arcadius did not even listen, but the Cyrenian ambassador was satisfied at having fulfilled his mission and had no doubts but that for the future all would go well with Cyrenaica.

Having finished his business with the emperor, Synesius felt himself free to give his attention to astronomy, of which he was very fond, and he made a kind of map of the heavens, marking the sun's path through the constellations, and the places of the different stars. In the midst of this fascinating study, he was rudely reminded that something else existed besides the sky, by an earthquake that frightened the people of Constantinople out of their senses. The churches had never been so crowded before; everyone wanted to confess his sins and obtain absolution for them. Synesius, however, was of another mind, and he rushed down to the sea, where he got on board a ship that was sailing for Alexandria. When he was safely out of the harbor — although the voyage was so bad that he only exchanged one danger for another — he remembered that he still owed money to various tradesmen in Constantinople, and this he carefully paid as soon as he arrived at Cyrene.

After the bustle of his life in Constantinople, Synesius settled down for some years in his native province, passing the summer on his country estate.

He could always make himself happy wherever he was and find enjoyment in little things. He could forget the bad harvests and dark tales of what the Goths were doing in Italy, in the lively talk of his friends, in the books he was writing, in the wonders of the desert that bordered Cyrenaica, and in the supreme joy of a short visit to Athens. Then, when he was twenty-eight, he went over to Alexandria to be married to a girl whom he had probably met at the time he was living there. We do not know very much about her, not even her name, but she seems to have made Synesius quite happy and to have looked well after their children. One thing we gather about her, in spite of his silence: she was a Christian, for the ceremony was performed by the bishop of Alexandria, although Synesius himself was as yet unbaptized.

There was soon a large nursery of children in the house, for besides his own boys and girls, Synesius took charge for some time of his nephew Dioscurius, the son of Euoptius, and also of a daughter of his sister, Stratonice, who had married as her first husband a man named Theodosius, an official of the imperial court. Synesius might have made the acquaintance of this little niece when he had gone there on his embassy, but at any rate he was so fond of her that one of his letters is full of lamentations, when, at the end of her visit to him, he was obliged to give her up to his brother Euoptius, then living on the seashore a few miles from Cyrene.

"I shall often come to see you," he said, as he put her into her litter with her nurse and ordered his slaves to watch over her until she reached the end of her journey. Phycus, the home of Euoptius, was only a few miles from Cyrene, and Synesius could easily have walked over there in the afternoon, and *would* have done so if he had been alive now. But the only time he spoke of walking, his whole household looked at each other in speechless horror.

"As if any gentleman would *dream* of going on foot beyond his own garden!" they whispered to each other in hushed voices, and somehow when Synesius called for his cloak to protect him from the night air, it had mysteriously disappeared. He had known by experience the chills that come on in the south at sunset, and dared not venture without his cloak, and for that day he was obliged to stay at home.

Although he was always ready to join in the children's games, Synesius looked after their education himself and did not entrust it entirely to tutors. Most likely he told them in the evenings the tales of Greece that he had learned as a little boy from his own mother — the beautiful fairy stories as well as the things that really happened; how Leonidas and his three hundred Spartans defeated the Persians in the Pass of Thermopylae; how the rulers of Carthage, the town they should someday visit westward beyond the setting sun, had sent forth Hannibal, one of their bravest generals, to conquer Rome, and how he had failed in consequence of their wicked treatment of him. These and other tales they heard, and listened to them with breathless interest.

"If you want to know the saddest story in the whole world," he would say, "you can read it by and by in this roll containing the book of Thucydides, with his account of the Sicilian expedition, and if you wish to hear how Egypt appeared to a Greek traveler eight hundred years ago, you will find all sorts of funny things in Herodotus." He also took pains that, young as they were, they should learn the most splendid passages in the Greek and Roman poets, and every morning Dioscurius, who seems older than the rest, came to his room and repeated to him fifty lines of poetry.

In Cyrene, Synesius had many slaves to do the work of the estate. The greater number of these had been born in the service of the family and were quite as much interested in seeing that everything was well done as was Synesius himself. "Ah! if that man had always lived here, he would never have dreamed of running away," he said once of a slave who had disappeared, and when another, who had come from a distance proved too drunken to keep, his master merely sent him home with the remark that vice always brought its own punishment.

Great was the rejoicing among the children — his own and probably some others also — when the time arrived for them all to go into the country. It was not only the change and the freedom that they liked, but the people were an endless amusement to them as well as to their father.

"Just fancy! They have never seen fish before!" they shrieked with delight, on watching the farmers and laborers crowding around a barrel of salt fish that had just arrived from Egypt.

"Come near," whispered one of the band, "and let us listen to what they say."

"Why they seem quite frightened," cried another, "at the idea of anything living in water!"

"Well, of course," answered the eldest, who had read more and traveled more than the rest, "there are no rivers *here*, and it would never do to have things living in *wells*. But you are too small to know anything about *that*," and he moved away with his head in the air, leaving the little boys much subdued behind him.

∽

Although Synesius was always happy in the country, whether he was ostrich-hunting or observing the bees in their hives, or drilling his children or studying some new question of the day, he was not a very successful farmer, and it was lucky for him that the soil was so rich that the crops almost grew of themselves. The slopes were covered with olives, which gave them oil for their lamps; grapes grew on trellises or trees; the fields were yellow with barley; figs were everywhere. Goats, from which they got their milk, jumped about and tried to butt the passersby, while camels, horses, and cattle were proudly shown off to Synesius's visitors. He made a collection, too, of the arms used by the various tribes in the district, and spent many hours practicing with them. On wet days, he shut himself up with his books and wrote a great many letters and pamphlets that we still have, and at these times he was happiest of all.

During the year after his marriage, some of the barbarians who dwelt in the surrounding country flung themselves, as they frequently did, upon the rich Pentapolis, or district of the Five Cities, and laid waste the crops and drove off the cattle. They also besieged some of the towns, in one of which Synesius was for a time shut up. We do not know what became of his wife during this time. Perhaps she had been sent back at the first hint of danger to her relations in Alexandria, and Synesius would certainly have felt freer without her.

From the besieged town he managed somehow to get a letter conveyed to a friend in Syria, begging for some of the native arrows, which were far better than those of Egypt, and also for a horse called Italus, which had some time before been offered to him, probably as a wedding present. In all ways, he did his utmost to spur the citizens to resistance, but does not appear to have been very successful, as they were extremely reluctant to wield the lances, swords, axes, and clubs he provided for them. Happily the enemy melted away this time, although another soon sprang up, and the blades of the weapons were never suffered to grow rusty if *he* could help it.

∞

The year 409 was the most important in the life of Synesius, for it found him a country gentleman, a farmer, a student, a philosopher, even a soldier; and left him, as yet unbaptized, the chosen bishop of the city of Ptolemais.

"I would rather die than be a bishop," he writes to a friend at the end of the eight months allowed him by the Patriarch of

Alexandria to make up his mind, for he knew that his consecration would mean the giving up of almost everything he cared
about, if he was to do his duty. Yet there was a general feeling, not
only amid the bishops and patriarch of the Egyptian Church, but
also among the people of the Pentapolis, whose consent was
needed, that he was the only man who could stand between them
and the barbarians from the south — every year more daring and
troublesome. It was thought too, and not without reason, that his
word would have influence with the men in power at the court of
Constantinople, many of whom were his friends. So the result of
these considerations was that one day Synesius received a letter
saying that he had been appointed bishop by the voice of the
clergy and of the people.

It came to him as a great surprise, although, of course, he knew
of many instances — as, for example, that of Ambrose — in which
a man who was not even in orders had been compelled to undergo
consecration. He turned over the matter from every point of view
for some time, and at length wrote an answer to his brother, then
in Alexandria, which was also to be shown to his friends in the
city and to the Patriarch Theophilus.

He had all his life been a learner, he says, and how does he
know that he is fitted to become a teacher? Although he has loved
the society of his fellowmen, his happiest hours were those which
he passed alone. As a bishop he will have to be at the beck and call
of everyone, and he will hardly find a single moment in which to
examine his own soul. Still, if it is his duty to accept office, he will
be ready to set aside his studies, and to relinquish the amusements
that have been so great a pleasure to him; he will consent to let his
hounds pine in vain for a hunt, and his bow rot upon the wall. But
one thing he will never give up, and that is his wife, and more than
that, he will suffer no compromise such as others have made with
their consciences, and will live openly with her as before. He
closes the letter by pointing out certain subjects on which he

desires more teaching and explanation, and leaves the decision to the electors.

In reply, the patriarch bade him take eight months to weigh the matter, and at the end of this period, Synesius gave in to their wishes, although holding fast to his own principles. "If he finds that he is unfitted to do the work demanded of him," he says, "he will resign and go to Greece." So, with a firm intention to fulfill the duties thrust upon him, he accepted Baptism and immediately after was consecrated bishop of Ptolemais.

∽

The three years of life remaining to him were spent in laboring for his people and in trying to forget in his work the troubles and sorrows that crowded upon him. To a man who had always felt that others had as much right to their own consciences as he himself, it was painful as well as tiresome to be continually inquiring into the particular religious principles of the dwellers in his diocese; to pass hours deciding their quarrels and in writing to officials either at Alexandria or Constantinople, to complain of the exaction of a tax-gatherer or the corruption of a magistrate. Yet he had to do all these things, besides conducting the services in his own church, watching carefully over the men who were allowed to preach in his diocese, and making visitations to every part so that he might see with his own eyes how his rules were carried out. If he could sometimes have had a day's hunting or a few hours alone with his books, he would have gone back rested to his work, but there was never a moment he could call his own.

He had counted the cost when he accepted the charge, and he paid the price in full.

∽

Synesius and his family no longer lived in Cyrene or in the country. Those two homes had to be parted with, as well as other things, when he was made a bishop; and Ptolemais, further to the west, and once the port of Carthage, was where they now lived. But no sooner had they settled there than one of Synesius's little boys fell ill. Every instant his father could spare was, we may be sure, spent with the dying child; but besides the duties demanded of him by the Church, the bishop was engaged in a hard struggle with the newly appointed governor of the Pentapolis, Andronicus by name, who was grinding down and oppressing the people. At length a meeting was called, and after Synesius had spoken on the difficulty of his position in having to keep order in the land as well as in the Church, he read out the sentence of excommunication passed by the clergy against "Andronicus of Berenice, born and bred to be the curse of the Pentapolis," whereby he and those who went with him were cut off from God and man.

The tyrant was not strong enough to stand for long against the power of the bishop, and shortly after the resignation that was forced upon him, he died miserably.

Scarcely was this affair settled than another of the children fell ill and died in a few days. But again Synesius was forced to put aside his private grief and take thought for the defense of the country, which was harassed by the raids of some tribes of barbarians, who took delight in kidnaping the children in order that they might be taught to fight against their own countrymen. The skillful young general Anysius beat them back for a while; but after he was recalled by order of the prefect of Constantinople, things became worse than ever, for the new leader was old and useless. In this desperate state of things, Synesius not only used all his influence to obtain a larger army and a better general, but worked hard himself at the defenses, and often shared the duties of the common soldiers.

His work and his sorrow together proved too much for him, and a letter to his old friend Hypatia, in the year 413, tells a sad tale of weakness that is fast overpowering him. We do not hear anything of his wife, and it is uncertain whether at that moment she was alive or not, but the death of his third son gave him the final blow. He had no strength and no wish to continue his labors as bishop, and there are signs in one of the last letters we possess, that he intended ending his days in a hermitage. Whether he lived long enough to do this we cannot tell, but this much we know, that in the year 413 a severe illness overtook him, and after that his history is a blank. It is better to think that he died then, for he had been taken from the life that suited him and thrust into a place for which he was not fitted, and the effort to live up to what was required of him wore him out.

From Sinner to Saint

Perhaps you have read about Augustine the monk, who was sent over to Britain by the Pope, Gregory the Great, to convert Ethelbert, King of Kent, to Christianity. This Augustine was a very famous person, no doubt, but you must not confuse him with a yet more famous St. Augustine, who was born two hundred years before, in a North African town called Thagaste, in the province of Numidia, and passed his youth in the old town of Carthage.

He has left a book of confessions, wherein he tells us all about himself, from the first things he could remember when he was a baby, the bad as well as the good; indeed, the bad much more than the good. And besides what he recollects of himself, he puts down the ways he has noticed in other babies and how naughty they can be, and he takes for granted that he was just like them, as no doubt he was.

When he had been fed, he was happy and comfortable, and "began to smile; first in sleep, then in waking; for so it was told me of myself, and I believed; for we see the like in other infants, although of myself I remember it not." Then gradually he moved his head and looked about, and certain things, such as the window, or the blazing logs on the hearth, would fix themselves on his mind. Very likely he thought how nice it would be to have the sunbeams or the flames to play with, and gave little coos and cries and stretched out his arms toward them, and Monica, his mother, or his nurse, would come and take him up from his cradle and show him a bright jewel or a pretty toy to content him. But often he would not be satisfied with these, and was, he says, "angry with them for not serving me, and avenged myself on them by tears. Such," he adds, "have I learned infants to be from observing them, and that I was myself such, they, all unconscious, have shown me better than my nurses who knew it."

After a while, he ceases to be a baby and becomes "a speaking boy," and he writes from his own memory of how things happened to him.

"It was not that my elders taught me words, but when they named any object and looked toward it, I saw the way their eyes went and remembered the name they had uttered. And by constantly hearing words as they came in various sentences, I understood the object that they signified, and having broken in my mouth to these signs, I thereby gave utterance to my will."

∞

Now Augustine was getting to be quite a big boy, and Monica's friends all told her she must send him to school. She did not want to part with him even for a few hours a day, but his father agreed that it must be, so she was obliged to yield, and perhaps Augustine himself was anxious to go, like his playfellows. But he very soon wished himself at home again, even though the other boys might laugh at him for being a baby.

"I was put to school to get learning, in which I, poor wretch, knew not what use there was; and yet, if idle in learning, I was beaten. For this was judged right by our forefathers; and many, passing the same course before us, framed for us weary paths, through which we were fain to pass." Then Augustine, "although small," began to pray "that he might not be beaten at school," but this prayer was not always answered. Yet he admits that "the torments" he and his schoolfellows suffered from their masters were not altogether without excuse. "We wanted not," he says, "memory or capacity, but our sole delight was play, and for this," he observes, "we were punished by those who themselves were doing the like." Yet whatever St. Augustine might have thought at the time, teaching naughty little boys lessons they will not learn is not a very amusing occupation; and if any boy fancies it is, let him try it in earnest for an hour. "Will any person of sense," complains Augustine, "approve of my being beaten because by playing at ball I made less progress in my studies? And if he who beat me was worsted in some argument with another tutor, he was more angry than I when I lost a game."

∞

In spite of these reasonings and grumblings, when Augustine was a few years older, he allows that the beatings had their use. "I loved not study," he confesses, "and hated to be forced to it. Yet I was forced; and this was well done toward me, for unless forced I had not learned." He told endless lies to his tutors and his parents, to enable him to shirk school and play instead, or "see vain shows." He was greedy too and stole fruit and sweet things from the dinner table at home, not always to eat himself, but to give as bribes to other boys to let him win in their matches; in fact, he never minded cheating, if he could not gain the victory fairly, so eager was he. This is worse than anything he has yet told us, and it is to be feared that even after sixteen hundred years, little boys, and even little girls, still sin in this way. Augustine knew all the while that he ought to be ashamed of himself, but if he was found out, he "chose rather to quarrel than to yield." And after a while, shame did its work, and he "learned to delight in truth" and to practice it.

Perhaps Augustine's parents might have been anxious to take him away from bad companions, as they sent him for a year to study grammar and public speaking in the city of Madaura, intending him to proceed to Carthage. But at the end of the year, his father, always a poor man, found he was not able to afford the money, and so Augustine, now fifteen, was kept at home in idleness. His father, at this time preparing for Baptism, does not appear to have given up many of his heathen ideas, for, according to his son's own account, he allowed the boy to do just as he liked and to drift back into evil ways, without attempting to stop him. Yet some of his misdeeds, such as stealing, were undertaken through sheer love of fun and danger, and not from any desire to keep the spoil.

"I stole," he writes, "that of which I had enough, and much better. Nor cared I to enjoy what I stole, but joyed in the theft and sin itself. A pear tree there was near our vineyard, laden with fruit, tempting neither for color nor taste. To shake and rob this, some young fellows of us went late one night (having, as was our custom, been idling in the streets until then), and took huge baskets of pears, not for our eating, but to fling to the hogs, after we had just tasted them. And this," he adds, "we enjoyed doing, merely because we knew it was wrong; and if the taste of the pears were at all sweet, it was only because they were stolen."

Many years have passed when Augustine writes about the theft, and grieves over the sinfulness of his state when he took pleasure in such doings; but he has worse tales to tell of his life in Carthage, where he spent the three following years. He loved chariot-racing, the fights of the gladiators, and most of all the theater. Here he wept and laughed with the actors in the plays as if their joys and sorrows had been real ones.

But in spite of this, he never thought of giving up his own amusements to help other people, and spent his hours in gambling and drinking and playing rude and unkind tricks upon the people he met. Yet, happily for Augustine, he was saved by the very ambition he thought so great a fault, and "joyed proudly and swelled with arrogance," when he was chief in the school of oratory, or as it was then called, "rhetoric."

∞

Neither as boy nor as a man could Augustine be persuaded to learn Greek. Latin he confesses that he loved, when he had gotten over the first stages of grammar, which were "as much a penalty to him as any Greek!" He laid up in his memory the wanderings of Aeneas and "wept for Dido dead, because she killed herself for love." "But why," he asks, "did I hate the Greek classics which have the like tales? For Homer also curiously wove the same fictions, yet is he bitter to my taste. Difficulty in truth, the difficulty of a foreign tongue, dashed, as it were, with gall the sweetness of a Greek fable. For not one word of it did I understand, and to make me understand I was strongly urged with rewards and punishments."

Latin, of course, although not the language of the common people in the province of Carthage, was that spoken by the Romans who had conquered Hannibal at the battle of Zama nearly six hundred years before, and Augustine had heard it around him from his cradle, although he was forced later to study the grammar. "This," he says, "I learned without fear or suffering, by mere observation, amid the caresses of my nursery and the jests of friends, smiling and encouraging me. I learned words, not of those who *taught*, but *talked* with me."

It was, strangely enough, the study of a Latin book called *Hortensius*, by Cicero the Roman orator, that turned his thoughts to better things when he was nearly nineteen. It contained a passage on the love of wisdom, which deeply struck Augustine, who had read it, because it was needful, if he was to become a lawyer, to be acquainted with the writings of the master of Roman eloquence. "To sharpen my tongue did I employ that book; but it did not infuse into me its style, only its matter."

With his interest in philosophy aroused, he resolved to turn his mind to the Holy Scriptures, in order to see what they were. But, like Naaman, he did not understand simple things: "they seemed to be unworthy to be compared to the statements of Cicero." What Augustine wanted was great swelling words and high-sounding phrases. Instead, he found plain facts and humble comparisons. "They were such as would grow up in a little one," and as yet Augustine "disdained to be a little one." By and by that would come to him; at present, "swollen with pride," he "took himself to be a great one."

Still, disgust with his past life began to stir now and then within him, and although for some years he was dragged back by the chains of the habits he himself had forged, in the end he burst them and was free.

∞

While Augustine was at Carthage, his father died, and his mother, left alone in her home, mourned day and night over the stories that reached her of her son's wickedness. But her prayers "drew his soul out of that profound darkness," for she wept for him to God, "more than mothers weep for the bodily deaths of their children." And a dream was sent to comfort her in her grief, as one night, when she was sorrowing, "a shining youth" came toward her and inquired of her the causes of her constant tears. "I lament lest my son's soul should be lost by his sins," said she, and the young man answered, "Where you are, there is he also." And as she looked, she beheld Augustine standing by her side, and after that she received him into her house, which she had been loath to do before, and he ate with her.

The years went by, and outwardly Augustine's life was little different from what it had been ever since he went to Carthage, but it did not satisfy him as it once had done. The pleasures, formerly so exciting, often seemed flat and stupid long before they were over; the fine speeches that sounded so grand at the moment appeared so empty when he came to think about them that he felt ashamed such folly could have gained him the prize; the wrestling matches in which he delighted, things too trifling for a grown man to spend half his time over. To win, by fair means or foul, had ceased to tempt him, and he rejected with scorn the proposal of a wizard to enable him by spells to overcome his antagonist, if Augustine would bestow on him a large enough bribe. "Though the garland were of imperishable gold, I would not suffer a fly to be killed so as to attain it," he exclaimed, on hearing that a sacrifice was to be offered, and he indignantly turned his back upon the man, trusting to nothing but his own strength for victory.

The loss of his dearest friend was his first real sorrow, and for a long while, "his heart was utterly darkened"; death seemed everywhere. As far back as he could remember, the young man, whose name we are not told, had been part of his life. "He had grown up as a child with me, and we had been both schoolfellows and playfellows. But he was not yet my friend as afterward." Kindred studies appear to have brought the two together, and for a time, indeed, Augustine's influence drew his friend away into the adoption of certain false doctrines, and of "superstitious fables." Augustine took a deep interest in all these questions, to the great grief of Monica, but she knew it was vain to speak to her son and had to content herself with praying for him.

Then the young man fell sick of a fever and for some days lay totally unconscious, until the priest insisted on baptizing him in this condition, lest he should die a heathen. Thus it was done, and, to the surprise of all, the unconscious invalid regained his senses, and it seemed as if he was about to recover. Augustine had remained at his bedside throughout his illness and, as soon as he was able to listen, tried to cheer him by making him laugh and even talked lightly of the baptism his friend had just received. But with a sternness that was quite new, the sick man shrank from him, and bade him cease from such speeches, if they were to remain friends.

Filled with astonishment, Augustine obeyed, and feeling quite sure that in a few days the invalid would be well again, left the town on some business. He came back in a week to hear that the fever had returned, and that the man he loved so much had sunk under it.

Augustine's account of his feelings at this time reminds us of the break-up of another close friendship of the ancient world: the death of Horace's friend, Quintilius. Like the Roman poet, the man who was afterward to become a great Christian was only conscious that for him life had come utterly to a standstill.

"My native country," he tells us, "was a torment to me, and my father's house a strange unhappiness: whatever I had shared with him, wanting him became a distracting torture. Mine eyes sought him everywhere, but he was not granted them, and I hated all places, for he was not in them. Well did one, Horace the poet, call his friend, 'Thou half of my soul,' for I felt that my soul and his soul were 'one soul in two bodies.'" Nothing soothed him; neither books nor music nor games. Augustine tried them all, and found them all "ghastly." He could not stay at Thagaste and went back to Carthage.

Here he got on a little better. He had still other friends, although they could never take the place of the one who was gone. But they were sorry for him and were kind to him, and drew him at times away from his grief to talk about books and poetry and the things that were happening around them. He began to write too, on all sorts of subjects, and this, more than anything else, healed his wound.

But his friend's death had not only caused him bitter sorrow; it was gradually working the great change of which there had been faint signs long before. The noise and lack of order among the students of Carthage disgusted and wearied him. What had seemed amusing while he was one of them was hateful now that he himself was a teacher. He was quite helpless in gaining obedience to any rules, and at last he resolved to leave Carthage and go to Rome, where the young men were not allowed to be lawless.

As soon as Monica was told of her son's resolve, "she grievously bewailed it." Even on the seashore, she clung to him and would not let him go until he lied to her, saying that he had a friend on board the vessel with whom he had promised to stay until the wind blew fair, and the vessel could sail. Still she would not return to Thagaste, and with much difficulty — and no doubt after many more lies — Augustine persuaded her to sleep in an oratory near the spot where the ship was anchored.

In the morning when she looked out, the vessel was gone, notwithstanding her prayers that the winds might be contrary.

∞

After recovering from an illness that seized him on his arrival in Rome, Augustine took a house and proceeded to look out for pupils who wished to learn rhetoric and the art of public speaking. He soon found, however, that although the students did not commit the particular offenses that had driven him from Carthage, they had plenty of faults of their own. One of these was specially inconvenient to a man who had to earn his living, and that was their custom of avoiding the payment of fees due to their master by going in a body, after they had heard a certain number of lectures, to learn of someone else. Glad, therefore, was Augustine to hear that a teacher of rhetoric was wanted in Milan, and he at once applied to Symmachus, the Roman prefect, to put him through an examination and, if he was found satisfactory, to give him the post.

The test was passed successfully, and Augustine started for Milan, where he was received with great kindness by Ambrose, the bishop, himself a famous orator.

As soon as her son was settled in Milan, Monica hastened to join him and was happy in listening to the sermons of Ambrose and in sharing in his good works. She still watched anxiously over

Augustine, but wisely kept silence on what she saw that made her sad. For ambition still reigned in his heart and ruled his will; he "panted after honors and gains"; those who do that are seldom satisfied.

Two friends he made, of whom he was very fond, and one of these, Alypius, was a native of Thagaste and an old pupil of Augustine's, both there and at Carthage. Alypius loved learning and had many good qualities; like his master, he took a great interest in the doctrines of the heretics called the Manichees, and had a passion for the circus and for the cruel games of the amphitheater.

∞

Nebridius, another old friend, followed Augustine to Milan, as well as Alypius, and "sought wisdom" also, but in spite of their example, their teacher could not give up the sins that were so dear to him and grieved his mother so much. He wished often to deliver himself from their bondage, but he had been their slave too long for this to be easy, although little by little the study of the Bible, the prayers of his mother, the sermons of Bishop Ambrose, and the talks with his friends did their work. Again and again his sin seemed hateful to him, and again and again he fell back into it. But at length a day came when he was "laid bare to himself" and was "gnawed within." After a fierce struggle with himself in the garden behind his house, the victory was won. He had conquered the *will* to sin and, in company with Alypius, sought his mother, and by his confession "turned her mourning into joy."

At this time, Augustine was about thirty-two years old and had great fame as a teacher of rhetoric, but for some months he had been suffering from a pain in his chest, and speaking was difficult to him. It was therefore all the easier to carry out his intention of resigning his professorship and devoting his whole remaining life to the service of God. After bidding farewell to his pupils, who were much grieved to part with him, he retired into the country with Alypius to prepare for Baptism, which they both received at Easter, at the hands of Ambrose himself.

Monica's prayers were answered, and her vision of long ago fulfilled, for "where she stood, Augustine stood also." Her life had no further cares, and she was ready to be done with it, when her call came. For a time she had her son with her and rejoiced to watch him passing his days in writing two books intended to contradict the heresies to which before he had inclined. In the evenings they talked together, and Augustine opened his heart to her and told her of his desire to sail to Africa and to preach to those whom he had once led astray.

"It is well, my son. I will go with you," she said, and as soon as the books were finished, they set off to Ostia, the port of Rome.

It was a long and tiring journey over the Apennines, and Monica reached Ostia much exhausted. It was needful she should rest a few days before attempting a sea voyage, and they found rooms looking out on a garden, where the noise of the busy seaport did not come to their ears. Here they had many quiet talks, and Augustine learned more in those few hours of his mother's sufferings in his behalf than during his whole life before.

Suddenly, one evening, as they were sitting together, gazing over the sea, she began to shiver. Augustine drew her inside, and closed the lattice, but it was too late. A fever had seized upon her, and she became unconscious. When her senses came back to her, she said to Augustine, "Where was I?" and then added, "Lay my body anywhere; do not disquiet yourself about that. Only remember me at the Lord's altar, wherever you may be."

The ship sailed without them, as on the ninth day Monica died. The grief of Augustine was terrible, for it was mixed with remorse for the years of agony he had caused her. But gradually, happier and more peaceful thoughts took possession of him, as he resolved to live as she would have had him do. Then he crossed over to Africa, where he was ordained a priest and finally made bishop of the town of Hippo. He spent his time in hard work and in writing many books, among which was his *Confessions,* from which this story is taken. Forty-three years after his baptism, he died at Hippo, encouraging his people to the last to hold out against the Arian Vandals who were besieging the city.

St. Germanus

The Governor Who Became Bishop

When, at the end of the fourth century after Christ, the boy Germanus was growing into a young man, his parents, the noble Rusticus and Germanilla, thought it was time he should go to Rome to finish his education. Like the sons of other rich parents, he had been well taught, and we may be quite sure that very few Roman fathers allowed their children to play when they should have been doing their lessons. For although Rusticus lived with his family in Auxerre, a little Gaulish town on the river Yonne, he counted himself nonetheless a Roman and the subject of Gratian, emperor of the West, when Germanus was born.

By that time, there were two emperors, one reigning in Constantinople and the other in Rome; and both empires were, in name, Christian, although many country districts in both empires were really as heathen as ever. Auxerre, however, was, like other places in Gaul, a Christian city and had a bishop; and Rusticus had seen that Germanus was duly baptized and that he had learned something about his religion, as well as grammar, astronomy, geometry, and literature.

Still, Rusticus had no intention of making the boy a priest; Germanus was to be a lawyer, and as he was not only fond of arguing, but also quick to see what was to be done in matters of daily life, his father hoped he might become a great man someday. And so he did.

It was a long way from Auxerre to Rome, but that made it all the more exciting for a boy of fifteen or sixteen. We are not told exactly how he traveled, but most likely he was put under the charge of some merchant or priest returning to the Holy City, who would ride with him and two or three servants as far as the river Rhone, and there they would take a boat that would carry them down to Marseilles. At Marseilles they would find plenty of ships sailing for Italy, one of which would undertake to land them at Ostia, the port of Rome, at the mouth of the Tiber.

Once Germanus was in Rome, Rusticus had no further anxiety about his son, for the students were carefully looked after. They were obliged to bring a written declaration of the date of their births, the names of their parents, and a statement of the profession they had chosen. These particulars were all set down in a book, and then the students were sent, under the charge of an inspector, to the rooms allotted to them. From time to time the inspector visited them to see that they were getting on well and attending their classes and lectures. But in no case did the law permit the strangers to stay in Rome after they were twenty, as it was considered that by that age their education ought to be finished, and if they remained longer, it was only to idle and get into mischief.

Germanus made the most of his years in Rome, and then, when they were over, returned to Auxerre and began to plead in the law courts. He loved his work and threw himself, heart and soul, into it. He spoke well and easily and gained many cases for his clients and much money for himself.

Soon his fame reached the ears of the prefect of Gaul, who ruled over the fourth, or western part, of the empire, and he, like a true Roman, always ready to detect and make use of the best tools, offered the successful lawyer a post under government. This Germanus gladly accepted. He quickly rose from one office to another and must have been quite a young man when he become "duke and governor of the provinces of Armorica and Nervica," which included the greater part of modern France; only the prefect and the vice-prefect were above him.

∞

Shortly before he obtained this higher honor, Germanus had married a girl of a noble family, who was rich and good, called Eustachia. He bought a country place a few miles out of Auxerre, and whenever he felt he could allow himself a holiday, he moved there with his wife, in order to enjoy some hunting.

In this way several years passed, when an event took place that changed the whole course of the life of Germanus.

In the midst of the town, there was a wide-open space, where a very old pear tree grew, under which the citizens used to assemble to talk over their affairs, or to gossip in the summer evenings. Now, it was the habit of Germanus, from time to time, to hang one or two dried specimens of game upon the branches. It seems to us a harmless thing enough, but it greatly displeased the bishop, who, in those days, was the ruling power in most of the cities. He thought it would remind the people of the heathen custom of decorating the branches of this very tree with hideous masks of men and beasts, as scarecrows or even as charms. So he wrote to Germanus to beg him to give up this practice, but the governor paid no heed. Then he went to his house, and still Germanus would not listen. At length the bishop, whose name was Amator, resolved to settle the matter himself, and when Germanus, who had been away on business, returned to his country house, the news met him that the old pear tree had been cut down to its roots and burned, and the beasts that were on it were thrown outside the walls.

The governor's face grew white with anger at the tale.

"Cut down the pear tree, has he?" he cried, when his wrath permitted him to speak. "He seems to have forgotten that I have power of life and death in my province! I will teach him how to defy me!" And he hastily ordered a large body of men to be ready to ride with him to Auxerre as soon as he had finished some urgent business that awaited him.

But although he was as quick as he could, he was yet too late. One of his household managed to warn the bishop, who was loved by all, and Amator declared himself happy in being permitted to die for what he believed to be the truth. Yet even as he spoke, a secret voice said to his soul that although his life on earth would not last much longer, it was not Germanus who would kill him, and — strange as it appeared — it was that very Germanus who would succeed him as bishop.

When Amator understood these things, he knew what was required of him; and he set forth instantly to ride to Autun, where the prefect happened to be, for it was the law that no office could be conferred without his leave, and it was fortunate that at this moment he was so near at hand.

The prefect received Amator with great honor and asked for his blessing; then he begged his guest to explain the reason for this sudden visit. In a few words, Amator told him all that had occurred and of the revelation of his approaching death.

"But will the people, who have the right to elect their bishop, be satisfied with Germanus," inquired the prefect, "especially when they are aware he has quarreled with you?"

"Yes, if I choose him," answered Amator, "and they feel it is the will of God. But I wished to make sure that you would not oppose it."

"I am in your hands," replied the prefect, and with that Amator was content and returned to Auxerre.

By this time, Germanus had begun to understand the folly of his conduct, and as soon as he knew that the bishop had come back, he went with his attendants to Auxerre, curious to learn what business had taken Amator to the prefect. He found a large crowd pressing into the hall belonging to the bishop's house, to which messengers had summoned them, and he and his followers entered likewise. When place could be found for no more, Amator came in and stood before them.

"My children," he said, "I have somewhat to say unto you. God has revealed to me that the day of my departure from you is at hand. Therefore, while there is time, consider carefully whom you will choose to rule the Church after me."

The people heard with amazement and had no words to tell their surprise and sorrow; and Amator, seeing this, bade them lay down the arms they carried and go with him into the church, Germanus accompanying them. When all were within, the bishop ordered the doors to be locked, and walked himself to the upper end, where the nobles and chief men were standing.

"In the name of God," he cried, and suddenly taking a pair of scissors from under his robes, he seized the hair of the astonished Germanus with one hand, while he cut it off with the other. Without giving him time to recover from his surprise, he slipped off the governor's mantle, and threw a bishop's dress over him, uttering the few words necessary to ordain him priest.

"Know, dear brother, that God has willed that you should succeed me as bishop of this place," he said. "Strive to keep holy the charge committed to you."

We do not hear that the governor made any resistance to these extraordinary proceedings; indeed, he seems to have been half-stunned by their violence and unexpectedness. But as soon as Amator had accomplished his desire, he went back to his house, for he felt the symptoms of death upon him. Still, ill though he was, he never ceased to preach to his people the duty of electing Germanus, which at last they agreed to do. Then he bade them carry him to the church, and place him upon the bishop's throne, and there, in the midst of the multitude who loved him, he gave up his soul on the first of May 418.

∽

Although, in obedience to Amator's wish, the nobles, the clergy, and the people with one voice proclaimed Germanus their bishop, he himself hesitated long before accepting the post and, in fact, at one time made up his mind to refuse it altogether. Although a just man and a Christian in name, he had been entirely occupied in fulfilling his duties as governor and had given little attention to matters belonging to the Church. But the more he hesitated, the more resolved were they all that he, and no other, should fill Amator's place, and at length he yielded.

Like St. Ambrose, in a very similar case, once Germanus had decided to accept the bishopric, he allowed nothing to stand between him and his office. He resigned his governorship, gave away the rich furniture and the possessions he had always enjoyed, and, hardest of all, parted with his wife, Eustachia. But although, as was the custom in those days, she retired into a convent, they seem always to have remained friends and even to have seen each other from time to time.

At the date of his election, Germanus was forty, and for thirty years he ruled the Church of Auxerre, reverenced throughout the empire for his wisdom and holiness. Henceforth, the manner of his daily life was entirely changed. He ate no meat, and only at Christmas and Easter could be prevailed on to touch wheaten cakes, wine, or salt. Barley-bread was his common food, and that he prepared himself, but before eating it, he sprinkled ashes in his mouth, lest it should taste too nice. Winter and summer, night and day, he wore a hair shirt under his only garment, which was a long woolen tunic, with a small hood added to cover his thick hair, while his bed consisted of four planks and his mattress of a compact mass of cinders. For blankets he had a coarse strip of cloth, yet when his labors were ended, he slept as soundly as he had ever done in the governor's palace.

The Governor Who Became Bishop

∞

Now, although the actual work of a bishop was quite new to Germanus, the qualities and the training that had made him a just and wise governor stood him in good stead in his present position. Men were no less quarrelsome, no less ready to take advantage wherever they could get it, no less given to cheat and to lie in the fourth century than in the twentieth, and the bishop needed to be able to see through made-up stories, to be just in his judgments, to be courageous in dealing with those in power, and to control his temper when acts of tyranny and wickedness were brought to his notice. Germanus had learned these things in a hard school, and it was not long before the people felt that they had done well for themselves in listening to the entreaties of Amator.

Very soon after Germanus had become bishop, a tax collector named Januarius appeared before him in great distress. The bishop asked him what was the matter and promised to give him all the help he could when he had heard the story. So Januarius, with a faltering voice, poured forth his tale.

It was his business, he said, to accompany the governor when he made the tour of the province, in order to see for himself the condition of the people, while Januarius collected the taxes that were due, and, when all were gathered, paid them into the treasury. He was returning from one of these tours, when, as they were passing near Auxerre, Januarius thought that here, at length, was the chance to visit the famous Bishop Germanus, of whose election he had heard so much. Therefore, without asking leave of the governor, he secretly left the party and took the road to Auxerre. He was so busy thinking of the great man he was about to see, and wondering how he would be received by him, that he quite forgot all about the money, and the fastening of the bag containing it becoming unloosed with the jogging of the horse, it slid down, unperceived, to the ground, just at the very moment when a lunatic, or a man possessed with an evil spirit, was coming out of a wood by the roadside. Waiting until Januarius was safely around a corner, he picked up the bag, and the tax collector knew nothing of his loss until he dismounted at the door of the bishop's house.

"No one will ever believe me," he ended, almost weeping with fear. "And death is the punishment. If you cannot help me, I am lost indeed."

"Do not be cast down," answered the bishop kindly. "Speak to me as to a friend, and tell me what it is you want me to do."

Januarius looked down and hesitated. The bishop watched him, but said nothing, and at length the tax gatherer murmured that he knew it was a great deal to ask, but that the only way to save him was for the bishop to replace the money.

"Well, this I will do," replied Germanus, "but first I will search the town, and, perchance, I may find the thief."

For three days the search continued, the bishop causing a close examination to be made of everyone whose character was not above suspicion, but all in vain; no trace of the money could be found. At the close of the third day, Januarius was nearly beside himself, for the following week the taxes were due to be given in, and his loss would be discovered. But the bishop did not despair.

"We have searched the sane men, and now we must try those who are possessed with devils," said he, "and that I will do myself." Then he ordered these unhappy creatures to be brought before him, and strangely enough, the first led into his presence was the thief himself, although the bishop did not know it. Very cunning was the man, and he betrayed nothing, so the bishop bade his attendants follow him to the church, bringing the accused with them. Thus it was done, and a great crowd entered the church after them. The bishop then gave a solemn greeting to the people, and, falling on the ground, prayed earnestly that the truth might be brought to light. As he prayed, the man with the evil spirit was gradually drawn out of the hands of those who held him and raised upward, floating in the air in the midst of flames, and shrieking in torment.

"I confess, O Germanus, I confess!" he cried. "It was I who stole the bag and hid it under a great stone in the edge of the wood."

When he heard this, the bishop bade the evil spirit leave the man, and he left him. Then the man stood upon his feet again, whole, and the messenger sent by the bishop to the hiding-place brought back the money, and Januarius departed, rejoicing.

Some time after this, Germanus set out upon a journey to visit a distant part of his diocese. It was winter and very cold, and at length the bishop became chilled to the bone, and when they reached a deserted ruin near the road, he declared he felt so ill he could go no farther. His companions looked at each other in dismay. The place, they knew, was said to be haunted by ghosts, and, although they did not like to admit it, even to themselves, they were horribly frightened at the idea of spending the night there. However, they dared not say so to the bishop and tried to comfort themselves by thinking that they were quite safe in the presence of such a holy man.

For a while all went well. They lit a fire and cooked their supper, and while they were eating it, a monk read, as was the custom, some pages out of a book of prayers. Germanus, worn out with pain and fatigue, fell asleep, lying wrapped up in cloaks under the shelter of a projecting wall. Suddenly the reader felt an icy wind blowing and, glancing up, beheld a pale figure standing before him, with chains about his legs. With a bound, the monk reached the side of the sleeping bishop and shook him violently.

"What is it?" asked Germanus, lifting his head, but the reader could not answer, and only pointed to the ghost.

"Tell me wherefore you are here, and why your body is not reposing in peace beneath the earth?" said Germanus, and the ghost made reply: "Great crimes did I and another commit when we were in the world, and as a punishment Christian burial was forbidden

*The man with the evil spirit was raised upward, floating
in the air in the midst of flames, and shrieking in torment.*

us, and we were compelled to wander until we could find someone to take pity on us. And therefore, O Germanus, I have come to you." And so he vanished.

Then Germanus rose, and without more ado, he bade his trembling followers search the ruins by aid of their lanterns and the full moon, he himself standing by to give them courage, and also to see that they were not fainthearted in their search. In silence and in dread, the men peered into the dark corners, and at length one gave a cry.

"What is it?" asked the bishop, hastening to the spot. "Have you found them?"

"Yes, truly," was the answer, and there, with stones piled over them, lay two skeletons, having chains about their legs.

"Leave them until sunrise," said the bishop, and at sunrise the chains were struck off, clothes were placed upon the naked skeletons and a grave was dug outside the walls. So at last their wanderings were done, and Christian burial was given them, and the bishop himself read the prayers and implored forgiveness for their misdeeds.

∞

Germanus had been for eleven years bishop of Auxerre when he paid his first visit to Britain, and this is how it came about. A heresy had broken out in the country, which was still governed by the Romans, and was spreading far and wide. The bishops and clergy preached against it in vain and finally resolved to send to Germanus and beg his help. By command of the pope, who had been informed of the state of the British church, a council of the bishops of Gaul met at Troyes, and it was decided that Germanus was to start at once on his mission, and that Lupus, bishop of Troyes, should accompany him.

They seem to have traveled partly on horseback and partly by water, but they could not have gotten on very fast, for at every town, crowds assembled to ask their blessing. Amidst the throng that awaited them at Nanterre, a small place just beyond Paris, Germanus's eye was caught by the radiant face of a little girl of six, and he asked her name.

"Geneviève," they told him.

"Ah," said the bishop to her parents, as he laid his hand upon her head. "One day the name of this child will be known throughout the land, and her life will be an example to us all," and picking up a small copper coin marked with a cross, which was lying on the ground at his feet, he gave it to her, bidding her wear it round her neck in remembrance of him.

And for hundreds of years after, when Geneviève was reverenced as the patron saint of Paris, the canons of her order distributed on her name day little cakes, each marked with a cross.

On a cold winter day, the two bishops embarked on board a small ship for Britain. The sea was smooth until they reached the middle of the channel, when a great gale sprang up and the waves washed over the side of the tossing vessel.

"The evil spirits are fighting against us," said the sailors, as the wind whistled through the sails and tore them to shreds, and in their terror, they deserted their posts and let the ship drift as it would, while they aroused Germanus, who had slept through it all, and told him they were lost unless he would pray for them. As he prayed, the storm subsided, and with a fair breeze behind them, they finished their voyage, landing at Richborough, a town lying to the north of Dover, not far from the mouth of the Thames.

All the way to London, and on to St. Albans (so called after the first British martyr), the two bishops preached against the heresy of Pelagius, to the multitudes who came to listen to them. At St. Albans — or Verulam, to use the old name — they stayed some time and then proceeded toward the northwest. It was during this journey that Germanus had the happiness of seeing his old friend, the Irish St. Patrick, who had formerly spent many years as his pupil at Auxerre. The mother of Patrick was a native of Gaul, and for a long while his family dwelt in the part of the country called Armorica, which was under the rule of Germanus while he was governor.

∞

Now, at the time of Germanus's first visit to Britain, the Romans had been settled there for four hundred years and were shortly to be replaced by the Saxons. But, although the famous conquest under Hengist and Horsa did not occur until twenty years later, bands of Saxon pirates were constantly sailing across the North Sea from the lowlands beyond the Elbe and laying waste the farms and villages along the banks of the rivers. At the date when Germanus was going from one town to another preaching against the heresy of Pelagius, they had become more daring than usual and had coasted around Cornwall and the Bristol Channel, and past Wales, until they had reached the river Dee — for the Saxons never lost sight of land if they could possibly help it. Here they were joined by the Picts from the southwest of Scotland, and the Scots from the north of Ireland, and together they proceeded up the Dee in their light ships, which could always find some place of shelter in rough weather. To check them, the Roman governors had ordered flat boats, which could float in shallow water, to be moored on the banks, and bridges to be built across the rivers, taking care to keep them so low that no masts could get under the arches. Yet, in spite of these precautions, the invaders did much harm, and the Britons, who did not feel strong enough to attack them, remained in their entrenchments.

This was the state of things in Lent 430, when Germanus and Lupus were baptizing large numbers in the county of Cheshire, on the other side of the Dee. They were having service as usual one morning, when a messenger, hot and breathless, interrupted the ceremony.

"Come over and help us, O Germanus!" he cried, as the Macedonians had cried to St. Paul. "The Saxons from across the seas, and the wild men from the north are advancing up the river, killing and burning as they go, and none can stop them."

"Return. I will follow," answered Germanus, and, accompanied by Bishop Lupus, he hastened to the British army, which was encamped beside a small stream called the Alen, not far from the town of Mold.

The arrival of the two bishops raised the spirits of the Britons, and they were at once hailed as commanders of the force. The duties of a general were not entirely new to Germanus. As duke and governor of Armorica, it was his place to lead the army in battle, and, although we do not know if he had actually done so, he was not the man to be found unprepared for any duty he might have to fulfill. So we may feel certain that he had studied Caesar's book on war, and talked with the generals who had faced the hordes of Goths and Barbarians at that time pouring into the empire, even if he had not spoken with the great Aetius himself.

It was on Easter Day that the enemy were actually seen leading their boats and making ready for battle, and, at the first intelligence of what was happening, Germanus sent out scouts to watch and to report to him the direction the allies would take to reach the British camp. When news was brought that they were moving toward a valley surrounded by high hills, he rejoiced greatly, for he knew they were delivered into his hands. He posted his men behind rocks and in ravines along the mountainsides, and gave strict orders that no one should stir until he gave the signal. The Picts and Saxons advanced cheerfully, feeling sure of victory, and passed through the narrow entrance into the valley itself, which to all appearance was empty. As soon as they were fairly within it, a voice cried, "Alleluia!" "Alleluia" was echoed from every rock, and the mountain was alive with a great host rushing down the slopes shouting, "Alleluia!" In their surprise, the Saxon leaders lost their heads. They turned and fled, followed by the whole of their army, leaving everything behind them.

Thus the "Alleluia" battle was won without an arrow being shot or a spear thrown, and the valley is known as the Field of German unto this day.

∞

Right glad were the people of Auxerre to welcome their bishop back a few months later, for things were going very ill with them. The Roman empire had for long been falling into decay, and the barbarians from the east and the north were establishing themselves within her boundaries. In order to meet the expenses of the constant wars, fresh taxes were imposed, but as the rich were not bound to pay them, they fell doubly heavy on the poorer people. Indeed, the plight of some was so wretched that they actually sold themselves into slavery to obtain food and clothing.

Auxerre, being on the more eastern side of Gaul, toward the battleground where Goths, Huns, Alans, and Franks fought in quick succession, was perhaps worse off than the towns farther west, and no sooner had the bishop entered the city than a deputation of the citizens appealed to him to save them. There was only one way to do it, and that was to visit the prefect of Gaul, now living at Arles, and obtain from him a decree by which, for the future, the town should be freed from all taxation. In our eyes, it seems hardly just that one city should pay heavy taxes imposed for a special purpose, and another should pay none, but such was the custom, and it does not appear to have occurred to Germanus that there was anything wrong about it. At any rate, after making hasty preparations, he set off with a few attendants on the long journey to Arles.

It was a wet day when he started, and toward evening, as the little company was drawing near its first resting-place, it passed a man who had neither shoes nor coat. Struck by his miserable plight, the bishop reined in his horse and began to talk to him; and, finding that the beggar had nowhere to go, invited him to spend the night in the house where they were to sleep. The man eagerly accepted and shared the supper that was provided for the bishop's followers, but when the others were engaged at their prayers, he managed to creep out unperceived and to steal the bishop's horse. The theft was, of course, not discovered until the next morning, when they were ready to depart, and the horse of one of the attendants was brought around for Germanus to mount.

"What beast is that? And where is my own horse?" asked he.

"The rascal that you sheltered yesterday has stolen him, O Germanus," they answered; and when he heard, the bishop looked grave and silently mounted the horse that was held for him.

For some distance they rode on, until at length the bishop turned in his saddle and said to the man nearest him, "Soon you will see that the thief has not profited by that evil deed, so let us pause for a while, until he comes up to us." And the word was given to halt under a grove of trees. In a short time, the thief came toward them, leading the horse.

"All this time, since I took the horse from the stable, have I been trying to flee," cried the man, as soon as he was near them, "but once I was out of sight of the house where you slept, the beast would not stir one step, pull his bridle as I might. Then I knew that this was the punishment of my crime, and I resolved, if I could, to restore him to you. And as if the creature could see into my mind, at that very moment, his feet were loosed and he hastened down this road, and, behold, I give him back to you without hurt."

"Arise, my son," said the bishop, for the thief had fallen on his knees. "If yesterday I had given you a cloak, you would not have stolen the horse. Now, therefore, take this mantle and steal no more."

After that, he bade his company continue the journey, and in due time they arrived at Arles, where he was welcomed with great honor by St. Hilary, the bishop, and by the prefect, to whom he at once explained the business that had brought him. The prefect readily promised that the people of Auxerre should suffer no more from the extra taxes, and Germanus hastened home with the joyful tidings.

∞

In 446, Germanus was again summoned to preach against heresy in Britain, where Vorti O'ern was now king, but he did not stay many months, as affairs in Gaul were in a very disturbed state and his presence was needed as peacemaker. This time it was the inhabitants of the northwest, who, under the name of the Armorican confederacy, had banded themselves together against the Romans and their allies, the Alans, and revolted against them. Now, when the hosts of barbarians were about to be let loose upon them by the General Aetius, a panic seized them, and they implored the help of the bishop, himself once governor of those very provinces. Contrary to their expectations, Germanus succeeded in obtaining a truce from the Alan king, and even consented to cross the Alps into Italy, and to lay the matter before the Emperor, Valentinian III, or to speak more truly, before his mother, Placidia.

During the months he spent in the town of Ravenna, the city on the Adriatic that was then the seat of government, Germanus worked hard to help all kinds of distressed people, as well as those distant tribes for whose sake he had come. But in the midst of his labors, and of his pleadings with the powerful empress-mother, the news arrived that the Armoricans had again broken into revolt and that the rising had been put down with much severity. Deep must have been the disappointment of the bishop that all his efforts had proved so useless, but he was not given long to lament, for his day of rest was at hand, and it was revealed to him in this wise.

One morning he had been talking over the affairs of the Church with some of the Italian bishops, when he suddenly broke off and remained silent. They waited respectfully, guessing from his face that he had something of importance to tell them, and at last he began to speak again. "In the night, during my sleep, I dreamed that the Lord visited me and gave me provisions for a journey.

" 'What journey must I take, Lord?' said I, and the Lord answered, 'Fear not. I send thee to no foreign land, but to thine own country, where thou shalt have eternal rest and peace.' And well I know what that country is which God promises to his servants."

Well, the bishops knew also, although in their grief they refused to believe, and sought to put another interpretation on the dream. But a few days later Germanus was taken ill, and when it became plain that death was near, hundreds flocked to take leave of him and to beg his blessing. Among these was the Empress Placidia, who fell on her knees by his bed and asked if there was nothing she could do for him who had done so much for the world.

"Yes, one thing," he said. "Let my body be carried back to Gaul and buried at Auxerre with my people." So at the end of seven days, he died, having ruled over his diocese thirty years.

Very unwillingly the empress gave orders that his last request should be fulfilled. His body was embalmed and covered with a magnificent cloak, on which the imperial arms were embroidered. It was then placed in a cedar-wood coffin, and, followed by an immense multitude, set out on its homeward journey across the Alps. From time to time, some of the mourners fell off, and others took their places, but five women walked on foot beside the corpse, never faltering. Three of them died on the way, worn out by fatigue, but the other two arrived at Auxerre safely. At the end of fifty-three days, the city was reached, and on the first of October 448, the bishop was laid to rest, as he had wished, with his own people.

St. Malchus

Captive Monk

When the learned St. Jerome was living in Antioch with Evagrius the priest, he heard much of a holy man named Malchus, dwelling in a village three miles away, and Jerome was filled with desire to go to see him. On his side, many tales of the wonderful knowledge of Jerome had reached the ears of Malchus, and gladly did he welcome his guest and answer his questions.

"Tell me somewhat of yourself," said Jerome at last, "and how you came here," and Malchus answered in this wise.

In Nisibis I was born, and as my parents had no other child, they set great store by me, and thought I deserved great riches and honor. When I came to be a man, they wished me to marry so that they might have grandchildren to play with in their old age, but my heart was not with them. "Let me become a monk," I said, "and serve the Lord." But to this they would not listen, and even threatened me with imprisonment and punishment. For a while, I tried to prevail with them to grant me my wish, but all being of no use, I departed secretly in the night, carrying with me only what money I needed for my journey.

In the beginning, I had resolved to go into a monastery of the East, but, as the Persians were about to make war on the Greeks, I changed my mind and turned westward beyond the river

Euphrates, to the south of Aleppo. There, in that desert country I remained for several years, and the monks in the house held me to be a holy man, because I obeyed the rules and fasted often and prayed much. But in this they were mistaken, for the love of money, which is the root of all evil, held its place deep in my soul.

This no one guessed, least of all I myself, until it was made known to me after this manner:

News came to me of my father's death, and the evil one put it into my heart that it was my duty to return home and comfort my mother and look after the property that had come to me, lest any of it should be wasted; and that after his death I should have the more to give to the poor. And more than that, I might even build a monastery myself and die an abbot.

These thoughts took possession of me, but for long I kept silence concerning them, until at length the abbot of the monastery perceived that all was not well with me, and questioned me about the matter.

When I told him that I desired to return home, he shook his head and warned me against listening to the voice of the tempter. But finding my resolve to go was still unchanged, he ceased to urge me, saying sadly, "My son, I see that the love of money has brought this evil. You will not hearken to my words, yet know that the sheep which strays from the flock, straightway falls a prey unto the wolves."

∞

So we parted, and the next day I set forth and journeyed as far as the town of Edessa, where I stayed, hoping to hear of a company of travelers going toward Nisibis, for greatly was that road infested with robbers.

After some weeks, seventy people were gathered together who were desirous of making the journey, and we set forth. But we had not gotten very far when we perceived a band of the terrible Arabs approaching us, and we were forced to surrender so as to save our lives. I was seated by order of their leader upon a camel, with a woman behind me, and much we both feared that we should fall off, for we were not used to these awkward beasts. Thus we traveled back to the camp, and there the Arab chief led the woman and me into his tent, and commanded us to obey his wife and to look on her as our mistress. Then woolen garments were given me, and I was sent to tend the sheep and the goats, which rejoiced me greatly, for I was alone and felt myself treading in the steps of the sons of Jacob and of David the king.

Now, it often happened that for the space of a month I was left to do as I would, but if my master was passing near the place of pasture, he would stop to see how his sheep might be. And when he found them fat and healthy, he knew that I had tended them faithfully, and he praised and rewarded me.

In this manner I lived for some time, eating goat's cheese and drinking milk, and in my solitude I had much time for pondering on the past, as well as on the future. It was my own fault that I had fallen into captivity, and often did I seem to behold the face of the abbot of the monastery that I had left, in my willfulness and greed of gain.

I was sitting thus one day, thinking thoughts of sadness and shame, when my eyes fell upon an ant's nest, close at my feet. Busily the little creatures came and went, and as I watched them day by day, it appeared as if they had some purpose in their goings and did not wander idly to and fro. They had made a narrow passage that led into the nest, and although multitudes were hurrying up and down it, none got in the way of his fellows. Some carried seeds they had picked up from outside to store them in their garner so that they might not be without food in winter; others were bearing on their backs their comrades who had met with accidents in the world that was so full of great big creatures, and these they seemed to be taking to some spot where they might be healed.

And as I looked, I observed that at the entrance a crowd of ants that had settled themselves, as I guessed, unlawfully in the nest, were being thrust out to make room for those whose home it was, while others again were loaded with grains of dust, perhaps to strengthen the walls of their nest, so that these might not be washed away in the rains of winter.

All this and more I saw, and wondered at the wisdom of those small insects, and marveled not that Solomon had bidden us learn from them.

∞

So the days went by, and more and more I longed to leave the tents of those Arab thieves and to be once more among my own people. And one evening I went to the woman who was my fellow captive, and was employed by the chief's wife to make cheeses out of the milk of the beasts of the tribe, and told her that it was in my mind to escape. On hearing this, she besought me to take her also, that she might seek a nunnery in which to end her days; to which I consented.

Then I killed two large goats, and fashioned their skins into water-bottles, and roasted the flesh, so that we would not be without food on our journey, and as soon as it was dark, we set forth. In spite of our terrors lest we should be pursued, the road seemed short, for were we not free? And quickly we went until we came to a wide river.

"How can we cross this?" asked the woman. "It is no use. We must turn back, and they will assuredly kill us."

But I soothed her and bade her be of good courage, for a way had been made plain to me. And this was the way.

I took the water skins, and blew them up until they were quite tight, and tied the necks tightly so that the air could not escape. Then I placed them in the water, and we sat upon them, holding each other's hands and paddling with our feet until we got toward the middle of the river, when the current carried us down and swept us to the other side.

Deep was our joy at finding ourselves on dry ground again, and we drank of the river, not knowing when we might again taste water; then we started afresh with hope in our hearts, although we were ever looking behind to see if the Arabs were pursuing after us.

For this cause, and also by reason of the burning sun, we hid ourselves in the day and traveled only when night had fallen.

We had gone five days in this manner, and were beginning to feel ourselves safe, when on turning our heads, as we had grown used to do almost without thinking of it, we beheld the Arab chief and one of his men riding after us, with naked swords in their hands. Heretofore we had kept ourselves concealed until the sun had set, but we had become somewhat careless, and besides, our water had failed us, and we were anxious to reach some wells not very far off. Therefore when we beheld our enemies and knew that they had seen us, so great was our agony that the sun itself appeared to grow dark. Escape seemed impossible, yet we were thankful to note a cave among the rocks, in which all the snakes that dwell in the desert had taken refuge, for they like not the heat of the sun. The woman who was with me had at most times a great dread of serpents, but now she heeded them not at all, in her fear of the Arabs. Hardly able to walk from the trembling of our legs, we staggered toward the cave, saying to each other, "If the Lord help us, this cave shall be unto us a house of deliverance, but if He leaves us to our captors, it will be our grave."

Our master and his followers had no difficulty in tracking our footsteps to the cave's mouth, where they alighted from their camels and prepared to enter. Crouching in the dark, we watched and felt that only a few moments of life were left us, and already the sharp edge of the steel seemed to strike cold against our throats.

"Come out, you dogs!" cried the chief, but our tongues were as if frozen, and we could not have spoken had we tried.

"Do you think I do not know that you are there?" he shouted again, but as we were still silent, he turned to his comrade, and said, "I will hold the camels; you go in and drive them out with the point of the sword." And the young man did his bidding, and entered the cave about five paces. There he stood still, for the light of the sun was yet in his eyes, and all appeared black darkness inside the cave. So near were we that he could have touched us with his hand, had he been able to see us, but he could not; and we scarcely dared to breathe.

"Come out, O wicked ones! Do you think you can escape me?" he cried, but even as he spoke, something large and yellow flew past us in the air, and knocked him on the ground, and there was silence, save for the sound of the lioness dragging his dead body over the floor of the cave, to where her cub was lying.

Now, his master outside supposed that we had overpowered the young man, so that he was unable to cry out; therefore he drew his sword and ran to the mouth of the cave, calling to us. But the light of the sun was in his eyes also and what had befallen the young man befell him likewise.

And having slain the Arab chief as well as his comrade, the lioness took up her cub in her mouth, and went forth into the desert.

∽

So close had death been to us that we seemed to have no strength left to move, and it was not until dawn the next day that we ventured forth, to where the camels were lying, with food and skins of water on their backs. After eating and drinking, we felt strong again, and mounting the camels, we rode across the rest of the desert, until we reached a camp that had been pitched by the Greeks. Here we told our tale, and the officer in command of it

The lioness took up her cub in her mouth and went forth into the desert.

sent us with an escort of armed soldiers to one Sabinus, then duke of Mesopotamia, in whose country we were at last safe. Sabinus gave us the price of the camels, and we set forth to the nearest convent, where I placed the woman who had shared so many dangers with me.

As for myself, the love of money had departed from my heart, and with it my wish to go to Nisibis. So I returned to my own monastery, where I dwelt for many years, until in the end I came hither. That is my tale.

Saint on a Pillar

If anyone had told Simeon, the shepherd boy who was following his flocks over the Syrian mountains in the early part of the fifth century, that he was, by his own choice, to spend most of his life on a pillar, and die standing on it, he would have laughed in scorn. What! Give up wandering about the hills and throwing sticks into the rivers that came so swiftly down after the melting of the snows? Give up the games with his friends and the winter evenings in the cottage, when his mother sat and mended his clothes while he gazed idly into the fire? Oh, it was absurd! He might go away perhaps to be a soldier, or join one of the merchant's caravans that went to Persia or India and brought back the wonderful things his father had seen, although of course *he* never had. Yes, he might do *that!* But stand on a pillar! Yet it was this, and nothing else, that came to pass.

Would you like to know how it happened? Well, I will tell you.

Simeon's parents were Christians, like most of the people about them, but were terribly poor, and glad enough they felt when a farmer, who lived nearby, offered the boy a place as his shepherd. The child was delighted, and as soon as he held his first week's pay in his hand, felt himself a man, and hastened proudly home to give it to his mother. He was most careful of the sheep and drove them away from the edges of ravines where they might fall and break their legs, and from marshy places which were apt to make their feet sore, and from thorny bushes where they might get entangled, and kept them on the rich, dry grass of the upland meadows, where the flowers grew. And the farmer thought he had never had such a good shepherd, and resolved that when the boy grew older, he would give him work on the farm.

Thus passed the summer and autumn, and as winter drew near, the sheep were led into the lower pastures and grazed in the fields near Simeon's home. Then the snows began and fell so thickly that they had to remain in the fold, safe from the wolves that were driven by hunger down the mountains, and Simeon was free to do as he liked. It sounded very pleasant; but in truth, when he had done all he could to help his mother, he did not know how to employ himself. He strolled outside, but there was no one to be seen and nothing to be heard — nothing, that is, except the church bell. Ah! that was a good idea! Why should he not go to church? At any rate, he would be warm there, and it would pass away the time.

So he waded through the snow and entered the church and stood — for in the Greek church, they either stand or kneel — in a corner not far from the pulpit.

Perhaps he did not listen very much at first. His thoughts may have wandered as children's thoughts — and grown-up people's too — are apt to do, and he gazed idly up at the priest, who was an old friend of his father, as he gave out his text from the Sermon on the Mount.

"Blessed are they that mourn, for they shall be comforted; blessed are the pure in heart, for they shall see God." And as Simeon listened, something seemed to awake inside him: the trappings of the soldier, the vision of the caravan of camels moving across the Syrian desert, fell away from him. He did not want outside things anymore, and when the sermon was ended, he shook himself as if to make sure he was awake, and followed the priest into the sacristy, and with bowed head asked how *he* could grow pure in heart and someday "see God."

"Go into a monastery, my son," answered the priest, "where the world will be shut out; and if you spend years in fasting and prayer, all evil desires will gradually pass from you, and your heart will become pure."

Simeon bowed his head again and went slowly out, not knowing where he was going. He wanted to think over the counsel given him by the priest, for although he was only a boy, he felt that he was deciding the question of his whole life. Which was right, to obey the priest or to stay at home and work for his father and mother? It was very difficult; and he did not feel able to settle the matter himself. Suddenly, he looked up and saw that he had walked a long way, and quite near him was the little church of the next village. Quickening his steps, he entered the door, and flinging himself on his knees, prayed that he might be shown what to do.

After that he returned home and said nothing of what had happened. But his mother saw that he looked very tired and sent him to bed early.

Simeon was soon fast asleep, and in his sleep he dreamed that he was digging the foundations of a building when a voice spoke to him, saying, "Dig deeper, dig boldly; for the pit is not deep enough." So he dug and dug with all his might, and thrice the voice bade him go on; then it called him to cease, crying, "Enough. Erect the building, and now you will find it easy to build, for you have conquered yourself."

Then Simeon awoke and lay on his bed a long time, wondering what could be the meaning of the dream — for he was sure it had one. At last he interpreted the dream for himself and said that until he had dug out all evil and worldly things from his mind, he could build nothing that would stand against temptation. Now, he was certain he had received a sign that the priest had been right, so, dressing himself softly, he stole out of the cottage, and ran off to the monastery.

∞

Hardly able to speak from the haste he had made, he knocked timidly at the door and was admitted by one of the monks. After telling his story, he was left alone for a while, and then he was received on probation, as it was called, for a number of weeks, so that the monks could find out if he was suitable to the life. But watch as they might, they could discover nothing in the boy to cause them to reject him. For several days he fasted, and they looked on astonished that a being not yet full-grown could go so long without food and spend so many hours on his knees. He studied the Psalms too, until he could say them off without a mistake. At last he was told that he was accepted as a monk, and great was his joy.

For two years he remained in the monastery, and then one evening, when the monks came out from chapel, he asked the superior if he might speak to him in his cell. When the door behind them was closed, Simeon told how he longed to follow the example of many holy hermits and go himself into the desert, where he could have no distractions from prayer, such as had beset him since he entered the convent. Only thus could he become "pure in heart," he said. When he entered the monastery, he had thought it would be easy to shut out temptations — as easy as his dream had promised him — but he had found it was not so. In the desert, surely, he would have peace, and he looked up hopefully at the superior, for he was young and did not know that our temptations go with us wherever we may be. The superior was wiser, but he understood that Simeon must discover this for himself and that it was better not to put hindrances in his way.

A few days later, Simeon bade farewell to the monastery — perhaps also to his parents — and took up his abode on Mount

Corypheus, in the lonely monastery over which Heliodorus ruled as abbot. Here, by his own wish, he was given the lowest place, doing the work of a servant and eating only as much as served to keep him alive, for he fasted as long and as often as ever, and saved part of the food allowed him for the poor. But he persisted besides in scourging himself so violently that the abbot was afraid he would kill himself, and after many warnings, sent him away for a time, declaring he would not answer for his life.

After a while, brother Simeon returned to the monastery, but in a few months he again grew restless and went off to another mountain and built himself a small stone hut where he could live entirely alone and do exactly what he chose. Fasting became his rule and eating his exception, and at the end of three years, he vowed he had become so strong that he could stand all day and keep awake nearly all night. When things had reached this point, he left his hut and climbed to the very top of the mountain, carry-ing with him a chain thirty feet in length.

"What can Brother Simeon be going to do with that?" thought one or two men whom he met on his way, but brother Simeon never heeded them, if even he knew they had passed by, so full was his mind of what he was about to do.

On the mountainside was a sort of flat shoulder, which was exactly the place Simeon had been seeking. It took him a long time to collect all the stones he wanted, for many of them had to be brought from a distance, but at length he decided that he had enough for his purpose, and gazed at the two heaps he had made with something like a smile of content. "Now I can begin," said he, and he set about building a rough wall around an enclosed green space. His back was aching and his hands were sore before he had finished, but he did not care about that, and picking up the chain from where it lay, he fastened it around his waist and fixed the ends to each side of the enclosure, putting great stones over them, sufficiently heavy to hold them down.

He thought that by thus cutting himself off from mankind, and all that made life pleasant, he would grow closer to God and nearer to perfection, and everyone else thought so too. The fame of his holiness spread throughout Northern Syria and Asia Minor, and pilgrims to Jerusalem turned out of their way to receive Simeon's blessing.

Among his visitors, one of the earliest was the bishop of Antioch. The sight of the wild-eyed young man with long, matted hair made a great impression on the bishop. Simeon was, of course, very dirty — nothing but rain ever washed him — but in those days, dirt was usually considered necessary to the holy life. He was also very thin, for he ate only a little goat's milk and bread brought to him daily by a herdsman who lived on the other side of the mountain, but his face gleamed with joy as he told the bishop the story of his past life, and how much he had longed for solitude so that he might become holy. His listener was deeply interested. He had seen many hermits before, but they had been merely men living apart, in deserts, and none of them had dreamed of tormenting his body after the manner of Brother Simeon. Only one thing was lacking to him, in the mind of the bishop, and before he bade the hermit farewell, he spoke, "You have chained yourself, I perceive," he said. "But why? Only wild beasts need chains, lest they should escape into the forests; it is of your own free will that you remain where you are. Surely that will is enough?"

"You are right," answered Simeon. "I had not thought of that," and he begged the bishop to send him a man from the village as he went down the mountains, to strike off his chains, and leave him to stand there unfettered by anything save the vows he had made to himself and God.

∞

As time passed, the throngs of people who came to him daily increased. Some hoped to be cured by his touch or his prayers from the diseases that tormented them; others sat on the wall and poured out to him their troubles and asked his advice, which they always followed, thinking it was inspired by God. At first Simeon was pleased at their coming, but he soon began to tire of them and longed to push the crowd away from him, when it pressed too closely. It was then that he bethought himself of making a column that would raise him above their heads, and it was thus that he obtained the surname of "Stylites," by which he is known, from a Greek word meaning "pillar."

His earliest column was nine feet high, and on top was a platform three feet across, so that it was quite impossible for him, even had he wished, to lie down on it. Everyone believed, Simeon himself first among them, that he never sat at all, and even slept standing. No doubt, in the course of time, he was able from habit to balance himself more easily than other men, but we also know now that when people scarcely eat or sleep, and do not use their minds, they get into strange conditions and fancy many things that are not true.

However, Simeon was satisfied with the life he had chosen, and never for a moment suspected that he could have served God better in some other way.

We can tell how he spent his days from a history given of him by Theodoret, one of his most devout admirers. In the evening, he began, so said Simeon, his long course of prayer, which continued all through the night until noon the next day. On one occasion, a man, filled with awe and devotion, sat at the foot of the pillar, his eyes fixed on Simeon, who, if he saw him, paid no heed to his presence. The watcher counted 1,244 bows made by the saint — it must have been a moonlight night — in the course of his prayers, and then he himself grew tired of counting, or perhaps he fell asleep. When Simeon's prayers were ended, he preached to the crowds around the base of the pillar, and argued about his Faith with men of other religions, or with heretics.

He prophesied too and gave warnings of disasters that would come as punishment for sin, and bishops and kings, who had journeyed from far to ask his advice, rode away with bowed heads and shame in their hearts when he accused them of misdeeds they had thought were known only to themselves.

∽

Yet even to a man on a pillar temptations will come, and there was one that sorely beset the hermits of old, perhaps more than other men: that of thinking themselves holier than their fellows, because of the dreariness of their lives. It was natural enough, when they found their lightest word obeyed and their reproof taken by those whose right to give life or death to their own subjects was quite unquestioned; when, for instance, heathen monarchs such as Varanes, king of Persia, sent public marks of his esteem to the saint upon the pillar, which by this time was thirty-six feet high. But the sin of self-righteousness was, according to Theodoret, quickly brought home to Simeon, and swift was the penalty.

"I am not as other men are," he had said proudly to himself, and when he thought of the manner of his death, he was convinced that it also would not be in the manner of other men or even of other hermits.

One day when he was quite alone, for his listeners had just left him, a chariot suddenly appeared before him, and so real was the vision, and so confident was the saint that death would take strange shape for him, that he lifted one leg in order to step into it. As he did so, he made the Sign of the Cross and the chariot vanished, but his foot still remained in the air, and for a year he stood on one leg on the pillar, himself a warning against the deadly sin of pride.

Now, it happened that the hermits scattered about the neighboring deserts did not look upon the saint upon the pillar with the same eyes as the multitudes of his disciples, who flocked to see and hear him. However much they might call their feeling by other names, these hermits were jealous of his fame and declared that he was no holier than the rest of them. So they fixed a meeting place, where large numbers assembled and talked over the matter, discussing the best plan to expose Simeon and to show the world what an impostor he really was.

Of course, they were all aware that no one would listen to any tales of *theirs*, but a trap must be laid that he himself would fall into, and this was not so easy to find. First one thing was proposed, and then another, and each had some objection. At length a very old hermit stood up and said, "Brothers, I know what to do: let us choose two or three among us and let them go to the mountain and bid Simeon come down from his pillar. If he is willing to do so, we shall feel that he is a true man, if not . . ." and he paused, and the brethren nodded their heads and answered, "It is well," being quite sure in their own minds that Simeon would not obey them.

At sunrise the three hermits who had been selected by the rest started on their journey. It took them a long while, as for many years they had scarcely left the caves in which they lived and their legs were very stiff, while their feet soon grew tired. But they comforted themselves by remembering that, after all, the delay did not matter, as whenever they got there Simeon would still be on the top of his pillar, and their message would be delivered. So they did not hurry.

∞

The saint was standing on his pillar one hot day, preaching to a greater crowd than usual, when three men, even more ragged and dusty than hermits generally were, appeared around the shoulder of the mountain, and halted, watching and waiting until the sermon should be ended, and they could say their say before the people departed to their homes — they would take care of that! Of course, they protested to each other — and themselves — that they were only anxious the world should no longer be deceived, but their triumphant faces told a different tale!

Relinquish the faith that shone in those hundreds of eyes, and the admiration that overflowed in those hundreds of hearts, and confess himself a mere mortal like the rest, by leaving his post where he stood like a beacon, and mix unnoticed with those whom he now commanded! Was it likely Simeon would do this? And, hermits and recluses though they were, they judged aright.

But the minutes seemed to drag until the sermon was ended. Then whispering, "It is time," the three strangers pressed forward to a little knoll above the heads of the people, where they could be seen by all.

"Simeon, we are sent by the hermits of the desert to command thee to leave thy pillar and come down and be as one of us." So they cried, and paused; and the crowd held its breath, waiting.

"Am I here for my own glory? Of course I will come down. Let someone bring me a ladder." These were the words that rang out in answer from the pillar. The crowd gave a low gasp, and the hermits gazed at each other. This was not the reply they had expected; the man was a true man and servant of God after all; or else — for suspicion and jealousy are hard to kill — he was stronger than they. In either case, the victory lay with him, and with a sigh they made answer: "No, it is enough. Stay on thy pillar, and may thy preaching prosper."

∞

The story of that day's event spread far and wide, and Simeon was held in greater reverence than ever. Visions he beheld too, of coming disasters, and was thus enabled to warn both kings and people to repent while there was yet time. Sometimes they listened, and the threatened punishment was averted; more often they contented themselves with saying how wonderful were his words, and how terrible were the sins of which he spoke.

As to the rod he had seen one night hanging over the earth, foretelling, as the saint declared, the scourge of famine and pestilence, why, he described it all so beautifully that you felt as if you had beheld it yourself! And the warning was neglected and the sermon forgotten, until, in two years, the plague that he had prophesied came to pass.

Another time he predicted that grasshoppers, numerous as the locusts in Egypt of old would darken the face of the country, but that they would devour only the grass of the fields, leaving untouched the food of man. And just as he had foretold, fifteen days afterward the air grew black with grasshoppers; and people sat in their houses trembling with fear, until a strong wind arose and blew them away, and only the bare earth, where once the grass had been, bore witness to their passing.

Henceforward until his death, the life of the saint was divided between preaching and prayer, and people never grew weary of hearing him. But at length men began to notice that the little basket he let down daily for them to fill with food often remained for hours without being drawn up, and although he preached as before, his voice grew weaker, and sometimes he seemed to forget the words he wished to speak. "The chariot will come for him soon," they whispered, remembering the story of days gone by; and a few days later (January 5, 459), he died in their midst, standing on his pillar.

Great was the cry that echoed over the mountains when the news was told, and it resounded, men said, for seven miles around, so deep was the grief at his loss. His body was taken to Antioch and there buried, while a church was set up to his memory on the site of the pillar.

Apostle of Northumbria

In the middle of the seventh century after Christ, the island of Britain was a very different place from what it is now, and great tracts of land that are at present covered in the summer with corn, or rich grass, were then wide lakes. Cities lying on the East Coast, which were at that time rich and prosperous, have for hundreds of years been buried under the waves; and dark forests, sheltering wolves and other fierce beasts, covered the moors of the north, in these days dotted over with villages. Still, there were plenty of fields and meadows for the children to play in, and the games of children are always much the same.

A number of little boys were gathered on the banks of one of the rivers in the country south of the Tweed, which we now call Northumberland, but was then part of the kingdom of Northumbria. They were of all ages, from three to ten, and were chattering fast and eagerly, apparently settling some races to be run and choosing the ground where they might try who could throw a ball the farthest. By and by, when everything was arranged, each boy went to his place. The two who were judges sat on a rock that was to be the winning post; the two who were to see that the winners started fairly were at the other end of the course; and the competitors themselves were drawn up in a line.

"Now," cried the starter, and off they went, heads well up and their feet lifted.

"Cuthbert, Cuthbert!" was the cry as one of the smallest boys shot ahead of the rest and sank panting on the rock that was the winning-post.

"It is always Cuthbert," muttered one of the beaten runners, and he was right; it always was, both in racing and in climbing trees, and in wrestling, where the child's quickness of eye and hand made up for his lack of strength. He loved all such things and, after a morning spent by the riverside, would go home proud and happy to his mother, and tell her of his victories, and how very, very nearly one boy had caught him up, and another had *almost* succeeded in throwing him.

But Cuthbert's pleasures were not to last long. He was only eight when a tiny creature not half his age, who had watched the races solemnly from a little hillock, came up to Cuthbert, and, pulling him aside from the other boys as they were planning a new game, begged him not to waste his time in such idle play, but give heed to the things of the mind. Cuthbert stared, as well he might, and paid no attention to him.

"Let us try how many of us can bend ourselves backward, until we can kiss the trunk of that tree," he said, running off to his friends. "And after that we can see if we can hold one leg out stiffly, and bend the other till the stiff leg almost touches the ground. It is easy enough to go *down*, but the difficulty is to get up again without tumbling over. My father can do it; he showed me yesterday." And, forthwith, they all began to practice, with much laughter and many falls, while the solemn-eyed boy looked on disapprovingly.

Suddenly a loud cry made them stop and turn around; the child had flung himself down on the ground and was sobbing bitterly. The others did not trouble about him. "Babies like that were better at home," they said; but Cuthbert, who always tried to help anyone younger or weaker than himself, ran up to the little fellow and asked him what was the matter.

"It is *you*," gasped the boy as soon as he could speak. "The rest may do as they like, but the Lord has chosen *you* to be His servant — the teacher of others — and you will not listen!"

Cuthbert did not answer. It seemed so strange that such words should come from so small a creature, too young to run or jump, or to play a game of any kind. How could he have gotten such notions into his head? Yet there was no doubt that he was very unhappy. So Cuthbert stooped down and whispered, "Well, don't cry. At any rate, I won't play any more today," and he patted the child's head and walked slowly away, in spite of the shouts of his friends to come back and join them.

This was really the end of Cuthbert's childhood. From the day the little boy had spoken to him, he put off childish things and was as thoughtful and serious as a man. But no one can tell us how he actually spent those years, and when next we hear of him, he was grown up.

All his life, Cuthbert loved walking and would go for miles across the mountain or along the seashore, visiting the dwellers in the scattered huts and preaching to them. It was, therefore, a terrible trial to him when at length a large lump formed itself on his knee so that he was unable to bend the joint and was continually in pain. For some time he still dragged himself about, but of course this only made his leg worse, and soon the pain grew so bad that he was obliged to be carried. At this period, he appears to have been living in some sort of a monastery, which had servants or porters to help with the work.

The air of the small, close cells was hateful to Cuthbert, and every day some of the servants took him in their arms and laid him down under a tree on the edge of the forest. One morning he was set in his usual place, from which he could see far away to the south and watch the clouds casting shadows over the hills and the moors. As he was gazing before him, trying to forget the pain he suffered, he beheld a man dressed in white, mounted on a white horse, riding toward him. When the rider drew near, he stopped, and, as Cuthbert did not rise in greeting, he asked with a smile whether he would not welcome him as a guest.

"Yes, indeed," answered Cuthbert. "Right welcome you are to me and to all of us, but I cannot rise to greet you as I fain would do with all civility, for I am bound and tied by a swelling in my knee, and although I have been examined by many a physician, not one has been able to heal me."

"I have some skill in such matters," said the man, dismounting from his horse. "Let me look at it, I pray you," and taking Cuthbert's knee between his hands, he put some questions to him.

"If you will do as I bid you, you will soon be cured," he said at last. "Boil some wheaten flour in milk, and spread it on a cloth; and while it is hot, lay it on the swelling, and in a short time the swelling will disappear and the pain depart, and your leg will be whole again. And now, farewell." With that he mounted his horse and rode away over the hills, and Cuthbert was persuaded that an angel had visited him.

Now, there was a monastery on the south side of the river Tyne, and it was the custom of the monks to send out flat boats or rafts to bring timber from some of the forests near the sea for their daily use. It happened that on one occasion, the little fleet had returned with its cargo and was just about to unload opposite the monastery, when a westerly gale sprang up, and it was blown out toward the ocean. The monks, beholding this disaster, ran out of the monastery to the riverbank and launched some boats to help the fast-disappearing rafts, but the boats were blown out to sea before they could get on board them. Then they fell on their knees and prayed amid the mocking of the crowd assembled on the other bank, who taunted them with thinking themselves holier than their neighbors. But Cuthbert, who stood among these people, checked their evil words and asked them if they had no pity for those who were drifting to their death, and called on them to pray also.

"Let no one pray for them," answered the mockers, "for they have taken away our old worship, and given us that which is strange to us."

On hearing this, Cuthbert bowed himself on the ground and prayed for the lives of the men in peril. And as he prayed, the wind changed, and the rafts and the boats were blown up the river again; and when they saw this, a silence fell upon the unbelievers, and they were converted.

∞

As time went by, Cuthbert made up his mind that he would lay aside the layman's dress and spear he still used and live altogether in a monastery, whereas before he had only dwelt in one for a short while, to rest from his journeys. His days were spent in going hither and thither, and often he would help with his work any who needed it, sometimes keeping sheep with the shepherds, sometimes sowing wheat with the ploughmen, or aiding the reapers to gather in the harvest.

One cold winter's day, he was riding alone to preach at a small village some distance off, when his horse began to hang his head and to show signs of weariness, for they had already come many miles. Cuthbert looked about for a place in which the beast could find food and rest, and perceived a farmhouse a little way off. Here he was gladly welcomed, and, after leading his horse to the stable, he entered and sat by the fire. But he would not eat, even though the farmer's wife pressed him, for it was the rule of the Church to fast that day until the evening. In vain the woman told him that if he would not eat now, he would be likely to fast until the morrow, as the country was desolate and bare of houses; but he would not listen to her, and when, toward sunset, his horse was rested, he took leave of her and rode on.

It was growing dark, and nothing was to be seen but a wild waste of moor, and Cuthbert was wondering whether he and his horse would not have to pass the night under some sheltering rock, when he noticed a little to the right a group of half-ruined huts, once inhabited by shepherds.

"Here we can rest well," he said to himself, and dismounting, he fastened his horse to a wall and gave him some hay that the wind had blown thither. But the horse had come far and was hungry, and the hay was not enough to satisfy him, so when he had finished it, he pulled some of the straw from the thatched roof, and as it fell, a folded-up linen cloth fell with it. Cuthbert, who was singing the day's psalms, heard the noise made by the horse and turned around, and when his prayers were ended, he went to see what was in the cloth, as it was a strange place for it to come from. Little he guessed that he should find wrapped up half a loaf of hot bread and some meat, and when he beheld them, he suddenly felt that he, as well as the horse, was exhausted for lack of food; and after this miracle had happened to him, he was even more ready than before to fast on the days appointed.

Some time later Cuthbert journeyed to the Abbey of Melrose, for, as has been told, he wished to leave the world and to be received into the priesthood by the man whom all held to be the holiest in the kingdom of Northumbria: Boisil the abbot, after whom the town of St. Boswell's was afterward called. He stayed at Melrose for some years, going for a short while with Eata, who was made abbot on the death of Boisil, to the new Abbey at Ripon, but right glad was he to return to Melrose and the country that he loved.

Still, it would be a mistake to think of him as shut up between walls and doing nothing but praying. He kept up his old custom of visiting the scattered houses and villages and preaching to the people, many of them yet pagans at heart, and he would be absent from Melrose for days or even weeks at a time.

It happened one day that he received a message from the abbess of Coldingham in Berwickshire, entreating him to come down and give some teaching to herself and her nuns. Cuthbert lost no time in setting out, for the ride was a long one, and he bade the abbot of Melrose not to be surprised if his return was delayed for many days. After his arrival at Coldingham, he walked, while it was light, to the fishers' huts gathered on the shore; and in the night, when the nuns slept, it was his habit to steal down to the sea and to sit on the rocks, where he prayed silently for hours.

Late one dark evening, when all was quiet, he went out as usual and took the path down to the cliffs, followed, although he knew it not, by a monk, curious to find out whither he was going. Right to the edge of the water Cuthbert went, the monk keeping in the shadow behind him; but what was the man's surprise when he saw the saint enter the sea and walk forward until it reached up to his neck. Thus he remained until dawn, chanting aloud the praise of God. With the first streaks of light he sank on his knees on the sand, for the tide was ebbing fast, and two seals swam toward him from a rock, and breathed over his cold feet to warm them, and rubbed them dry with their hair; and Cuthbert stroked their heads, and thanked them and blessed them, and they lay on the sands in the sun's rays, until the tide rose again and they returned to the island where they dwelt.

When the monk saw these things, he was filled with shame at having thought evil of so holy a man, to whom the very beasts offered service. Indeed, so great was his penitence that his legs shook with grief, and they could scarcely carry him home to the monastery. After morning prayer, he hastened to Cuthbert and besought pardon for what he had done, never doubting but that it had been revealed to him already. But in that he found he was mistaken, for the saint, beholding his distress, said gently, "What is it, my brother? What is the ill-deed that you repent of? Is it that you spied upon me last night when I prayed upon the seashore? Be comforted, for you have my forgiveness; only see you tell no man that which you saw, for I would not be thought holier than I am."

So the monk promised, and departed homeward, after Cuthbert had blessed him.

The years were going by fast, and Cuthbert was no longer as strong as he had been in his youth, and his long walks tired him. But still he would not let another monk take his place, for the people loved him and looked for his coming.

On an autumn morning, he left the monastery to visit a distant spot, taking with him a boy as his companion, and after walking many miles, they sat down to rest, for the way had been steep and rough.

"The village is still far off," said Cuthbert. "Tell me if there is any house on the road where they will give us food, for you are of the country, whereas this part is strange to me." Yet, although he spoke in this way to his companion, he himself knew what would happen.

"I was wondering as to that also," answered the boy, "for I know not a single hut near our path, and we have brought no food with us. Yet if we eat nothing, we shall faint from hunger."

"Fear not, but trust in God," replied Cuthbert. "Behold that eagle flying through the sky above us. It is she that will feed us, so let us continue our journey with a good heart." The boy's face brightened as he listened, and he jumped up eagerly, and with light feet went by the saint's side along the road until they came to a river.

"Look!" said Cuthbert, standing still and pointing to a rock at a little distance. "Do you see where our handmaid the eagle is sitting? Run, I pray, and search and bring back quickly whatsoever the Lord may have sent us." And the boy ran and brought back a salmon, which the eagle had caught and laid on the bank. Now, the salmon was so large the boy could scarcely carry it.

"Why have you not given our handmaid her share, my son?" asked the saint as the boy staggered toward him. "Cut it quickly in two and give her the half she deserves." Then the boy did as he was bid, and they took the other half with them until they beheld

"Why have you not given our handmaid her share, my son?"

a cottage, where they entered; and the woman of the cottage cooked the fish for them, and there was enough for them all, and to spare.

∽

Opposite the coast of Northumberland there is a small island, called Lindisfarne, or Holy Island, which you can reach on foot when the tide is out. It was to this place that Cuthbert was sent in 664 to teach the brethren afresh the rules of the Church and of the holy life, for they had grown careless, and each followed his own will. It was hard work, for not only did he instruct the monks of Lindisfarne and the poor, and those who took advantage of their riches and strength to oppress them, but he visited the sick people as he had done from his boyhood, and was as strict as he had ever been in fasting and in denying himself all that was not absolutely needed.

At first the monks of Lindisfarne declined to obey the new rules of discipline that Cuthbert introduced, and followed the old ones, if they followed any at all, but he was much too wise to quarrel over it. When he saw that they were in a bad temper and likely to be troublesome, he would quietly break up the meeting without taking any notice of their ill-behavior, and at the next assembly began the same discussion and repeated the same things, just as if he had never said them before. In the end, this method, and still more his example, gained his point. The monks ceased to be angry if anyone woke them from their sleep at night, or roused them from their rest at midday, and as Cuthbert's dress was woven of the natural color of the sheep's wool, by and by the brethren were content to lay aside their brighter gowns and wear it also.

As time went on, Cuthbert grew more and more anxious to lay down the burden that he found so heavy and devote a few of the years that remained to him to thinking about his soul. With the consent of the abbot, he had chosen one of a group of seventeen small islands, which lay to the south, as the place of his retirement, and when the monks left him on the little beach, he was perfectly happy — happier perhaps than he had ever been before. For one thing, he was alone. His only companions were the multitudes of wild birds that built their nests in the island rocks. He knew he must not run the risk of making himself ill by sleeping out under the sky as he had often done in his youth, so he began at once to scoop out from the ground a little cell with two rooms in it: one an oratory, the other a living room. This he thatched with straw, and surrounded it with walls of loose stones, which he brought up from the beach. Down by the shore he afterward built a larger house, so that the monks who came over from Lindisfarne to see him might have somewhere to sleep if a sudden storm prevented their getting back to the monastery.

For a short time after he first took up his abode in Farne Island, he had no bread, save what the monks brought to him in a boat, but soon he began to feel that he ought not to put them to that trouble, so he begged them instead to give him some tools and some seed of wheat, that he might get bread for himself. It was spring when he sowed the wheat, but it never came up, and he thought that the soil did not suit it.

"Bring me, I pray you, some seed of barley," he said to the brethren when they next paid him a visit, and the barley when sown sprang up apace, and soon its ears waved in the wind, and the birds beheld it and came in flocks to eat it. But Cuthbert was angry that his toil should be wasted, and he spoke in wrath to the birds: "Begone, you thieves! What do you here? Do you think to reap that which you have not sown? Begone, I say," and the birds departed with a great flutter of wings, as hastily as the asses did from St. Anthony's garden.

No more feathered robbers were seen trying to steal St. Cuthbert's corn, but he was not to live in peace for all that, for one day he perceived two crows who had settled on the island pulling out bits of straw from the roof of the monks' house, in order to build a nest for themselves. Then Cuthbert was moved to anger at them also and forbade them to touch the roof, but, although they flew away for a moment, they returned to their task as soon as they thought the saint had departed. This he had expected, so was watching, and, finding the two crows busily employed as before, he suddenly appeared before them, and commanded them in the name of the Lord to cease spoiling his thatch and to go, which they did sorrowfully.

Three days after, when Cuthbert was digging near the spring, one of the crows alighted on a stone before him and, spreading its wings, bowed its head twice to the ground, uttering plaintive cries. Cuthbert at once understood that it was asking for pardon and answered, "O, bird, I forgive you for your thievish tricks! Return if you will."

On hearing this, the crow flapped its wings joyfully and flew off, returning shortly with its mate, both carrying between them a large piece of fat, which they laid at his feet in token of gratitude.

This fat the saint kept to grease the leathern gaiters of the monks, his visitors.

∞

It was in the year 684 that Cuthbert, much against his own wishes, was made bishop of Lindisfarne; but, when once he had accepted the office, he worked hard and faithfully for his people. Many were the journeys that he took, and the holy men that he visited, even traveling as far as distant Derwentwater to take counsel with St. Herbert, the hermit, in his cell on one of the islands in the middle of the lake. In that same year, a plague was raging in Northumbria, and whole towns and villages were left desolate. Some of the monks feared the infection and shrank away; but, whenever it was possible, the bishop was to be found at every bedside, praying and comforting the sick and dying.

Men shook their heads as they looked on his worn face, which yet was full of peace and joy; and when the plague was over, the bishop felt that his work was done, and he might now leave it for someone else to carry on.

Yet a great deal remained to be gotten through before he could resign his bishopric, and he had to go around to the houses and monasteries of his diocese, to encourage his people to persevere in holiness, and to see that all was set in order as far as he could do it.

It chanced that he was summoned by the abbess Elfleda to consecrate a church, lately built near her monastery in Whitby, on the coast of Yorkshire. It was a long journey for a man as weak as Cuthbert now was, but he did not hesitate, although he was very tired by the time he arrived. There was a large gathering of monks from all the neighboring monasteries, eager to see the famous bishop, and supper was spread on the day of the consecration, in the big refectory; but, while he was speaking of the condition of the Church in the North, and the number of monasteries that had increased so greatly during his lifetime, Cuthbert's knife dropped from his hands, his tongue grew silent, while his face became pale and his eyes stared before him.

The company looked on in wonder; something, they felt, was taking place that they did not understand, and at length a priest leaned forward and said to the abbess, "Ask the bishop what he has seen, for I know that not without cause do his hands tremble so that he cannot hold the knife. His eyes behold a vision that is hidden from us."

The abbess touched the bishop's sleeve and begged him to tell her why he had ceased to eat; for, said she, "of a truth something has happened," to which Cuthbert answered with a smile, "Do you think I can eat forever? It is time that my knife had a little rest!" but she urged him all the more. Then he said gravely, "I have seen the soul of a holy man carried up to the kingdom of Heaven."

"From whence did he go?' asked she.

"From your monastery."

"But what is his name?" she inquired.

"That you will tell me tomorrow when I am celebrating Mass," answered he. But the abbess, not satisfied with this saying of the bishop, sent over to the larger monastery to know if anyone was dead.

Now, when the messenger had reached this monastery, he found all in it alive and well; but as it was late, they besought him to spend the night there, which he did. In the morning, he was returning to the abbey, when he met some men driving a cart containing the dead body of a shepherd, who drove the abbess's sheep daily to find pasture.

"Who is that, and how did he come by his death?" said the messenger, and the men answered, "Hadwald is his name, and he fell last night from the branch of a high tree, and we are taking him to his burial."

When he heard that, he hastened to the abbess; and she, overcome with amazement at the strange tale, entered the church where the bishop was performing service.

"Remember in your prayers, my lord bishop," she cried, interrupting him, "my servant Hadwald, who died yesterday from a fall from a tree."

Thus was the bishop's prophecy fulfilled, that during Mass she should tell him the name of the dead man, which had not been revealed to him.

∞

The moment had now come when Cuthbert had finished his work and could resign his office. A small ship was ready to carry him over to Farne Island, and a crowd of monks and poor people were gathered on the shore to bid him farewell.

"Tell us, my lord bishop," said one, "when you will return to us?" The bishop paused as he was about to enter the boat, and, looking the man in the face, he answered, "When you shall bring my body back to its burial." So he passed on and came no more alive to Lindisfarne.

∞

During the first two months of his stay on the Island of Farne, he was well and content, rejoicing in having no cares to distract his thoughts from the next world, which he was so soon to enter. After that, he suddenly fell ill, and when the abbot of Lindisfarne happened to visit him, he was shocked at the paleness of his face. But Cuthbert made light of his sickness, so the abbot did not understand that he was stricken to death, and only asked for his blessing, as he might not delay, having much business to do at Lindisfarne.

"Do so," Cuthbert answered, "and return home in safety. But when the Lord shall have taken my spirit, bury me in this house, near my oratory, toward the south, over against the eastern side of the holy cross, which I have raised there; and know that there lies under the turf, on the north of the oratory, a stone coffin, given me long ago by Cudda, the abbot. In the coffin is some linen woven by the abbess Verca; in that, wrap my body and place it in the coffin."

"O father!' cried Herfrid. "I cannot leave you ill and alone. Let some of the brethren remain, I beseech you."

"Not now," said Cuthbert. "But when God shall give you a sign, then come."

∞

For five days a tempest raged and the waves reared themselves high, and no boat dared put to sea; but when at last Herfrid, the abbot, contrived to reach the island, he found the bishop sitting in the monks' house by the shore. Bidding the brethren sail back to Lindisfarne, the abbot stayed to tend him, and at Cuthbert's own wish, a priest and sundry of the other monks returned in the morning and were with him when his soul departed to the Lord.

"I will that I am buried here," he said again, shortly before his death. But the monks would not have it so and, with one accord, begged that he would let them carry him over to Lindisfarne, so that his body might lie among them.

Cuthbert did not answer directly, but at length he spoke: "It was my wish to rest here, where I have fought my little battles for the Lord, and whence I hoped to arise and receive the crown of righteousness. And I think that for you too it were better, for at Lindisfarne many evildoers may fly from the mainland to my tomb for refuge, and much trouble would you have with their lords. For, humble though I am, I know full well that I have the name of a servant of Christ."

The words that he spoke were wise, but the monks would not listen to him, and in the end he gave way to their urging. Yet one more counsel he did give: "If you will really carry me to Lindisfarne, then bury me inside the church, so that, although you can visit my grave when you please, you can shut the doors, and prevent, when it seems needful, others from doing so."

A great multitude awaited the boat that bore the body of their bishop back to Lindisfarne, and followed it to the grave, which had been dug by the altar of the Church of St. Peter. Since early morning they had known that he was no longer upon earth, for before the sun rose, they had beheld the light of two candles that one of the monks had carried to the highest rock of the Island of Farne, and there kindled them, as had been agreed, and all men read the tale they told and mourned deeply, as if each had lost his father; for so indeed they felt.

For eleven years Cuthbert's body was left at peace in the church, and then the monks asked the consent of their bishop to gather his bones and to place them in a high tomb they had built on the floor of the church itself. But when the coffin was opened, they fell on their knees, for the saint lay as if asleep, and the vestments wherein they had wrapped him were fresh and unspotted. By command of the bishop, the vestments were taken off and kept as relics, and new ones brought to clothe him; and in this manner the body was laid in a chest and placed in the tomb on the pavement.

∞

Nearly two hundred years went by, and a horde of Danish pirates swooped down upon the northern coasts, burning and murdering as they went. The monks at Lindisfarne had warning of their coming and fled, carrying with them the body of Cuthbert and all his relics. These they left for a time in Chester-le-Street and, as soon as that was no longer safe, conveyed them to Ripon, and finally to Durham, and in 1104 Cuthbert's body was placed in the new cathedral, where it still lies. Simeon the Chronicler assures us that, although more than four hundred years had gone by since his death, the saint still bore the semblance of life.

Dead as well as alive, Cuthbert was strong to protect the weak, for, as he had foretold, there was a right of sanctuary at his grave, until Henry VIII suppressed the monasteries and did away with all such privileges, forgetful how his own mother in her childhood had sought refuge in the sanctuary of Westminster. No doubt, as the bishop had said, many criminals *did* escape by reason of such places, but on the whole they saved the lives of a multitude of helpless people in those lawless times.

The Exiled Monk

It is always very hard to understand the lives led by people in our own country hundreds and hundreds of years ago, when they had none of the things that are so common with us that we do not even think about them. We can picture quite easily the manners in which the Greeks, the Romans, or even the Assyrians passed their time, for the customs of the dwellers in cities are really much the same in all ages. But as for knowing the ways of the wild men who had their homes where Belfast or Glasgow or Aberdeen now stand — why, that is a very different matter!

If you had been traveling slowly and painfully through the British Isles fourteen hundred years ago, in the sixth century after Christ, you would hardly have recognized it to be the same country you know so well. The sea is the only thing that is quite unchanged. On the East Coast of England even that has advanced nearer and nearer, until the base of the cliffs has been eaten away, and rocks have fallen, and whole towns have been swallowed up by the waves. The mountains too might not have worn exactly the same shapes that we look at. Snow and ice have torn great holes in their sides, and the rocks, slipping down, have changed the courses of the rivers. Instead of turf and heather, forests then often grew up to the top; and the swampy lands, at that time bright in the summer with forget-me-nots and yellow water-lilies, are now golden with corn and pretty dancing oats.

∽

Thus it was into a world strange to us that Columba was born in the year 520. His parents were kinsmen of some of the proudest Irish kings, and his mother's name, Ethne, or Enna, as it is called, is still to be found among Irish children. They had their home in a wild part of Donegal, on the northwest coast of Ireland, where you can lie on the great cliffs all day and look far out across the Atlantic, while clouds of seabirds flutter and screech around you. Sea-trout and other fish were to be had for the asking, and wild duck and game abounded in the marshes and forests further inland.

We are not told how Columba passed his boyhood, but we may be sure that besides fishing, and shooting with his bow and arrow, he was taught the Christian Faith and heard tales from his mother of the manner in which the saints of old had died rather than sacrifice on the altars of the pagans.

By and by, Ethne noticed that the boy spent less and less time in the sports that once had filled his thoughts, and more and more time alone brooding. Now and then Columba would ask her a question, but for the most part he was silent. She guessed what was working in his mind, but said nothing and waited until he should speak.

At length the moment came. He wanted to be a priest. Would his father and mother tell him what to do?

∽

A few months later, Columba set out and walked over the mountains, and across what we now call Ulster, until he reached Strangford Lough, on the eastern coast of Ireland. On the shores of the bay, which is almost a lake, dwelt Bishop Finnian, whose fame for holiness had spread even into Donegal. On hearing the youth's errand, the bishop gave him a warm welcome and promised to teach him all he knew. So for several years, Columba remained in this quiet place, where, when the bishop thought him fit, he was ordained a deacon.

After that, St. Finnian thought that Columba had stayed with him long enough and that it would be better for him to learn from other teachers. So with great sorrow he bade the young man farewell and commanded him to take counsel of his friend Gemman and to follow his advice. This Columba promised to do, and the advice Gemman gave him was to go into a monastery, where, after a while, he was made a priest.

The monasteries of those days were not the big stone buildings they became many centuries later, but in general were nothing better than a collection of huts, with an oratory for the monks to pray in. Columba wandered from one to the other, until at length he began to weary of new faces and strange speech, and to long for his native country; and one day he said goodbye to his friends, and in 545, when he was twenty-five years old, he turned his face northward and once more entered Ulster, then known as Scotia. This is very confusing, as in reading of those days we must never forget that the "Scots" are really the men of Ulster.

Now, Irishmen have always gotten the character of being fond of fighting, and there are no better soldiers in the whole British Army. But when they carry their love of a fight into their daily life, they are apt to get into trouble. At that time, everybody fought in Ireland. Even the women were expected to take their part in a battle, just as the Amazons did in the Greek stories. Bishops and priests, holy as many of them were accounted, were foremost in all the quarrels and, for hundreds of years, formed with their followers a large portion of the armies all over Europe.

It is no surprise, therefore, to learn that after a while Columba, who had been traveling about, founding churches and monasteries, was accused of stirring up strife between some of the Irish kings, which ended in bloodshed. For this he was excommunicated — that is, forbidden to say Mass or perform any of the church services; and as life was very painful to him under these circumstances, he resolved to cross the water and take up his abode in the new lands to the north, where he might be free.

One morning he set sail in a small boat and, with a fair south wind behind him, landed at the island of Hy, or Iona, where he spent his remaining thirty-four years, although he visited Ireland more than once and loved it more than any place on earth.

∞

The island of Iona, forever bound up with the name of St. Columba, lay on the border between the Christian Scots, who had previously come over from Ireland and had settled in the country, and the pagan Picts, whose territory was on the north and east. It was necessary to obtain the consent of both nations before Columba made his home on the island, so he lost no time in visiting the Pictish king, who bade him welcome. They had many talks together, and in the end, Columba succeeded in converting the pagan chief and also gained permission to found the famous monastery on Hy.

But he did not always stay on the island. On fine days, he would get into one of the curious little wicker-boats covered with skins, called coracles, and sail to the opposite shore, where he preached to the people and made friends with them. Far and wide he wandered, and many were the churches he built and the adventures that befell him.

One day, as he and a small company of monks were walking through a glen, he noticed some wild-looking men crouching behind the rocks, apparently lying in wait for him. Find Uigan, who was with him, saw them also, for the sun above caught the glint of their spears. He snatched the cowl, or loose hood, that covered St. Columba's head and put it on his own, hoping thereby to deceive the strange men into thinking that he himself was Columba, so that they would take his life instead of his master's. But quick as he was, their eyes were quicker still. Find Uigan was pushed aside, and the spear thrust past him. Columba fell with the shock of the blow, and the murderer went away satisfied that he had killed his enemy, and never knowing that the weapon had not so much as torn a hole in Columba's garments, which were as hard to pierce as if they were made of polished steel.

Greatly was Columba loved throughout the land, yet he was feared a little too, for he could speak sternly if need be, and expected men to obey him. And tales were told by one and another of the marvelous deeds he had done, and to the faith of his followers nothing seemed too marvelous for St. Columba. He loved birds and beasts too and was grateful to any creature that showed him kindness, which he never failed to repay in some way or another.

Once he reached Lochaber, the home of the fairies, very wet and tired, for he had sailed early that morning from Iona and, after beating about the long narrow sea that divides the island of Mull from Morvern, had nearly been wrecked on one of the rocks on the eastern shores of Loch Linnhe. Scarcely able to crawl, he entered the hut of rough wood, with its covering of woven twigs, which belonged to Nesan the crooked. Now, Nesan was a very poor man, but his door was open to all, and he bade the saint welcome and set before him milk and coarse bread.

"How many cows have you?" asked Columba when he had finished his supper.

"Five, counting the black one," said Nesan.

"I will bless them, and they shall become a hundred and five, neither more nor less," said the saint. And so they did, but if a calf happened to be born into the herd, a cow died to make up for it. And thus it was always with the herd of Nesan.

∞

Columba had returned to Iona and was sitting alone in his cell when one of the brethren passed by on his way to catch some fish.

"Listen to me," said Columba, "and see that you hearken unto my words. On the morning of the third day from this, you must go down to the shore on the west side of the island and sit on a rock and wait there. By and by you will behold, blown by the winds and very weary, a crane that is a stranger to the country of the Picts and has come from the north of Hibernia, where I myself dwelt in my infancy. Far out of its course the winds have taken it, and after the ninth hour of the day it can struggle no longer and will sink on the sand at your feet. Treat that crane tenderly, and warm it in your bosom, and carry it to some neighboring house, where they will be good to it and tend it carefully for three days and nights.

"When the crane is refreshed, and its strength has come back to it, it will flutter its wings and long to return to the pleasant land it has left. See, therefore, that you do not then hinder it, but set wide the door so that it may fly south."

So spoke Columba, wishing perhaps in his heart that he might fly back with the crane, for seldom indeed had he trodden the soil of Donegal during the years since Hy had been his home.

"As you say, so will I do," answered the monk, and he waited on the western shore until the crane was borne to him by the wind, as Columba had foretold.

∞

"My crops are ruined by the rain and the stones that the great storms have swept down from the mountains into their midst," said a poor man one day, throwing himself on his knees before Columba. "My wife can make no bread, and the children will starve unless you will help me."

Columba looked at him and knew that he spoke truly, and pity filled the heart of the saint.

"Take this. It is all I have," he said, holding out some coins. "But hurry swiftly to that wood yonder, and cut a branch from a tree, and bring it back to me." The peasant hid the money in his wallet and hastened to cut the branch, which was straight and supple as a wand, and held it out to Columba, who sharpened one end with a knife.

"Have a care of this stake, my friend, for as long as you keep it, never will you be without food. It will harm neither men nor cattle, but a fish or a wild beast that touches it will die. And now, farewell," and without waiting to hear the peasant's words of gratitude, Columba entered the hut.

The poor man forgot his miseries, in the joy of knowing that they were ended, and he went at once to the depths of the forest near his home, where the wild beasts came in numbers to drink from a pool. Here he drove in the stake with a firm hand and then, returning to his wooden hut, told his wife of the wonderful thing that had happened. All that night he lay awake, counting the hours as they went by, and when the grey light stole in through the hole in the roof, he arose and ran like the wind to the forest. There, sure enough, lay a dead stag, pierced through the heart by the stake, and gladly did he tie together some branches of trees and, placing on them the body of the stag, brought it home to his wife.

"This will give us meat for many a day," he shouted as she hurried out of the hut. "And the skin will make me a warm coat, which I need sorely."

For some time, things prospered greatly with the peasant. Each day a deer was found lying dead in the forest, and when the man's wife did not want it to cook for themselves, she gave it to the neighbors in exchange for other things.

But at length the woman grew so used to having plenty to eat, that she quite forgot the words the saint had spoken to her husband, and one day she said, "Throw away that stake. We can do quite well without it, and if one of the king's men or his cattle were to get hurt by it, of a certainty we ourselves should be taken as slaves or put to death."

"Not so," replied her husband. "Remember, the holy Columba bade me keep the stake in the ground if we wanted food. Do you wish to starve, as we did before?'

"That is but talk," answered the wife. "But now that we have grown rich by selling the deer for meal and wool, the stake is no more good to us." And although the man was not persuaded that she was in the right, at last he grew weary of listening to her and, taking up the stake, brought it up to the hut, and leaned it against the wall, while he considered what to do with it. Then there was peace for a while, until one of the children tripped over the root of a tree, and staggered up against the stake, which, in falling, ran him through the body so that he died.

Terrible was the grief of the woman when she saw her dead son lying on the ground with the stake beside him, but she would not confess that the saint had spoken truly, and that the fault was hers. Her husband indeed knew, but by long talking his wife had made him also half-afraid of the wrath of the king if his beasts were slain, and he put more faith in her than he did in the holy Columba. Therefore, when sobbing, she bade him never let her see anymore the stake that had caused her such sorrow, he hid it in a clump of bushes so thick that he thought no beast could get through them.

As before, he rose early next morning and went to the place, no longer hoping, but fearing that he might find a dead deer awaiting him. And so it was. Then, stealthily looking round to make sure that no one was watching, he snatched the stake from the ground and pushed his way through the bushes to the bank of the river. Here he stooped down and laid it carefully under the water, in a line with the bank, wedging the end between two stones, so that it might be held fast.

With a lightened heart he returned to the hut and bade his wife be easy, for he had gotten rid of the stake forever, and there was nothing more to be feared from the king.

"You are sure that you have fixed it firmly?" she asked. "For the salmon are caught here for the king's table, and if one was to be killed by anyone else, heavy would be the punishment."

"Have no fear," answered the man. "You can come with me and make certain," and after dinner they went together to the riverbank.

"Did I not say so?" cried she, pointing to a huge salmon transfixed by the stake against which it had swum blindly.

"Well, nought will make it alive again, so you had better carry it home, and I myself will bear the stake and put it on the roof, where it can harm no one." And so he did, and that same evening a crow flew against it, and fell dead down the chimney hole into the hut.

"It might be one of the king's falcons next," muttered the woman, turning pale. "Let us make an end of it," and she seized a hatchet, and chopping the stick in pieces, threw them on the fire.

"What are we going to have for dinner today?" asked one of the children, when the big salmon had been cooked and eaten; and the father and mother looked at each other, for suddenly they understood how great had been their foolishness, and how, by burning the magic stake, they had of their own free will turned themselves again into beggars. Even the saint could do no more for them. They had thrown away the gift he had bestowed, and for the future they must find their own food, or go without it.

∞

Columba had left Lochaber and crossed the mountains, preaching as he went, until he reached the place where the town of Inverness now stands. There the river Ness is broad and swiftly flowing, but Columba and his brethren had to cross it, as they had business to do on the other side. No boats were to be seen within reach, but on the opposite bank lay one called a coble, and Columba was about to order one of the monks to swim across and fetch it over, when he beheld the body of a man floating on the water, with blood flowing from his thighs.

"Cast a rope over him and bring him to land. Perhaps he is not dead," cried the saint, but a boy who was passing shook his head.

"He was swimming in the river when the monster who dwells in the bottom rose up and bit him, and none who is bitten by that monster escapes." And the boy's words were true, for when the man was brought to shore, there was no breath left in him.

"Cross we must," repeated Columba. "Who will bring that coble across? Lugne, you are a strong swimmer. Will you go?"

"Willingly," answered Lugne, throwing off his cloak, but his plunge disturbed the water, and the monster wakened out of his sleep, came up to the surface, and, roaring until the monks shook with terror, dashed after Lugne.

"He is lost too, our comrade," whispered one to another, as with a rush the huge beast swam to within a spear's length of Lugne, but Columba stepped out from among them and held up his hand.

"Go back with all speed whence you came," he said, "for this man is safe from you." And with another roar, louder than the first, the monster dived beneath the water and was seen no more.

After his business was ended, Columba returned to Iona, and there in a vision he beheld his friend Cormac, who had sailed away to discover a desert in the ocean in great danger, together with the men on board his ship. For the space of fourteen days, a south wind had blown, which had driven him northward, far away to the land of silence, amid mountains of glittering ice. A few days more, and his boat would be stuck fast, and even now loathsome insects as large as frogs appeared — none could tell whence — and pressed in armies over the prow and sides and stern of the little ship until Cormac dreaded lest the leathern covering should be pierced through, and crowded on the handles of the oars, stinging the hands of those who grasped them. All this Columba saw, and he called to his monks, and told them of his vision, and they knelt together and prayed that the wind might blow from the north, and send Cormac back to them. And at that hour, the wind changed, and the horrible creatures disappeared in the cracks of the ice, and in due time Cormac was among them again.

∞

Thus passed the years, until Columba counted thirty winters since he had left his home for Iona. He had done much work, had preached all over the land, had founded churches, and had sent forth missionaries like himself, and now he was tired and longed to go to his rest. But although he was more than seventy, he was strong and well, and this he took as a sign that the day of his death was not yet at hand, and that other tasks awaited him.

He was sitting one morning with some of the brethren in his little hut, planning out what each one was to do. In the midst of telling them how to reach a distant church on the mainland, he paused, and a bright light shone on his face. In an instant it faded as suddenly as it had come, and a deep sadness took its place.

"What is it?" asked his friends. "Why do you look first so glad and then so sorrowful?'"

Columba did not reply for a moment. Then he said, "If I tell you the reason, you must all hold your peace, for the world may not know it yet. Thirty years and more have I spent in Iona, and now I long that death may come and fetch me. Here, in the presence of you all, I have had my answer: 'Your prayers, O Columba, have been heard.' This it was that filled my heart with joy; but my joy was speedily turned into grief, for the voice, for which I alone had ears, continued: 'Be patient, and in four years a messenger will come for you.' So in patience I must abide, but the time seems long."

"Your sorrow is our joy," replied the brethren; then, at a sign from Columba, they went out.

These last years were spent much like the others, and only those monks who had been that day in the hut knew that Columba, even when full of thoughts and plans for others, was secretly counting the minutes until they were ended. At length they saw by the brightening of his face that his time on earth was nearly over, and as far as he would let them, they never left him, and treasured up his few words.

"Get me the cart," he said early one morning, "for I must visit the settlement on the other side, and let two of you go with me."

Silently the journey was made, and when they reached the halting-place, the saint went from one brother to the other, giving counsel as to the work they had to do and bidding them take heed to his words, as it was the last time he should be among them. He looked so little like a dying man that hardly would they believe him, but when he had finished giving counsel to each one, he mounted the cart, and, standing up, blessed them and the island and all that was in it, and promised that forever after, their dreaded enemy, the snakes, with the three-forked tongues, should have no power to hurt them.

∞

The day before he died, he went out into the fields and entered the barns where the corn was stored.

"It will last throughout the year," he said to his followers and gave the corn his blessing. Then he left the barn and turned homeward, but feeling suddenly tired, he sat down to rest, where a cross was fixed into a millstone. While he sat there, a horse, used by the monks to carry milk pails from the cowshed to the monastery, passed by and drew near to Columba, and laid his head on the saint's breast and wailed loudly, tears running from his eyes.

"What ails the creature?" cried the man who was following, and he would have driven him away, had not Columba stopped him, for the tears were in his eyes also.

The horse laid his head on the saint's breast and wailed loudly.

"Let the horse alone, that he may pour his grief into my bosom, if he will. For he loves me and is wiser than many men, and knows that I am about to leave him."

So, his waiting time over, and caring to the end for those who loved him, whether man or beast, the death that Columba had prayed for came to him.

Sailor Saint

In reading the lives of the Irish saints, we are amazed and almost confused at the number of wonderful things told about them. The Irish are always fond of marvels and of turning everyday events into a story, and when they began to tell about their holy men and women, they were not contented unless they surrounded them with strange signs and gave them gifts and powers beyond those of common people. This is the reason every Irish saint is a worker of miracles from his cradle and that prophecies showing his future greatness attend his birth. A saint would not have been a saint at all in their eyes if he had been a baby like other babies, so his father and his mother and even friends at a distance see visions concerning him, and one person repeats the tale to another and, like most tales, it grows with the telling.

∞

Now, the morning after Brendan was born, somewhere about 490, a rich man, who lived a long way off, arrived at the house of Finnlog, father of Brendan, driving thirty cows and thirty calves before him.

"These are for the baby who will be a great saint," he said, kneeling before the cradle. "For thus it was made known to me last night in a dream." Then Finnlog feasted him and bade him rest awhile, but Airde, the giver of the cows, would not listen to him.

"I have far to travel," he answered, "and many rivers to cross. I must be gone in haste lest night fall and the waters drown me." So he took farewell of them.

Hardly was he out of sight when Finnlog beheld someone else climbing the hill to his dwelling. "It is the holy Bishop Eirc," he thought, "and great honor it is that he does me." Then Finnlog went to meet him and bowed low before the bishop.

"O Finnlog!" said the bishop. "Last night as I slept, I beheld a wood in the midst of fire, and in the fire angels in bright and white garments passing up and down. Such a sight I have never seen, no, nor heard of, and a voice within me told me to arise and come to you, for in your house I should find the infant who someday will be the glory of Ireland."

"Enter then," answered Finnlog, "for the voice spoke truly," and the bishop entered and did homage to the baby.

"I will baptize him," he said, and Finnlog and his wife gladly consented thereto, and when that was done, the bishop returned whence he had come.

For a year Brendan remained with his mother, who nursed him and watched over him. But at the end of that time, she delivered him up with many tears to Bishop Eirc, and Ita, who herself had watched over the childhood of Eirc, tended Brendan also. Greatly she loved him, and often she saw him surrounded by angels whom no other could see, and Brendan himself did not know it. For five years Ita took care of him, and weary seemed the hours to her when he had left her side and was in the house of Bishop Eirc, reading the Psalms and learning about holy things.

∞

"I am thirsty," said Brendan one morning, for the sun was hot and the walk from Ita's house felt longer than usual.

"By the grace of God you shall quench your thirst, my son," answered the bishop, and on looking up, Brendan beheld a hind approaching, with a little fawn trotting behind her. At a sign from the bishop, a woman came near and milked the hind and gave Brendan to drink of the milk. And every day, the hind appeared with the fawn trotting after her, and when Brendan had drunk as much milk as he wanted, they returned to the mountains, whence they had come.

"I would learn to write," said Brendan another day, when he was older. So the bishop taught him, and after he could write quickly and well, Eirc sent him away, first to this person and then to that, teachers of the rules of the church, which every man had to know if, like Brendan, he wished to become a priest. And when he knew them, he returned to Eirc, who received him into the priesthood.

∽

For a while, he stayed quietly with Bishop Eirc, until on a Sunday a sermon was preached in the place where he was, and this was the text: "Everyone that hath forsaken father or mother or sister or lands for my sake shall receive a hundredfold in the present, and shall possess everlasting life." As he listened, the will grew strong in Brendan to gain that which was promised, and in his prayers he begged to have a land given him where he might dwell apart from men, at peace, and hidden. As he slept, a voice came to him and said, "Arise, O Brendan! Your prayers are heard, and the Lord has granted what you have asked, even the Land of Promise." Then Brendan arose, as he was bidden, and, with the holy voice still sounding in his ears, went up a high mountain from which he beheld the sea, and in the midst of the sea, hanging like a cloud, an island like a pearl, and from the island angels flew up to and down from Heaven.

During three days he stayed on the mountains, and most of the time he slept. And again an angel spoke to him and said, "I will go beside you forevermore and will guide you to the island."

After that Brendan came down from the mountain and went back to Finnlog's house. Long it was since his mother had seen him, but he told her that he could not abide with her, for he was going far out into the ocean if only his father would build for him three large ships with sails made of skins, and three rows of oars, with ten men to each row. This Finnlog did gladly, and the men to row the ships were found; some of them were monks and some were not.

For five years Brendan sailed the "awful bitter ocean," and they passed many islands, fair and green, but Brendan would not suffer his men to land. Strange wonders they saw as they rode over the sea: great whales tossing pillars of water into the air, porpoises tumbling and vanishing under the waves, red-mouthed monsters hideous to look upon.

As they went, the skies grew clearer and the air warmer, and by and by, Easter was at hand.

"Where are we to keep our Easter?" asked the monks, and Brendan made answer, as the angel had bidden him: "Yonder, on the island that lies there."

Now, he knew, for the angel had told him, that it was no island, but the back of a huge whale, but the men did not know it. So they landed and heard Mass, and then they made a fire and put on a pot to boil so that they might roast a lamb for their Passover. But when the fire began to blaze, the island began to move under them, until their hearts grew frightened and they ran, every man as fast as he could, down to the water. And scarcely had they gotten on board their ships again when the island vanished in the sea. But still they knew not that it was a whale, but thought it was enchantment. Then Brendan told them it was no island, but so large was that whale that its head and tail could never meet, although it often tried to make them do so. From this time they returned to that place every year at Easter for seven years, and always the whale was awaiting them.

∞

Many were the wonders that Brendan and his men beheld while they sailed over those seas, and often they thought that the ship would be sucked down in the black whirlpools or driven onto the bare, sharp rocks, but in the end they always escaped. Once they beheld a thick cloud hanging before them, and when they drew nearer, they saw through the cloud a man sitting on a rock. Before him hung a cloth that flapped in the wind on his face, while icy waves broke over his head.

"Who are you?" asked Brendan, marveling at the sight. "And what do you here?"

And the man answered, "I am that most wretched Judas who made the worst of all bargains, and once in seven days grace is given me to escape from the fires of Hell and cool my burning soul in the sea."

As they listened, awe and pity fell upon the men, and they rowed away in silence.

After they had left the rock of Judas behind them, they passed an island whose cliffs were bright with flowers and whose waters were blue and sparkling. But there was no place for them to land between the cliffs, even though for twelve days they rowed around searching for one. Only men's voices were heard singing praises to God, and at the sound a deep sleep fell upon Brendan and his companions. When they awoke, a tablet of wax was lying in their ship, and on it was written, "Waste not time in trying to enter this island, for that you will never do. Return now to your country, for there is work for you there, and in the end you shall come to the land you are seeking." And when Brendan had read the words he commanded the men to row back to Ireland.

Seven years had now passed since Brendan sailed away, and glad were the people to see him once more. They pressed around him, eager to hear all that he had seen and done, and they brought

"I am that most wretched Judas."

him gifts and besought him for help in their troubles. He stayed with them for a while, and then he left them and went to Eirc, the bishop, and to Ita, his foster-mother. And Ita bade him go into Connaught and build a ship large enough to withstand the waves of the ocean and to carry him to the Land of Promise.

A long time that ship took in building, but when it was finished, he placed in it his monks and his servants who had voyaged with him, and not knowing whither they might be going, he ordered them to take seeds of corn to sow and plants that they might put in the earth, while some carpenters and blacksmiths came and begged that they might sail in that ship also. At length all was ready, everyone had gone on board, and Brendan was about to follow them, when the king's fool was seen hurrying down the hill, and he made signs to Brendan to stop.

"What is it, my son?" asked Brendan when the fool drew near, and the man fell on his knees and answered, "O Brendan! Have pity on my misery and take me also, for I am weary of my life at the king's court."

"Come then," said Brendan, and the man climbed over the ship's side and made one with the rest. Now there were sixty men on board that vessel.

First they sailed north, toward the Isle of Arran, and then the tiller was put about, and they sailed west. Soon they reached a lofty island down whose sides the rushing streams made music, but they could not land by reason of the sea-cats that sat in crowds on the rocks, waiting to devour them if they should go on shore, or to swarm on the ship if it approached near enough.

"What do these sea-cats want?" said one to another, and Brendan answered, "To eat us have they come." Then he spoke to the fool, saying, "I hear the angels calling to you to go and enter into eternal life," and Brendan's words seemed good to the fool, and he stood on the prow of the ship and leaped ashore, his face shining with gladness at the thought of giving his life to save his friends, and the sea-cats rushed at him and devoured him, while the ship rowed away and the men were unharmed.

∞

Westward they went again, until they beheld another island and on it was a church and, by the church, an old man praying. Now, the old man was so thin that he seemed to have nothing over his bones. He rose from his knees at the sight of the ship and hastened to the shore and called loudly to Brendan, "Flee swiftly, or evil will overtake you. Know that in this island is a great sea-cat, tall as a young ox or a three-year-old horse, for it has grown a monstrous size from feeding on the fish, which, as you may behold, abound in these waters; and the sea is as much its home as the land." With that they quickly took their seats and grasped their oars and rowed away as fast as they could into the broad ocean, but in the distance behind them they saw a speck, and the speck grew larger and larger as it swiftly drew nearer.

"It is the sea-cat," said they, and the sea-cat it was, with a boar's tusks in its head and its eyes bright as a brazen pot; and its strength was the strength of a lion, and its appetite that of a hound. As the men looked, their hearts melted with fear, and even Brendan shrank at the sight of it, so they all prayed that they might be delivered from that monster; and while they prayed, there appeared a huge whale right between them and the sea-cat. Then a fight began, such as never before had been seen in that ocean, and sometimes one got the better and sometimes the other. But at length the teeth of the sea-cat were so firmly fixed in the body of the whale, and the whale's tail so tightly wrapped round the legs of the sea-cat that neither could swim anymore, and they both sank to the bottom and were made fast in the crack of a rock, so that they died.

When Brendan and his men beheld that, they gave thanks and rowed back to the island, where the old man stood on the shore.

He wept tears of joy at the sight of them, for he had watched the sea-cat start in pursuit of the ship and knew not what the end would be. So he made them welcome, and sitting beside them on the rocks, he told them how he had come there.

"There were twelve of us," he said, "and we set out from Ireland to sail on a pilgrimage, and we brought that monstrous sea-cat with us, for it was then small as a little bird and very dear to us. After that it ate of the fish that lie under the cliffs and grew large and strong as you beheld it, but never did it harm any of us. One by one, eleven of us died, and now that you have come to listen to my confession, I can die also."

Then he made his confession, but first he showed them how they should come to the Land of Promise that they were seeking, and after that he died, and they buried him with his brethren.

∽

In those seas, the islands are many, and often did Brendan cause the anchor of the ship to be dropped, so that he might land, lest anyone should be living in that place, needing help or counsel. Sometimes he would sail across the ocean so far that not so much as a bare rock could he behold, nothing but water around him and the sky above, unless indeed the prow of the vessel was set northward, when wonderful pillars of glittering ice would float toward them, showing colors of red and green in the sunlight, and blue in the shadows as the night came on. But well the helmsman knew that he must keep far away from those mountains of ice, or they would break his ship in pieces and drown all who were therein.

"Set the ship's course to the southward, for the holy St. Gildas has summoned me in a dream, and we must needs go to him," said Brendan. For many days they sailed, until at length a rough wild coast appeared before them.

"Tomorrow we shall be there," said he, "if the wind is behind us."

And the men were glad, for they had come from far and were weary. That night Gildas in his monastery had a dream also, and he saw in his dream Brendan and his companions drawing near the shore. Then he bade much food to be prepared and ordered the porter to shut fast the great door with iron bars and bolts so that none might enter.

When Brendan and his monks stepped on land, it was all covered with snow, and thick, soft flakes were falling still, but none fell upon Brendan and his friends. Greatly were they amazed to find the door bolted and barred instead of standing wide, so that all who would might enter. From within the porter heard their voices and cried to them, "I may not let you in, but at the word of so holy a man the door will open." At that Brendan bade Talmach, his follower, to stretch forth his hand to the door, and as he did so, the bolts withdrew of themselves and they all passed into the monastery.

Three days Brendan spent in that place, and then Gildas, the wise, spoke to him: "In the wilderness nearby dwell a number of fierce wild beasts, which are dreaded by all the people and are so bold that they even venture up the gates of the monastery itself. No man has been able to slay them, although many have sought to do so. So now help us, and by the power given you, subdue those beasts so that they do no more hurt." Then Brendan, with Talmach, his follower, went into the wilderness, and men on horses rode after them, to see what would happen.

After walking for a while over the wide moor, with gorse and heather about them, they reached a cluster of rocks and beheld a lioness asleep in the sun, with her cubs about her.

"Go and arouse her, O Talmach!" said Brendan, and Talmach went. Softly though his feet sounded on the grass, the lioness heard him and sprang up with a roar, which was echoed from the throats of the other beasts, which rushed to the spot where the man stood. But as they came, Brendan looked at them and said:

"Follow us now quietly, and let the cubs follow also," and in this manner they returned to the town that lay outside the monastery. At the gates, Brendan stopped and spoke to the wild beasts again, saying, "From henceforth you will guard the sheep and the cows when they go out to feed, and will watch that no wolves come near them."

And this the beasts did forevermore.

∞

After this it was time for Brendan to sail northward again, and he took farewell of Gildas and entered his ship. And near the Irish shore he stopped at a little island, where an old man dwelt alone, and right glad was the old man to see Brendan.

"How came you here?" asked the saint. "You are so old that many years must have passed since you quitted your country."

"You say truly," answered the hermit. "And now you have come to give me your blessing, I shall be suffered to depart in peace, for I am tired of this life and would fain be finished with it."

"Have you always been alone?" asked Brendan.

"No, verily," answered the hermit. "Once we were three — young men all — who set out on a pilgrimage. A cake for each was all the food we brought, but I took my little cat also. For a while after we left the shore, we rowed our boat, but then we cast away our oars and let it drift as it would, knowing that the Lord would guide us; and the waves rocked us until we found ourselves in a harbor where green slopes ran down to the sea. There we landed and looked about to choose a spot in which we could build a church, and at last we found one in the midst of the island.

"Then I looked around for my cat, which I had forgotten, but it was nowhere to be seen, which grieved me sorely, for much did I love it. In the evening, when the sun was sinking over the sea, I beheld a strange beast approaching from afar, but of a shape that I knew not.

" 'What beast is that?' I said to my companions, and the one whose eyes could reach beyond those of common men answered me, 'It is your little cat, and in its mouth it bears a salmon twice its own size.' And my heart rejoiced to know my little cat was coming back to me. And thrice each day the little cat brought us a salmon in his mouth.

"But at length the thought entered our minds that it was not the duty of a pilgrim to let himself be fed by a cat, although in our setting out, we knew not that so it would be. And one said, 'Although we brought no food with us, yet in bringing our cat, we brought plenty. We will therefore eat no more of the cat's providing, but he shall eat of the salmon himself. Yet, because he has been kind to us, we will be kind to him all the days of his life.' So we fasted for twenty-four hours, and then it was made known to us that on the altar of the church we would find every day a wheaten cake and a piece of fish for each man.

"Since that, many years have passed. My friends have died and my cat, and now give me your blessing, that I may die also."

Then Brendan blessed him, and he died as he had wished.

The ship sailed away until it reached an island known as the Paradise of Birds, for snow-white birds covered it from end to end, as many and as bright as the angels of Heaven. Thence they set the helm westward, and, when forty days were over, a thick cloud wrapped the vessel, so that the men could scarcely see each other. But after an hour, the cloud vanished; a great light shone round about them, and there lay before them the island they had sought for seven years.

"Rest here awhile, O weary ones," said a voice, "for this is the Land of Promise."

So they rested and ate of the fruits, and listened to heavenly music and gazed at the flowers, which were brighter far than those of earth. And when they were rested, an angel came to them and bade them return home, for their wanderings were done and the work of Brendan lay in his monastery among his own people.

But fruits and precious stones they were to bear with them, so that all might know whither they had come.

Charm Queller

Senan's parents had two farms, and sometimes they lived at one and sometimes at the other. Whenever they wished to change, they bade Senan go before to see that all was ready. Always Senan had a comfortable house for them, and sheds for the cattle they drove before them, and a yard for the fowls, and everything they needed. For he loved to give help, and none knew how to do it better than he.

But once it happened that Senan had not gone to the farm as he had been bidden, for a neighbor was in trouble and wanted counsel. As soon as his mother beheld him enter the house, when she thought he was far away, she was angry and spoke hard words, telling him that nought would be prepared, and the fault would be his.

"Small use you are to us," she ended in wrath. But Senan only smiled at her.

"Be at rest, O mother!" he said. "Fear not. You shall have what is needful." And as they journeyed toward the farm, they beheld the sheds and the house and the tools, which they had left behind, flying past them through the air; and the things settled themselves down, each in its own place.

Other miracles were done by Senan before he had yet reached manhood, but they are too many to tell. The time was now near when he should become a priest, although he knew it not, and this is how that came to pass.

Gergenn, his father, one day bade Senan take the oxen out of the farm in the west, and drive them toward the farm in the east, and Senan got ready to do his bidding. The way was long, and at nightfall they still had far to travel, for oxen go slowly. Senan was puzzled as to where he should leave the oxen until the morning, for the tide was full, and it would be many hours before he could drive them along the sands. Glad was he, then, when he perceived the fortress of Machar close by, for surely, he thought, there will be a courtyard there, where my beasts may shelter. So he commanded the beasts to lie down where they stood and await him, while he knocked at the door of the house.

Now, Machar was not in the fort on that night, and the steward whom he had left in charge spoke rude words to Senan and refused him entrance, and Senan returned to where his oxen lay and sat beside them until the tide should flow out again; and as soon as the sands were clear, he called the oxen to rise up and go, and he himself followed behind them, the waves washing his heels as he went. He was angry and sore at the way in which he had been treated at the fortress of Machar, and he said to himself as he followed his oxen over the sands, "I have done this work long enough. Henceforth I will do that of a priest." And as he spoke, he broke the spear he held in his hand to drive away the wolves, and he tied the two pieces into a cross and set it firmly in the ground beyond the high-water mark; then, kneeling beside it, he made a vow.

After that, he rose and went his way, not knowing that during the next night the fortress of Machar was plundered by robbers and the wife of Machar carried captive.

∞

Leaving the oxen with his father, Senan journeyed to a holy man named Cassidan, who made him a priest, and taught him his psalms and the rules that were to guide him through life. But if he expected to escape from herding cattle, greatly was he mistaken, for he found that every man in the school of Cassidan took his turn in driving the cows and calves that belonged to the church to pasture. And although the beasts went quietly enough with all others, as soon as Senan called them from their sheds into the fields, a spirit of evil seemed to take possession of them. When he collected the calves on one side to drive them into a meadow by themselves, the cows would follow after them and go each one to her own calf; and when he collected the cows on the other side, the calves would run after them, each one to its own mother. This they did many times, until Senan drew a line with his staff on the ground between them, and neither dare step over it.

Then he took out his psalter and learned his psalms, until the hour came for the cows to be milked.

In that year, a great famine fell upon the land, and robbers went about plundering the people. On a certain night, one robber said to another, "Let us go, when it grows dark, to the mill of Cell Manach, where a solitary man grinds corn; and easily can we slay him and bring home enough corn to last us many weeks."

"We will do that," answered his companion, and they set out forthwith. In the door was a hole, and through the hole the robbers peeped, and in the mill they saw not one man but *two*; and one was reading, and the other was grinding the corn. Now, the man who was reading was Senan.

"What shall we do?" the robbers asked each other. "Shall we enter and attack them?" but the wiser answered, "No, for if we are two, they are two also. Let us wait until the miller, who is grinding the corn, goes back to his home with the corn he has ground. We can then kill him and carry off his sack. As for the other fellow, I do not know who he is, only that he is of another household from the miller and will go his own way."

So they hid until the grinding was ended, and Senan, who was reading his book, lay down and slept. But the man who was grinding the corn did not sleep. By and by, the dawn broke and the sun rose, and still no one had left the mill. Then Senan got up and opened the door, and the robbers entered and spoke to him, saying, "Who was with you while you were reading and sleeping, and where is he?"

At that Senan looked at them and made answer: "He that keepeth Israel shall neither slumber nor sleep."

And the robbers understood that it was Christ Himself who had come there to protect Senan, His servant; and they repented, and left off doing evil.

∞

As Senan had passed his days in his father's house working on the farm, when he went to live with Notal in the school after he became a priest, he was given, as has been told, the charge of the beasts and of the daily food required for everyone. This was how he came to visit the mill on the night when the robbers went to attack it, for the owner, whom he had thought to find there, was a friend, and often Senan helped him in his work. In the house of Notal there was a mill likewise, and there Senan ground the corn to be made into bread. This he generally did at night, after milking the cows.

"Give me, I pray you, a candle," he said one evening to the cook. "I need one to grind the corn, and there are no more left."

"The new candlewicks are not yet dipped in the tallow," answered the cook. "But take this; it might serve you for the present," and Senan took the candle that he held out and went into the mill.

At the end of a week, the cook remembered about the candle, and thought to himself that it must have been burned out long ago, and he wondered how Senan had gotten another. So curious was he that he ran to the mill and looked through the keyhole and beheld Senan sitting by the candle, reading, while the mill ground of itself.

Great was his surprise, but he said nothing, and crept away; and the next night he came again, and again beheld Senan reading by the candle and the mill grinding alone. Thus it happened thrice, and the third time the grinding was finished, and Senan gave the candle to the cook, and the candle was as long at the end of the week as it had been at the beginning, which was truly a marvel.

By this time, the fame of Senan had spread far and wide, and many were the people who flocked to his presence, some for one reason and some for another, but mostly to ask him to come and live among them. When Notal, his counselor, knew of their desire, he sent for Senan and bade him listen to the words of the multitude and to choose a place where he might dwell, at any rate, for a while. So, much against his will, Senan obeyed the voice of Notal and went for a while to Inniscorthy.

∞

After Senan had preached some time to the people of Inniscorthy, he left them and journeyed from one town to another, founding churches. At Inis Mor, or the "great island," the monks drew water to be used for the church from a well that was in a rock nearby, and one evening they came to the bishop and told him that the water had been defiled by a woman who had washed her child's clothes in it.

"That is an evil deed," said the bishop when he heard of it, "and evil will come of it."

Then spoke Libern, the son of Dail: "The son of the woman has gone from her over the edge of Ireland," for the boy was playing on the cliff and his foot slipped, and he fell down into the water. As soon as the news reached his mother, loudly did she wail, and hastened to Senan and told him what had happened to the child, and Senan was wrath and went to the bishop.

"O Setna," said he, "it is you and Libern also who, in revenge for the defiling of the water, cast a spell on the boy and are the cause of his death. Go, and let Libern go with you, and leave him to do penance on a rock in the midst of the sea, and find the child and carry him to his mother." So with shame in his heart, the bishop did as Senan bade him, and left Libern on the rock, and sought the boy, whom he found at the bottom of the tall cliff playing with the waves, which laughed about him; and the child laughed too and gathered up the white foam in his hands and sucked it, for he thought it was the milk, fresh from the cow, which foamed and bubbled. The bishop was glad when he saw the boy and knew he was still alive and, lifting him in his arms, bore him to the boat and brought him to Senan, and Senan carried him to his mother.

"The Lord has forgiven Libern," said Senan to the bishop, "for the sea has left the rock dry. Fetch him, therefore, and bring him hither."

Thus Libern came off the rock, knowing his sin had been pardoned, and, humble of heart, stood before Senan.

"Can we find water here, O Senan, if the well is defiled?" asked he, and Senan answered, "Thrust the crozier that is beside your foot into the earth, and water in abundance will gush out." So Libern thrust in the crozier, and water gushed out as Senan had foretold, and the spring is called the Well of Libern unto this day.

∞

Senan was sitting on the flagstone in front of his house when Raphael the archangel appeared before him.

"Behold the island that is in the midst of the sea," said Raphael. "God has set there an awful monster to keep it, so that no sinner should enter therein; but now you are to go there and found a church, and the monster shall be cast out, lest it frighten those who follow you."

"What is timely to God is timely to me," answered Senan, and then the angels who were with Raphael took up the flagstone with

Senan upon it and bore him across the sea to a high hill in the middle of the island, and there they left him and went to seek the monster.

Greatly marveled the monster when it beheld the angels in the guise of men approaching, for never before had it seen a living creature upon the island; and as it went swiftly to meet them, the earth trembled under its feet. Fearful and wonderful was that beast to look upon: a horse's mane was on its neck, and in its head a single eye, crimson and angry. The feet of it were thick, and its nails of iron, so that sparks of fire flew out of the rocks as it passed over them, while its breath scorched the grass and flowers that grew in the cracks. Its tail was borrowed from a whale, and its body seemed as long as the island itself; and when it entered the sea, the water boiled and fizzled from the heat that proceeded from it.

The monster moved quickly past the angels and drew near to the place where Senan was awaiting it, its mouth open wide so that the saint could gaze right into the middle of it. But he raised his hand and made the Sign of the Cross, and the beast stopped and was silent.

"Leave this island, I command you," said Senan, "and see that you do no hurt to any, wherever you may go."

Then the monster turned and entered the sea and swam across to the land, and from that day forth, it harmed no one.

∞

When news reached the king of that part of the country that Senan was dwelling in the island, and had caused the monster to abandon it, he was very wrath and bade the brothers of Senan — Coel and Liath — go and cast out the saint. But when they landed and found Senan, he refused to do their bidding, saying that the king claimed what was not his and had no power to thrust him out.

"If you will not come for our asking, we shall have to make you," said they, and they took his hands and dragged him down the cliff. There Liath loosed the hand he held, but Coel dragged him over the stones of the beach until his bones were well-nigh broken.

"Why do you not help me?" asked Coel in anger, and Liath answered, "I will not do it, and I grieve for the harm I have already caused him."

"Why," asked Coel again, "should you forfeit your own lands — for the king will assuredly take them from you — rather than thrust this man from a place that is none of his?"

"Because it is easier even to leave Ireland than to do ill to Senan," replied Liath. And without him, Coel could not prevail over Senan, so he entered the boat with Liath and sailed away from the island to his home; and as he stepped through the door of his house, his foot slipped and he fell, striking his head against a sharp corner so that he died, and soon his children died also and his lands fell to Senan. When Liath saw that, he returned and told Senan what had happened, and of the death of Coel.

"You did well," answered Senan, "not to join Coel in his strife with the will of God, for had you done this, you also would be lying dead and your children likewise, as Coel's children are lying."

As soon as the king's steward heard these tidings, he hastened to tell his master, who was very wrath, and sent for his wizard to take counsel with him about the matter. And when it was laid before him, the wizard answered, "Be not troubled concerning this, O king, for I will cast a charm over Senan, and either he shall die or he shall yield the lands up to you."

"So do," replied the king, "and I will reward you."

After that, the wizard went to the island and to the spot where Senan dwelt, and chanted spells against him, bidding him give up the land, lest evil should befall him. But Senan cared nothing for his words and said that he had charms that were stronger than any the wizard could cast, and that he might do his worst. This angered the wizard, and he threw a spell over the sun, so that thick darkness settled on the face of the island; but Senan charmed away the darkness, and the sun shone bright as before. After that, the wizard conjured up a storm, and the air was rent with thunders and lightnings; but Senan caused the storm to cease, and it hurt no one. More spells the wizard cast, but never could he prevail against Senan, and at last he said, "I go out of this island to a place you know not, but by and by I will come again."

"You will never come again," answered Senan, "and it will not be lucky for you in the place to which you go," and his words angered the wizard a second time, and he charmed a mist to cover the land, so that Senan might not tell whither he went. Safely he reached an island that lay across the sea, but in the night, the wind blew the waves so that they covered the island, and all that dwelt in it were drowned and the wizard likewise.

∞

Donnan, the son of Liath — Senan's brother — came to the island to learn reading and the rules of the church in the school of the monks. One day Donnan was bidden by Senan to go down to the shore to cut seaweed for him. So Donnan called two little boys who were at the school also, and they climbed over the rocks, which stretched far out into the sea, where the seaweed grew thickest.

"I will go back now," said Donnan after a while, "for I have work to do; and when that is finished, I will return for you and the seaweed, which you have gathered."

Then he rowed back to the land, but as soon as he got out of the boat, a wave carried it away, and there was no other on the island.

On the rock the boys sat waiting, and they watched the sea creeping closer and closer until it touched their feet, and gently it floated them off the rock and they were drowned; and on the morrow, after the tide was high, their bodies were found lying on the sand, and they looked happy and peaceful, as if they slept.

When their father and mother heard this, they hastened to the shore, and raised a great cry, "Give us back our children, O Senan the saint!"

Then said Senan, "Go, Donnan, and bid the boys arise," and Donnan hastened to the sea and beheld the boys lying there, and called to them: "Arise, and speak unto your parents, for thus are you bidden by Senan." At his words, the boys stood up, and, turning to their parents, they said, "An ill-deed have you done, bringing us out of the land we had reached."

Wonderingly their mother answered, "Why? Would you rather stay in that land than come home to us?"

But the boys cried with one voice, "Though the whole world were given us, and all the glory of it, it would seem a prison after the land from which you have summoned us. Keep us not here; but it will be granted that, for our sakes, you shall suffer no sorrow."

So they died; and their bodies were buried before the convent where Senan dwelt.

∽

At length the time came when it was made known to Senan that the day of his death drew near. He kept silence and revealed it to none, but hastened to finish the work that had been given him, so that none might be left undone. When all was completed, he bade farewell to his friends and lay down, waiting.

"Let my body lie here until dawn," he said to his monks, and they did as he bade them; and in the dawn they rose up and carried it out and buried it with great honor.

Friend of Kings

Those of you who know the stories of the Knights of the Round Table will remember that when King Arthur bids farewell to his comrades, he passes in the black barge out of their sight to the Isle of Avalon. There he was to rest amid the meadows, "fair with orchard lawns and bowery hollows crowned with summer sea."

Now, perhaps many children have read the tale of Arthur's last farewell without guessing that there is a *real* Isle of Avalon, and that it was given its name by the Romans, nineteen hundred years ago. Avalon lies on the river Brue, just where, long ago, it broadened and stretched out almost into a lake. The water was so clear that the Britons who dwelt in the country gave it a name that means "the isle of glass"; and you could lie on its banks and watch the fishes playing hide-and-seek below you. If you landed on the island, you would find a tangle of flowering shrubs and, beyond, orchards white with blossom in spring and golden with fruit in autumn.

Altogether, Avalon was a very pleasant place, and a pleasant place it is still, even though the glassy waters have disappeared and streets stand where water-lilies and forget-me-nots once grew. On all sides you may see ruined arches or fragments of old buildings, which tell those who understand a tale of the former greatness of Avalon — or, as it was afterward called, Glastonbury. And besides the ruins you will be shown the tree of the Holy Thorn, which blossoms at Christmas and is supposed to have sprung from a hawthorn staff that St. Joseph of Arimathea, on a pilgrimage from Palestine, stuck into the ground when he threw himself down to rest. Of course it is *only* a story, for St. Joseph never came here at all, but it is quite true that the thorn comes into flower every Christmas, and for hundreds of years, pilgrims flocked to worship at the chapel, said to have been founded by the Jews.

By and by, a whole colony of Irish missionaries settled there and built themselves cells of wattles or twisted willows, which must have been very cold and damp to live in, and constructed a wooden church. In course of time, this was replaced by a stone one, and when in the reign of Henry II the existing church was burned down, a magnificent abbey was founded on its ruins.

∞

It was about the year 924, when the famous King Athelstan reigned over the whole of the South of England, then known as Wessex, that a baby named Dunstan was born in Glastonbury, not far from the royal palace. His parents, who were both noble, wished their little boy to be taught carefully everything that a gentleman ought to learn. He was a clever, eager child, always wanting to do everything other people did, and the Irish monks who kept a sort of school for the sons of the rich people in the neighborhood had no trouble with their pupil. As soon as he could read and write, his masters set him to study the Bible, and he was required to know the Latin poets and historians of the great days of Rome; the English poets, Caedmon and Beowulf; the stories of the saints (especially the Irish ones); and something about the Frankish kings who reigned across the sea, and the court of Charlemagne, where Athelstan's great-great-grandfather, King Egbert, had once spent many years in exile.

You might think all this was enough for one little boy to learn, but it was only part of Dunstan's lessons. There was one particular monk who taught him Latin, and another who was his musical teacher, while a third undertook to ground him in arithmetic and geometry, and took him out on fine nights to watch the stars. On wet days, he sang church music, or drew, or modeled figures out of clay, for Dunstan's hands were as clever as his head; and in after years, when he was a very great man indeed, the monks would probably show the precious manuscripts he had copied and illuminated, the vestments he had designed for the priests, or the iron crosses he had made for the church; while his mother was never tired of displaying the gold and silver ornaments that were her son's work. Even as late as the thirteenth century, bells fashioned by Dunstan were still hanging in the church at Abingdon.

So time passed on. The boy could not have been more anxious to learn than the monks were to teach him; and the end of it was that Dunstan got brain fever and became dangerously ill. The monks were very unhappy but never thought the fault was theirs, and for weeks his mother sat with him day and night, but he did not know her. At length he sank into unconsciousness, and the poor lady, worn out with lack of rest, fell fast asleep. When she awoke, Dunstan was missing. The delirium had returned, and in his frenzy, he had arisen and rushed out to the church; the doors were closed, but a ladder leaned against the walls, left there by some workmen. Mad with fever, Dunstan ran up it onto the roof, yet, in spite of the locked doors, when the church was opened next morning, he was found lying on the floor, faint and weak but without the fever.

It was after this that Athelstan invited the boy to come and live at the palace and be the playmate of his brother Edward, whose fast friend he remained through life. Dunstan was very handsome and had charming manners, but the young pages and nobles about the court did not like him, and mocked at his small size and delicacy, which prevented his joining in their rough sports.

"He is more than half a maiden," they would cry. "Let him sit by the hearth with a distaff." And with anger in his heart, which he felt it would be well to conceal, Dunstan sought the ladies' "bower," as their sitting-room was then called. There he was always welcome. Nobody could draw patterns for them to work like young Dunstan, and nobody was so good a judge of the evenness of the stitches, and of the way the colors were combined.

But an unlucky end came to his visits, and this was brought about by a piece of mischief of his own.

From the time Dunstan was quite a little boy, he had the power of imitating other people's voices, and of making them sound as if they proceeded from any direction he pleased. Nowadays, we call this gift "ventriloquism" and listen with interest and amusement to anyone who possesses it; but when Athelstan sat on the throne, it was held to be wicked magic, inspired by the Devil himself.

One morning Dunstan received a message from the lady Ethelwyn, begging him to give his advice as to the pattern of some new vestments that she and her maidens were embroidering. He entered the room and found them all bending over the work close to the window, for even when the sun shone brightly, so little light penetrated the narrow slits in the wall, that nearly the whole apartment was in shadow. He was apparently considering carefully the important question as to whether red or yellow would look best in a particular part of the pattern, when a sound of soft, low music was heard coming from the end of the room. For a moment the ladies gazed at each other in astonishment; then exclaiming that Dunstan knew more than any Christian ought to, Ethelwyn rushed from the chamber, followed by her maidens.

The story was not long in reaching the ears of the king, and Dunstan was formally accused of dabbling in witchcraft, and other unlawful acts. Young though he was, his talents and the favor they gained him had won him many enemies, and old tales were now whispered, all tending to prove him guilty. Sentence of exile from court was passed on him, but, as he still denied his crime, it was not to be carried out until he had first gone through one of the tests of innocence, known as the "ordeal of cold water."

Several kinds of ordeals were practiced at that time throughout Europe. There was the ordeal by hot iron, to which, perhaps you will remember, the mother of King Hacon had to submit, when a heavy weight, white with heat, was withdrawn from the fire, laid in her hand, and held there until she was told to throw it down. A bandage was next placed on the hand and sealed by the priest, and left for three days. On the third day the bandage was publicly unwound, and as no scar was to be found on the palm where the iron had lain, she was proclaimed innocent.

In another kind of ordeal, the accused person was forced to plunge his arm into boiling water and to draw out a bar of iron without being scalded.

But, fortunately for Dunstan, the form of ordeal to which he was condemned was the easiest of all. He was merely to be thrown into cold water, to see if he would sink or swim, and his hands and feet were not allowed to be tied, as was the general custom.

A large crowd of idle and curious people were assembled to see Dunstan, mounted on a led horse, ride up to the pond where the ceremony was to take place. But before the arrival of the officials whose duty it was to watch that justice was done, the culprit was dragged from the saddle by some young men standing by and flung into the water.

Gasping with the shock, he managed to crawl to the further bank, and then ran for his life, hearing behind him the noise of yelping dogs, set on by his cruel persecutors. Luckily the beasts had not touched him when they were called off by the officers of the court, who decided that Dunstan had done all that was required of him and was free.

∞

Although Dunstan's life was safe, he was forbidden to return to court, and without delay he set out on a long ride to Winchester, to take refuge with the bishop. His heart was very sad, for he had left behind him a girl whom he loved deeply and someday hoped to marry. But his kinsman, Elfege the Bald, bishop of Winchester, who received him with great kindness, thought that it was a pity such abilities as Dunstan's should be lost to the Church. Elfege made constant appeals to the youth's ambition and pointed out that the road to power lay only through the vestments of the priest. At first his words made no impression. "But I can be a priest and be married too," argued Dunstan.

"That is true, but then you will never be anything but a priest," answered Elfege. "Whereas if you remain unmarried, you can — and will — rise to govern the state and be a king in all but the name."

"Yes, perhaps; still, there are other things in life besides power," murmured the boy in a low voice, and Elfege, who knew the value of silence, pretended not to hear him.

For some months, the struggle between the two went on. Dunstan held out longer than most boys of sixteen would have done, but his health, always delicate, broke down from the strain. He had no strength to fight anymore, and at length, to the joy of Elfege, he consented to do as the bishop wished. So, to prevent any further change of mind, Elfege at once ordained him priest and, as soon as he was fit to travel, sent him abroad to a Benedictine monastery.

When he returned, there was no more bitter enemy than he of the married clergy, several of whom had been his teachers in his childhood, not many years ago. It almost seemed as if he wanted to prove to himself that he was right when he gave up a home for ambition; and his first act after his appointment as abbot of Glastonbury by King Edmund, when he was twenty-two, was to expel them from their posts.

But all this happened later, for as soon as he came from Fleury, he built himself a tiny cell close to the churchyard, five feet long and two and a half feet wide, and far too low for him to stand upright in. In this cell he believed he would spend the rest of his days thinking about heavenly things.

When he laid down this plan for himself, he knew very little of his own nature. For a while, indeed, his cell contented him; he fasted until his mind as well as his body grew weak, and the visions he saw in this condition he took to be real. The Devil, he said to the friends who now and then came to see him, visited him continually and beset him with temptations. And, quite convinced of the truth of what he was telling, he convinced his listeners also, and they carried away wonderful stories of the Devil looking in at the window of the cell and disturbing the holy man with mocking words, until Dunstan seized his nose with a pair of red-hot tongs; the Devil's shrieks might have been heard at the palace.

If Dunstan had led this life for very long, he would probably have ended in becoming mad, but, fortunately, a lady who formed part of King Athelstan's court was one of those who came to his cell to consult him about the state of her soul. She was a sensible woman and saw that his mode of living was very bad for him in every way. Little by little she obtained great influence over him and persuaded him that it was his duty to go more into the world and seek out those who could not, or would not, come to him. After a while he listened to her and sometimes left his cell for her house, where he met again men of experience and learning.

The ambition that had been implanted in him by Elfege the Bald was awakened; he felt there existed another side to life than the monkish one, and when Athelstan died and Edmund sat on the throne, the newly appointed abbot of Glastonbury threw all his energy into his work.

∞

Dunstan was now a rich man. His parents had bequeathed him one estate, and his friend, the lady Ethelgiva, another; so that he was able to build a new church, and such buildings for his monks as he thought proper. He also drew up a set of rules, and every man who would not swear obedience to them had to seek shelter elsewhere. Their places were speedily filled by young, eager monks like himself, and these he forced to study, in order that Glastonbury should once more be the great school to which boys of all parts might come in far greater numbers than they had ten years earlier, when he himself was educated there.

Always busy, the devils who had persecuted him flew away, and if he dreamed now, it was of angels.

Few men can say that they have been the advisors of four kings, yet this was Dunstan's position. It is impossible to read the history of those times without noticing the youth of almost all the sovereigns of Wessex; and yet how wisely and well they governed, and how triumphantly they beat back their foes, the Danes, who were always pressing on them. On the death of each sovereign, the borders of the kingdom stretched a little farther, and a fresh monarch paid tribute to their overlord of Wessex. Much of this success was due to the counsel of Dunstan and the chancellor Thurketul; in spite of his delicacy, the young abbot seemed able to do everything and to know everything, but however greatly the king might need him, he never ceased for one moment the work of reforming the discipline of the Church.

∞

Edmund the king was keeping the festival of St. Augustine the missionary, at Pucklechurch, in Gloucestershire, and Dunstan was in his abbey of Glastonbury, many long miles away. The abbot was sitting alone in his cell, tired with a hard day's labor, and feeling strangely sad, although all was going well with him. Suddenly, the walls around him appeared to fade, and he beheld the banqueting hall at Pucklechurch where Edmund was seated. As he looked, he saw Leof the outlaw enter the hall, a man whom the king had banished six years before on account of his many crimes. Unnoticed, Leof crept up, and took his place at the royal table and, when the cup-bearer ordered him to depart, angrily bade him begone. The noise attracted the king's attention, and he sprang up and, seizing Leof by the hair, dragged him to the floor, falling with him. As they struggled together, Leof managed to pull out a dagger from his coat and struck Edmund full in the breast. The king died without a groan, and the dagger with which Leof had killed him was turned on him by the attendants.

All this Dunstan beheld, and as the vision faded away, he seemed to see the Devil's face dancing with mocking glee at the murder. Without losing a moment, Dunstan started off to Pucklechurch, hoping against hope that he might yet be in time to save the king. About halfway he met a messenger, sent to fetch him. "Tell me your tale," said the abbot, and when the tale was told, it was in all particulars what Dunstan had seen in his vision.

Edmund was only twenty-four at the time of his death, and it was quite plain that his two little boys must be passed over, and Edred, his brother, reign in his stead, and continue the fight for the supremacy of Wessex. Dunstan and Edred were nearly the same age and had known each other long before at the Court of Athelstan, where they became great friends. No sooner was Edred declared king than he sent for Dunstan and took counsel with him as to the government of his own kingdoms of Wessex and Mercia, and how best to subdue the tributary land of Northumbria, which was constantly in revolt. Edred was as ready to fight as his brothers, Athelstan and Edmund, or his father, King Edward, but he suffered all his life from a terrible illness that made it impossible to him for a long time to eat any meat, and for this he was heartily despised by his subjects, who loved nothing so much as eating and drinking.

Still, whatever pain he may have undergone, the king did not allow his delicacy to interfere with his duty to his country, and for ten years he devoted all his time and strength to conquering his enemies and improving the condition for his people. But in the end, the task proved too much for him, and after his death at Frome, in 955, his nephew Edwy succeeded him on the throne of Wessex, while to Edwy's younger brother Edgar was given the subject kingdom of Anglia, which we now call Essex.

∞

Edwy was only fifteen and had not the talent for governing that marked most of the kings of Wessex. Like many people weak in character, he was very much afraid of being thought to be influenced by anyone; and Dunstan, who was used to being consulted on every occasion by the two former kings, had little patience with Edwy's youth and folly. At Edwy's coronation feast, a quarrel took place, and, seeing that the married clergy were all ready to side with the king, Dunstan retired for a time to Glastonbury. Here, in the abbey he had built, and amid the folk who were so proud of him, he held himself to be safe, but Edwy's anger, kept alive by his wife and her mother, still pursued him, and armed men were sent to take him prisoner. But they little knew of what stuff the abbot was made if they expected to conduct him quietly into the king's presence. As the soldiers were in the act of forcing him through the church door, a fearful sound was heard, which some said resembled "the wheezy voice of a gleesome hag," and others "the bleating of a calf," but a calf that could never have grazed in earthly fields.

The grasp on Dunstan's arms was loosened, and the abbot stood still, making no attempt to escape, while those around him quaked and shivered, their foreheads wet with fear.

The soldiers fell back, not daring to touch him.

Then the silence was broken by the voice of Dunstan himself: "Foe of mankind, beware lest thou rejoice before thy time! For great as may be thy joy in witnessing my departure, thy grief will be twofold greater, when God, to thy confusion, shall permit me to return."

The soldiers fell back, not daring to touch him, and Dunstan, taking advantage of their fright, walked quietly away and hid himself, until he could sail in a ship to Flanders.

This time his gift of ventriloquism had served him better than in the bower of the lady Ethelwyn!

∞

Wessex soon grew tired of the misrule of Edwy, and after two years, his brother Edgar was proclaimed king of a large part of England — Mercia, or the Midlands, and Northumbria. Edgar's first act was to send for Dunstan, who gladly quitted Flanders and returned to pursue his old policy at home. Still he did not use his new power in avenging himself on Edwy and even tried, although vainly, to make friends with him.

On one point only Dunstan seems to have changed his mind during his exile. In Edred's reign, he had refused the bishopric of Winchester, although he had allowed the king to know that when Canterbury was vacant, he would consent to be primate of England. Now, however, at Edgar's request he suffered himself to be nominated bishop of Worcester and London without giving up Glastonbury. It was against the law of the Church to hold all these together, and no man knew it better than Dunstan. But Rome was far off, and many things might happen before the news reached the ears of Pope John XII. And before the news probably *did* reach the Pope, Odo, archbishop of Canterbury, was dead, and Edwy also; and at the request of Edgar, now king of Wessex, Dunstan set out for Rome to receive from the pope the robe or pallium of the archbishop.

The brilliancy of the reign of Edgar was chiefly owing to the counsels of Dunstan, although the king must be given full credit for listening to his advice.

When the younger son of Edmund ascended the throne, he was only sixteen, and loved every kind of pomp and splendor. So Dunstan, keeping himself all the while in the background — for in spite of his ambition, the archbishop was too great a man to care for praise — spent much of his time in gratifying this weakness of the king, and arranging progresses through the country and organizing reviews to test the soundness of his fleet and the skill of the oarsmen.

Not that these things were purely amusements. Dunstan was fully aware that the subject kingdoms would be all the more loyal if they could see and speak to the sovereign who was their overlord; and as for the reviews, why, the coasts on the East were infested with pirates from across the seas, who must be kept down at any cost. And, of course, without a good navy, this could not be done.

The most famous and the most splendid of these royal progresses was one that took place in 973, when Edgar had been fourteen years sole king, and just after his second coronation at Bath. Attended by his court, he traveled across the country as far as Chester and was met there by the eight kings who came to do him homage for their kingdoms. It was, perhaps, the proudest moment in the life of the "Bretwalda" — for this was Edgar's title among his people — when he sat at the prow of his ship and was rowed on the river Dee by his tributaries. They came from all parts: five kings from Wales, nearly as small in stature as Edgar himself; the tall Maccus from the isles of the North, Malcolm of Cumberland, and Kenneth of Scotland. Kenneth, at least, he knew well, for once when a meeting between them had taken place, the Scottish king had gone away and spoken mockingly about his overlord, saying it was a shame that grown men should pay tribute to a dwarf.

The idle words were carried by some tale-bearer to Edgar, and Kenneth was instantly summoned into his presence.

"Let us go into that wood. I have somewhat to say unto thee," said the king, and Kenneth followed him silently.

"Now," continued Edgar, when they had reached a cleared space, out of sight of all men, "draw thy sword, and we will see which is the better man, the giant or the dwarf, and who shall obey the other."

Kenneth colored; he was generous and not afraid to own himself in the wrong.

"I take back my words, O king. It was an ill hour when I spoke them," and Edgar held out his hand and forgave him.

∞

During these years the country prospered, the roads were improved, the robbers severely punished, and a payment given to every man who brought in the head of a wolf — for wolves were the terror of lonely villages during the winter. The peasants, like all Saxons, were heavy drinkers and, when drunk, very quarrelsome. Matters were made worse by the custom of having only one pot in each tavern, and the pot was passed from man to man. Many were the fights and brawls that arose from this habit, for everybody accused his neighbor of having swallowed more than his share. So Dunstan ordered pegs of gold or silver to be fastened at even spaces down the great pot, and no one, under pain of punishment, might drink further than his own peg. Besides this, the archbishop took care that the poor, who were oppressed by those who were stronger than they, should have the right of coming to lay their cause before the king himself, and they were always sure of a hearing.

But, notwithstanding all these things in which Dunstan thought and planned for the good of the people and Edgar carried out his ideas, there was a dark stain in the king's character, which the archbishop knew that it was his duty not to forgive, without real proof of penitence. Whether Edgar was really ashamed of his crime or not, we cannot tell, but he felt that he could not afford to quarrel with his minister, to whom he owed most of his power; therefore, like David, he humbled himself and offered to submit to any punishment Dunstan might inflict on him.

"You will have copies of the Bible written and placed in the churches," said the archbishop. "You will see that the poor have justice; you will make better laws; and you will not wear your crown for seven years."

The king's face fell as he heard the sentence. The three first conditions he was ready to fulfill; in reality they were Dunstan's business. But the last! This hit him in his weakest part, his vanity; and he felt it keenly.

Yet a glance at the archbishop's face told him that it would be useless to plead, so he merely bowed his head and murmured, "I obey."

And that is the reason Edgar was recrowned at Bath, in the year 973, two years before he died.

∞

We all know the sad story of Edgar's two children, Edward the Martyr and his half-brother, Ethelred the Unready. The country was divided into two parties, one of which was headed by the mother of Ethelred, Queen Elfrida; who had the support of the married clergy — still existing in large numbers — and the other by Dunstan, the upholder of Edward.

The archbishop was only fifty-one, but a life of unceasing work was telling fast on him, and he had never shaken off his childish delicacy, which yet he had kept at bay and not allowed to interfere with his duty. Still, with the waning of his strength, he was conscious that his power over men was waning also, slight though the signs might be.

Perhaps no one else perceived it, but Dunstan knew, and saw he must make the best of the time left him. The struggle between both parties had lasted three years, when the archbishop called a meeting of the chief men of both sides in an upper room of a large house. The subject they had met to discuss was the old worn one — the marriage of the clergy, and, as always when this was brought forward, words ran high and threatened to become blows. In the midst of the tumult, Dunstan held up his hand, and the noise ceased as if by magic.

"I am old and tired," he said, "and I long for peace. Many times have I spoken, and there is no need that I should speak further. My cause is the cause of Heaven, and Heaven will decide between us." He might have added more, but at that instant there was a fearful crash and a sound of wild shrieks. The floor had given way and those who had been standing on it were flung violently down below. Several were killed; some were injured; only Dunstan and his friends, who were sitting on a solid beam, escaped.

As usual on these occasions, there were two versions of the accident. At first the people exclaimed that the archbishop had been saved by a miracle, and that it was a proof of the righteousness of his cause; but later there arose whispers that his skill in carpentry and mechanics had enabled him to arrange for the collapse of the floor, although these wiseacres did not perceive that such a trick could not have been played without leaving traces behind, and of such traces there were none. Besides, even Dunstan could hardly have arranged that the fall should take place while he was making his appeal to Heaven. If the floor had given way before he was speaking, his plot would have failed of success.

∽

Another year passed. Edward was murdered — thrown from a window by his stepmother, it is said. Elfrida was imprisoned in a convent, and little Ethelred crowned at Kingston.

For some years, Dunstan managed things as of old, and all went well, but the young king, as he grew up, showed a violent dislike toward the archbishop, who left the court as often as he could and lived more and more at Canterbury. Here he led a peaceful existence, preaching sometimes, making laws for the good of the Church, working at organs, trying to heal quarrels. By the time he was sixty-four, he had grown very weak, and on Ascension Day 988, he gave his last sermon. He knew, he said, that he would never stand in that pulpit again and begged his listeners to think of him with kindness and affection. Twice his weakness forced him to stop, and once he was obliged to leave the pulpit; but he persevered, and even attended the usual state banquet, pointing out, as he returned home by way of the church, the spot where he wished to be buried.

Three days later he died; a great man and a good one, in spite of his faults; and one who must be judged, not by what we think right now, but what men held to be right a thousand years ago.

Queen of Scotland

If ever you pay a visit to Edinburgh, you ought to go and see the castle. If you are in the town, you cannot help *seeing* it, for it stands on a perpendicular rock, five hundred feet high, at the west end of the principal street, Princes Street; and if the rock is not *quite* five hundred feet high — well, the English said that it was, when they drew a picture of the siege of the castle in Queen Mary Stuart's time. The English then destroyed the old fortress. What you see now is not so old, but it has one ancient chapel. On the very center of the smooth black top of the rock is the little oratory of St. Margaret of Scotland, a dark round cell with round arches and columns ornamented in the style of the Norman builders. In this oratory, just before her sad death in 1093, St. Margaret used to say her prayers and make her offerings of gold and jewels.

∽

In her day, the castle and the view from the castle were very unlike what you see now. Where the railway line runs — at the foot of the tall rock and through the gardens of Princes Street — in Queen Margaret's time and long afterward, there lay a lake fringed with reeds, and full of trout and wild ducks and coots and water-hens. There was no huge town below the rock, only a few thatched cottages, but you could see from the top the Firth of Forth and its islands, and far away to the blue Highland hills. If you now go through the narrow gate into the castle, or if you look up at it from the gardens below, you remember the many strange things that happened there and the many brave deeds that were done in years long ago. You remember them, at least, if you have read the "Tales of a Grandfather," by Sir Walter Scott; and if you have not, the sooner you do, the better.

Just cross the bridge over the railway and walk to the foot of the rock. How far could you climb up it, even if there were no enemies on the top rolling down huge stones at you, and firing at you with bows or with muskets from behind the castle wall? I have tried that climb many a day when I was a boy at school, and I never could get up very far. Then think of making the climb in the dark at midnight! It seems impossible, but Randolph Earl of Murray and his men reached the top in the night, and surprised the English and took the castle during the wars of Robert Bruce against Edward II. Then again, the great Claverhouse, Viscount Dundee, climbed the rocks with his scented love-locks tossing in the wind and spoke to the duke of Gordon, who held the fort for King James II. After that Dundee climbed down again and rode away to the north to victory and death.

In the castle, the boy Earl of Douglas and his brother were treacherously murdered, and later Queen Mary's son, James VI of Scotland and I of England, was born there. In fact, an endless number of true stories are to be told about the castle, but the earliest is the story of the beautiful St. Margaret, Queen of Scotland.

Margaret was of the old Anglo-Saxon Royal blood of England, of the family that traced its descent from Woden, the heathen god. Margaret's father, Edward the Exile, was son of the brave, fighting English king Edmund Ironside. When Edward was a baby, it is said that the Danish king Canute (the king whom the waves did not obey) wanted to kill him and his twin brother, lest one or other should live to make war against the conquering Danes and take the crown. Now, if Canute had wanted to murder Edward, I think he would have done it. However, the story (which we need not believe) says that Canute sent the children to his half-brother, the king of Sweden, and asked *him* to put them to death. But the royal Swede was a good Christian man, and he sent the two little boys to a saint and king — namely, St. Stephen of Hungary — who acted to them like another father. In Hungary they were far enough from all the troubles and dangers of England, and with the example of a king (who was also a saint) before their eyes, they must have been naughty indeed if they did not learn to behave well.

When Edward the Exile grew up, he married a princess, a niece of the queen, the wife of St. Stephen, and their child was Margaret. Her brother was Edgar, called Edgar the Atheling, and Edgar, after Harold was killed at the Battle of Hastings, was chosen by the English for their king. But Edgar was not a great fighting man; he saw that he had no chance of defeating William the Conqueror and all his Normans. He never was crowned, but lived quietly enough on what the Normans chose to give him.

Now, we know nothing about what Edgar's sister, Margaret, did in Hungary; nothing at all is told about her childhood. She seems to have been born about 1045, so she would be twenty-one years old at the date of the Norman Conquest, and twenty-two or twenty-three when, in 1067 or 1068, her brother Edgar fled from England into Scotland. At this time, the king of Scotland was Malcolm, called in Gaelic, Malcolm Cean-mor or "Big Head." Everybody who has seen or read Shakespeare's famous play *Macbeth* knows about Malcolm, son of "the gracious Duncan," that good old king whom Macbeth murdered in his own castle. But the story that Shakespeare tells is a kind of fairytale about the witches that meet Macbeth on the blasted heath to Birnam Wood, which marched to Dunsinane. Duncan was not an old man, but a middle-aged man; and he, according to Scottish law, was not the rightful king, but a usurper, and Macbeth was really on the side of the rightful king, who was named Lulach. However, Malcolm, the son of Duncan, defeated and killed both Macbeth and young Lulach; and when the Atheling, with his mother, Agatha, and his sisters, Margaret and Christina, came to Scotland, Malcolm was settled on the throne. He himself naturally spoke Gaelic, like all of his people north of the river Forth, but his subjects south of the Forth spoke English. As Malcolm himself had an English or English-speaking Danish mother, he spoke English as well as Gaelic, so that the king and the exiles, cast by a tempest into his kingdom on their way to Hungary, had no difficulty in talking to each other. At this period, Malcolm's position was not easy, for, in his own opinion, his lands stretched far south of Scotland into England, while the kings of England believed that they were the superiors of the kings of Scotland. Thus each side did all the harm possible to each other, whenever they had the chance.

According to one story, Malcolm first met Margaret, and fell in love with her, in 1068. According to another story, he had invaded England and was burning the houses and the crops, and killing men, women, and children, near Wearmouth, when the ships of Edgar Atheling and Margaret entered the harbor. Malcolm came down to meet the wanderers, gave them a feast, and invited them to stay with him in Scotland as long as they pleased. Margaret was very beautiful, very good and kind, and having lived peacefully in the house of a royal saint, her manners were gentle and courteous. It was therefore natural for Malcolm to fall in love with her. Besides, Margaret was the sister of the rightful king of England and so was a fit wife for any king. Margaret was rather unwilling to marry him at first, but when she did consent, she became the best wife in the world. Being English, of course she found Scotland and the Scots very rough and began to introduce English manners and ways, which the part of the people who spoke only Gaelic did not like. But Malcolm saw that the English ways were going to prevail, and he helped Margaret as much as he could.

Her good deeds began at home; Malcolm was a rough, hot-tempered, fighting man, but Margaret, says a priest who lived at her court, "made the king most attentive to works of justice, mercy, and almsgiving," and it is said that he would pray all through the night and shed tears when he thought of his sins. His first wish was to please his beautiful wife and to do whatever she desired. "Although he could not read, he would turn over and examine her books, and kiss those that she liked best." Such books he caused to be bound in plates of gold curiously ornamented, and set with precious stones, topazes and sapphires and rubies. One of these books was a copy of the Four Gospels in Latin, with the capital letters in gold.

Now, St. Margaret, unlike most saints, is not famous as a worker of miracles. Still, the priest who live at her court tells about something very strange that happened there. One day, when they were on a journey, the servant who carried the book for the queen let it fall out of its bag into a river, which he was crossing by a ford. He did not notice that it had been dropped, and when the queen asked for her book, he looked into his bag, but found, to his dismay, that it was missing. Then there was a hunt all along the road by which the man had come. As the book had a cover of gold and precious stones, it was, they thought, certain to glitter in the sun, yet they were uneasy, for if any person picked it up, it was very doubtful that he would be honest enough to restore it.

Well, "at long and at last," the book was found in the bed of the river, open and rolling about among the pebbles. The waves had swept away the little squares of silk that covered the illuminated pictures on the margins, and as the priest that tells the story says, "Who could have guessed that the book would have been worth anything after such a drenching? Who could have believed that so much as a single letter would have been visible? Yet the book looked as if it had never been touched by the water, except that on the margin of the leaves, the least possible stain of wet might be detected." And the queen became fonder than ever of her book when it was brought back to her.

Now, this is a true story, for, if you go to the Bodleian Library at Oxford, you may see the very Gospels of St. Margaret, with the tale about the miracle written at the end. To be sure, the beautiful golden covers have been stolen long ago, perhaps at the Reformation, when all the gold and silver and precious things in the cathedrals and churches were scattered and plundered. The binding of the book has thus disappeared, but the book itself, somehow, came into a parish library in the country, and when the owners of the library sold their old books, they did not know anything about the value of St. Margaret's Gospels, so the Bodleian Library bought the book very cheap.

Margaret gave many vessels of pure gold to her new church in Dunfermline, and a crucifix adorned with gold and precious stones. This was not the cross called the "Black Rood" and said to contain a piece of the wood of the true Cross, which many years afterward Edward I carried away to England. To the church at St. Andrews, Margaret also gave a beautiful crucifix; but all these things, and many others, were probably melted down during the wars at the time of the Reformation. The queen's own bower was always full of ladies working at embroideries for the vestments of the priests.

She was very careful in educating her children, and the tutors had orders to punish the young princes whenever they were naughty, as frolicsome children will often be. One of her sons, named David, was the best of the old kings of Scotland and built many beautiful abbeys, such as Dryburgh, Melrose, and Jedburgh, which are splendid even in their ruins, for the English burned them in the old wars, especially under Henry VIII.

Margaret liked to see people well dressed, and she encouraged her subjects to buy bright-colored cloths and ornaments from foreign merchants. Some historians have thought that she brought in the tartans, but this is a mistake, as the Highlanders wore tartans many hundreds of years before her time.

∞

Margaret had a good deal of trouble with the priests who spoke Gaelic in Scotland. Their customs were different from the customs of the church on the Continent and in England. Of these, the strangest was that they did no work on Saturday, the Sabbath of the Jews, but worked as usual on Sunday. They fasted on only thirty-six, not forty, days in Lent, and they seem not to have thought themselves worthy to take Holy Communion. Margaret argued with these priests, and, as she did not know Gaelic and they did not know English, King Malcolm explained to each side what the other side was saying. Margaret had the better in the arguments, but the Gaelic-speaking people did not like to be taught English ways, and they did not want any of Margaret's sons, who all had English names, to be king when Malcolm should die.

But the poor must have been fond of her, for when she went riding about the country, she gave away all the money and pretty things she wore to beggars, and would even go to the king's treasures and take money for the poor, "and this pious plundering the king always took pleasantly and in good part," although he sometimes said that he would have her tried and punished.

Scotland was full of poor prisoners, carried out of England during the wars, and Margaret used to find them out, pay their ransoms, and send them home. The priest who wrote her life says that he admired her works of mercy more than miracles, for miracles may be worked by bad people (probably he means witches) as well as by righteous people, but mercy and kindness are good in themselves.

∞

At length, after she had been queen for nearly five-and-twenty years, Margaret began to feel very weak and tired, and those who

Margaret used to find prisoners,
pay their ransoms, and send them home.

loved her grew very anxious about her pale face and slow movements. One day she sent a messenger to fetch the priest to her oratory, and when he arrived, she told him in a few words that it had been revealed to her she was soon to die. The priest, as he looked at her, felt she was right, and she rapidly grew worse.

Unfortunately Malcolm, who, like most people, had been very ill-treated by William Rufus, was making war on him far away. Margaret could have no news from him, so the priest was much startled when one morning she said to him, "Perhaps this very day a great misfortune may fall on Scotland, such a sorrow as has not been felt for very many years." And it befell that on that very day, Malcolm and his eldest son were slain in battle.

But Margaret did not know that her words had come true and went for the last time into that little chapel on the crest of the castle rock in Edinburgh and received Holy Communion. Then she was laid in her bed, and, being in great pain, asked for the Black Rood. She remained quite still with the Rood clasped to her breast, when her son Edgar, who had escaped from the battle, knocked at her door and was allowed to come in. At first he could not speak; then in broken words he told his tale and how he had seen his father and his brother fall, sword in hand. And apart from his grief, his heart was sore, for well he knew that the Gaelic-speaking people would rebel against any king who was of English blood, and, as if all this were not enough, he beheld his mother dying before him.

The sight of her son roused the queen from her stupor. In a quiet voice, she asked some questions about her dead husband and her son, and Edgar tried to comfort her. "She had known before," she said, "what had befallen them and implored him to hide nothing from her." When he had finished, she made her last prayer, saying, "Deliver me," and so she left this world and all sorrow and pain.

She had desired to be buried at Dunfermline, but the rebels were besieging the castle, and but for a timely mist, through which her friends stole away, bearing her body, her wish would have been unfulfilled. Much later, in 1250, Margaret was acknowledged as a saint, and her body was placed in a silver shrine under the High Altar, at Dunfermline. There is a pretty story that her coffin would not be moved until that of Malcolm was also brought, and so these two were laid together to rest, as in their deaths they had not been divided.

The Pious Princess

A crowd of minstrels and poets were gathered in the castle of Wartburg, in 1207, under the protection of its lord, the landgrave of Thuringia, and great excitement reigned among them, as it had been agreed on that a prize should be for him to whose poem the palm was given, while death was the penalty that awaited the rest. But when all sung so sweetly, who could decide which song was the best? And at length they resolved to fetch from the court of Hungary to judge them the minstrel whose name rang through the world, the famous Klingsor.

So Klingsor came and was welcomed by everyone, great and small.

"What news is there from the land you live in? Travelers such as you are rare indeed!" cried the citizens and courtiers, who pressed around the minstrel in the garden of the inn, in the town of Eisenach. Klingsor did not answer them at once; instead he gazed up at the sky, and after a pause he said, "Know that this night a star has risen in Hungary whose brightness shall light the world. A daughter has been born to the king, and her name shall be called Elizabeth, and she shall be given in marriage to the son of your master, and she will become a saint, and be the wonder and consolation of Christendom."

Early next morning the knights who had heard the prophecy rode up to the castle to tell the landgrave of the words of Klingsor.

The landgrave listened with astonishment and with a grave face; but he said nothing, and in a few hours rode himself, escorted by his knights to fetch the minstrel, and brought him back to Wartburg. Alone in the landgrave's closet, they spoke long together about the affairs of Hungary, until Klingsor rose hastily, and, bowing low, begged that he might go, as he was chosen to preside at the singing tournament and decide on the victor.

The minstrels were so many and so good that judgment was not easy, but at length the prize was given to Henry von Ofterdingen, and as we hear nothing of the deaths of his unsuccessful rivals, we may hope that some way was found of sparing their lives.

∽

Stories of the goodness of the Princess Elizabeth were told almost from the day of her birth, and the landgrave of Thuringia, who managed always to hear what was going on around him, made up his mind that his eldest son, Ludwig, would be fortunate indeed if he could obtain the princess for a wife. So in the year 1211, he fitted out an embassy of knights and ladies and dispatched them to Hungary, where they formally petitioned for the hand of the princess. In this they were supported by Klingsor, who was a great favorite of the king, and the minstrel drew such a picture of the wealth and prosperity of Thuringia and the qualities of Prince Ludwig, that the king and queen consented at once to the marriage.

Now, the landgrave had charged his ambassadors to bring Elizabeth (then just four) back with them, in order that she might be brought up in his castle of Wartburg with her future husband. With a heavy heart the queen made ready the little girl for her journey across the mountains, and one fine day she kissed her for the last time and placed her with her own hands in the silver cradle in which the child was to travel, forcing back the tears that almost choked her, lest one should fall on Elizabeth's forehead and bring her ill-luck.

"I shall have plenty of time to weep after she has gone," thought the queen, and when the procession passed under the gate of the castle with the famous knight, Walter von Varila, riding by the side of the big strong horse that carried the cradle, the poor mother turned away from the watch tower and shut herself into her bare, dark room, alone with her grief.

Elizabeth slept during much of the long journey, for the horse went slowly over the mountains and her cradle was very soft and comfortable. At last, however, they reached the castle, and her arrival was splendidly celebrated with balls and banquets and songs. The landgravine Sophia slept during the first night by the side of Elizabeth, lest she should wake and be frightened at finding herself alone in a strange place, and the prince seemed delighted with his brown-faced little bride.

The next day the betrothal took place, and besides the courtiers, the citizens of the town of Eisenach and their wives were invited to the ceremony, and great was the pleasure of the good women at the sight of the young pair, for Ludwig was a tall, handsome boy of eleven, seven years older than Elizabeth.

The bride herself was quite happy and at her ease, and soon grew very fond of her "brother," as she called her future husband. There was no lack of children for her to play with, for she had seven maids of honor and Ludwig and his brothers and sisters, Henry and Conrad and Agnes, and another Elizabeth who, by and by, became a nun.

And when she was tired of games, the little princess would call one of her attendants, and they would go down the steep path that led from Wartburg to Eisenach, with its straggling streets and steep roofs — too steep for the snow to lie on — and into the meadows by the river where the flowers grew. For Elizabeth loved flowers and birds and animals of all kinds, and she learned to watch in the spring for the coming of the storks, standing on one leg on the chimneys, and to listen for the swallows on their return from their winter quarters, telling each other their adventures in their nests under the gables.

But among all the things that Elizabeth had to interest her in her new life, there was one that governed her thoughts and actions, as those who lived with her soon saw. She loved to pray by herself, but if she could not do that, she would pray somehow. Many tales are told of her childhood, when her very games would be made occasions of reminding her playfellows of God. If someone proposed a hopping race, Elizabeth would contrive that the winning-post was the chapel door. If it was unlocked, she would go in for a moment and kneel down; if it was shut, she had to content herself with kissing the lock.

"Let us see which is the tallest," she cried one day. "You all lie down on the ground, and I will come and lie by each of you in turn, and we shall see whose feet stretch farther than mine," and whenever she lay down, she said a short prayer or murmured an Our Father. When she grew up, she used to tell these childish tricks with a smile, but she was very serious at the time she did them.

"He prayeth best who loveth best / All things both great and small," sang an English poet a hundred years ago, and Elizabeth certainly "prayed well," for she loved everything and everybody, but especially the poor people around the castle. In the winter, when deep snow covered the mountains for months at a time, she would give them all the money she was allowed by the landgrave, to buy them food and warm clothes. Or she might be met with, in some of the passages leading to the great kitchens of the castle, laden with scraps of food she had found thrown away, which she carried herself to the children. The stewards and cooks were very angry at this habit of Elizabeth, because they thought the unused food belonged to them, to do what they liked with; but they did not dare to complain, because the landgrave always let her do as she liked, and of course Elizabeth had not the least idea there was anything to complain about.

Unfortunately for the child, when she was nine and Ludwig sixteen, the landgrave Hermann died, and in him she lost a constant friend, who never failed to aid her in her plans for helping his people. But Elizabeth's mother-in-law, and her sister-in-law Agnes, who was famous for her beauty, thought very differently, and told her how silly it was in a princess to behave as if she were a servant; and as soon as her maids of honor saw how she was now treated, they began to laugh at her too. Even the officials of the court, who only wanted to please the landgravine as being the most powerful person in the state, were very rude to her. Ludwig alone took her side, but he was often away in distant parts of his duchy that he was learning to rule, or busy practicing sword-play or tennis in the court of the castle, or absent for two or three days on hunting expeditions; and as Elizabeth was always bright and happy with him, and never told tales, he did not guess the cruel way in which she was being persecuted. More and more she stayed in her own rooms with poor girls whose parents she had helped, for her companions.

For a long while, Elizabeth managed to avoid a quarrel with her mother-in-law. When one considers she was in years only a child still, it is a marvel; but things grew worse and worse, and at last the smoldering flames broke out into a fire. It was the feast of the Assumption, August 15, and it was the custom both of the court and of the people of Eisenach to keep the day as a holiday, and to offer gifts in church of fruit and flowers. By the command of the landgravine Sophia, Agnes and Elizabeth and their two maids of honor put on their richest dresses and golden circlets and went with her in state to the church. Sophia knelt down before the great crucifix, with the princesses on either side; but on seeing Elizabeth take off her coronet and lay it on a bench beside her, and then bow herself to the earth, the landgravine was filled with wrath, and, forgetting where she was, exclaimed loudly, "What is the matter with you, Elizabeth? Do you want to make everyone laugh at you?

Young ladies ought to kneel upright, and not fall down like old nuns or tired horses. Is your crown too heavy for you? Why can't you behave like us?"

Elizabeth rose to her feet at these rough words, and, although her face was flushed, she answered quietly, "Dear lady, do not be angry with me. How can I bear upon my head a crown of gold and jewels, when my Lord wears a crown of thorns?" Then, kneeling again, she covered her face with her mantle to hide her tears.

At length a whisper was heard at court that the marriage between Ludwig and Elizabeth would never take place, and that she would be sent back to her father. Her mother was dead, murdered four years before by a band of conspirators, which had given a terrible shock to her daughter. The king of Hungary troubled himself very little about Elizabeth, and the landgravine did not think he would resent the insult if Ludwig were to choose a richer, nobler bride.

"It had happened before," she said, "and would happen again," and Elizabeth would most certainly have been expelled in disgrace from Wartburg, had it not been for Ludwig, who turned a deaf ear to the counsels of mother, sister, and friends. The more pressing their attack, the more he turned to Elizabeth, and in her company there was always peace; and he never was absent for a day without bringing her back a little present to show that he had thought of her — a rosary of coral beads, a purse, a knife, a crucifix, a pair of gloves — and she received them all with gratitude, for she loved him as much as ever. Once only he forgot, and then her enemies openly triumphed and renewed their persecution, and Elizabeth — her spirit almost broken — poured out her heart to Walter von Varila, the knight who had brought her to Thuringia.

"Have patience yet a little longer," said Varila, "and I will speak to my lord."

A week later, Ludwig was hunting in the mountains not far from Wartburg, and Varila was with him. At midday, being hungry, they sat down in a wood to eat, and as the landgrave was in a particularly good temper, Varila felt that his chance had come. So he said, "Will you allow me to ask you a question, my lord?"

"Ask me anything you like," answered Ludwig.

"Well then, my lord, to be plain, what do you intend to do with the Princess Elizabeth whom I brought to you? Are you going to make her your wife? Or will you break your word and send her back to her father? People are talking, and it is right that you should know it."

At that Ludwig rose, and solemnly stretched his hand toward the Inselberg, the highest peak in Thuringia.

"Do you see that mountain?" he said. "Well, if it were made of gold from base to summit, and it were given to me on condition that I should send back Elizabeth, I would never do it. She is more to me than anything in the world."

"May I tell her that, my lord?" asked Varila.

"Yes, truly, and beg her to be comforted, and to accept this gift from me," and he drew from his wallet a little mirror on which was engraved the figure of our Lord.

After this Elizabeth paid no heed to rude words or unkind deeds until in 1220, on his return from his first war, Ludwig took her to wife with great pomp in the castle of Wartburg.

Elizabeth was then a tall, dark, well-made girl; while her husband, seven years older, was noted for his fair, handsome face, and his gentle manners. Still, he knew well enough how to make himself obeyed, and once married, Elizabeth was freed from her tormentors and was suffered to visit her poor neighbors as much as she liked.

Indeed, they may be said to have occupied all the thoughts that she did not give to her husband, and this sometimes caused her to seem forgetful and neglectful of the duties of her position, and her mother-in-law's rebukes were not always undeserved. It was hardly to be wondered at, that Sophia should be angry when at the marriage feast of her daughter the beautiful Agnes of Thuringia with the Duke of Austria, Elizabeth — who, according to custom, should have been ready to carry around the great bowl for each of the guests to dip their fingers in, as every hostess did on state occasions — could not be found.

"Where can she be?" said Ludwig to his mother, and then the seneschal stepped forward and told them that he had seen Elizabeth leaving the church, but on the steps she had been stopped by a half-naked beggar, who implored her to have pity on him. The landgravine, moved by his prayers, gave him her royal silken mantle and hastened back to the castle; but as it was against the rules that she should appear at a ceremonial banquet without one, she stayed quietly in her room.

"I will go and fetch her," exclaimed Ludwig with a laugh when he heard the tale, and he ran upstairs to her.

"Little sister," he said — it had always been his name for her — "we ought to have been at dinner long ago, but we have been waiting for you."

"I will do as you will, dear brother," answered she, "but I have no mantle, for I gave mine to a beggar. He was so cold." But as she spoke, one of her maids came forward: "Madam, your mantle is hanging in your closet. I will bring it in a moment."

Elizabeth and her husband looked at each other, and the same thought crossed their minds: "Inasmuch as ye have done it unto the least of these my brethren, ye have done it unto me." But they said nothing, and went down together to the banquet.

Another time Elizabeth's boundless charity might have had more serious results. Ludwig had gone away on some expedition, where he could not take his wife. She was very sad at being left at home, for whenever it was possible, she was always with him, galloping by his side, in snow and tempest, rain or sunshine. So to distract her thoughts, she spent more time than ever with her poor people, and one evening, while passing by a miserable shed, she heard deep groans and, entering, discovered a leper in the last stage of his dreadful disease. No one would come near him or touch him, but Elizabeth was not afraid.

"Lean on me," she said, "and I will take you where you shall be cared for," and in some way, she found strength to drag him up to the castle and laid him in her husband's own bed, so that she could always be at hand to nurse him, never thinking of what the consequences might be. When Sophia heard this, her fear and wrath knew no bounds. She dared not turn him out — to touch him might mean that she in her turn would become a leper — and she was aware that it was useless ordering a servant to move him, but her fury against Elizabeth was greater than ever.

Things were at this pass when Ludwig came home.

"See what Elizabeth has done now!" cried Sophia. "As if it were not bad enough for her to visit those wretched creatures in their homes. She has brought in a leper and laid him in your bed. Do you hear, in your *bed*!" But in her indignation she actually forgot her fears, and going before her son into the room, tore open the curtains! Ludwig looked down for a moment at the dying man.

"I see Christ Himself," he answered gently, and his mother was silent.

In spite of the unkindness showed her by Sophia, Elizabeth was perfectly happy. She had by this time two babies: Hermann, who died when he was eighteen; and Sophia, who afterward married the duke of Brabant. Later, two other little girls were born, and they became nuns.

It was during Ludwig's visit to the Emperor Frederick II in Sicily, in the year 1225, that a grievous famine broke out in Thuringia and many died of starvation. Elizabeth gave largely out of her own stores, but ten times the amount of corn she possessed would not have fed the people. With famine came sickness, and then she built a hospital below the castle, where twenty-eight of the most ill were nursed by her and her maids. Of course, Ludwig's mother and the steward grumbled at the expense, but Elizabeth went her way, only her heart sickened as she realized how little she could do, as she passed gaunt men in the road eagerly gnawing roots they had dug up from the ground, or seeking for berries to stay their hunger.

How thankful she was when Ludwig came back, and she could share her cares with him. As usual, the court officials and his mother tried to make mischief between them, complaining of how she had wasted his goods. But Ludwig sternly bade them be silent.

"Let her alone. She has done what she could," he said and gave orders that corn should be bought wherever it might be gotten and distributed among those who needed it so greatly. Afterward there sprang up a story too beautiful to be left untold, for it shows what her people felt about Elizabeth. The landgravine, says the legend, was walking down the path to Eisenach, her maid Ysentrud behind her, when she met her husband returning to the castle.

"You ladies seem heavily laden," he remarked, smiling. "What have you got hidden in your mantles? Nay, little sister, but I *will* see," he added, as Elizabeth hesitated, fearing he might think she was doing something unbecoming his wife, and he gave her mantle a little pull. As he did so, there fell out, not the long white loaves that were baked in the castle kitchen, but a heap of lilies and roses.

∞

But the happy days of Elizabeth's life were fast drawing to a close, and for the four remaining years of her life, she was to suffer pain of every kind, and even hunger and cold and everything that she had tried so hard to spare others. She was only twenty when, in 1227, her husband took the cross under the Emperor Frederick II and proceeded to set his duchy in order before starting for the

Holy Land. Elizabeth's heart was almost broken, but she did not try to keep him from fulfilling his vow. With a white face she gave him all the help she could, but she went silently along the dark passages of the castle, and even her babies could not make her smile. One thing only she was resolved upon. She would ride with him to the frontier and bid him farewell there. But at the frontier, she could not make up her mind to leave him. "I will go on to the next halting-place," she said, and when that was reached, she rode on again. At length her old friend Walter von Varila went sorrowfully up to Ludwig. "My lord, it must be. Her Highness must go."

Elizabeth heard the words and stood like a statue. Then a shudder ran through her; she threw her arms round her husband's neck and they clung together for a while. After a pause, Ludwig gently unwound her arms and spoke.

"Little sister," he said, and he called her so for the last time, "look well at this ring on my finger, with the lamb and flag engraved on the sapphire. When I reach my goal, I will send it back by one whom you can trust, and he will tell you if I am alive or dead. And now — farewell."

The Alps were crossed at last, and the noble company made their way through Italy to join the emperor at the state of Apulia. At Brindisi the vessels were anchored that were to carry the army to the Holy Land; but no sooner had both the emperor and Ludwig entered their ships than they were both seized with fever and had to put in to Otranto. Here Ludwig grew worse and worse and felt that he must die. He sent for his knights to hear his last orders, and choosing out one or two to bear the ring to Elizabeth, he begged the rest to carry his bones back to Thuringia, after they had accomplished their vow and delivered the tomb of Christ from the hands of the infidels. As he spoke, a flock of white doves entered the little cabin and flew around his bed.

"I must fly away with them," he said, and as the doves flew out of the porthole, he gave his last sigh.

The knights, charged with the terrible news, were a long time in traveling to Thuringia; and when at length they got there, Elizabeth was too ill to receive them. It was to Sophia they first told their tale, and when Elizabeth was fit to bear it, her mother-in-law broke it to her more tenderly than could have been expected. The landgravine listened without seeming to understand; then she leaped out of bed and ran wildly about the corridors of the castle as one that had lost her wits, until she flung herself against a wall, crying, "Dead! Dead!" between her sobs.

All Thuringia mourned with her — all, that is to say, but her two brothers-in-law, who took advantage of the condition she was in to seize the government and to drive Elizabeth and her children from the castle, refusing her leave even to carry away the things that belonged to her. Sophia, whose heart was softened by her grief, did her best to prevent Henry, the elder of the two, from behaving in this wicked way; but he would listen to nothing, and in the middle of the winter, Elizabeth bade goodbye to the castle that had been her home for twenty years, bearing in her arms her baby, then only a few weeks old. The other three were led by her two maids: Ysentrude, who had come with her from Hungary, and the faithful Guta.

Where to go they knew not, for Henry had forbidden the people of Eisenach to receive Elizabeth, and they, in spite of all that she and her husband had done for them, had not courage to disobey him. From door after door she was turned away, until the keeper of a miserable little inn took pity on the forlorn creatures and offered them shelter for the night. The next day a very poor priest sought her out and begged her to accept what he could offer; and thankful indeed was Elizabeth to go with him, and to put her babies to sleep on clean straw. She sold the jewels she had worn when she was sent from the castle in order to buy them bread, and

The keeper of a miserable little inn took pity on
the forlorn creatures and offered them shelter for the night.

after all were gone, she obtained a few pence by spinning. At length some friends came forward and besought her to give her children into their charge, and they would hide them safely from their uncles. It was agony for Elizabeth to part with them, but she knew it was best, and, sad and lonely though she was, it gave her peace to feel that the children were well and happy.

∞

It seems strange to us that some of the many German princes to whom she was related did not interfere on her behalf; but they were generally busy with their own little quarrels, and in those days, news traveled slowly. Sophia did all she could to help her, and at last she wrote to Elizabeth's aunt, the abbess Matilda of Kitzingen, who was filled with horror at her niece's sufferings and sent a carriage at once to fetch her to the banks of the river Main, where the poor princess found her children awaiting her. Here for a while was rest and peace, but in a few months the prince bishop of Bamberg, the abbess's brother and Elizabeth's uncle, interfered and declared that it was not suitable that she should remain in the convent, and urged her to return to Hungary. But this the landgravine at once declined. She had now no mother to welcome her, and her father, whom she had only seen once since her babyhood, seemed almost to have forgotten her existence.

Then the bishop insisted on her occupying a castle of his not far from Bayreuth, granting her a pension that would, he said, enable her to live comfortably, since she would not marry again, as he greatly wished. But Elizabeth would never "live comfortably" as long as there were any poor at her gates, and although she took up her abode in the castle, between prayers and almsgiving, her days were spent much as before.

One consolation she had at this time: the arrival of the crusading knights with the body of Ludwig, which had lain since his death in the town of Otranto. The journey was long and very difficult, but they were faithful to their trust, and at each town where they rested, the coffin was left for the night in a church. When they drew near Bamberg, a message was sent to the bishop, and he quickly summoned Elizabeth.

The whole of Thuringia was present at the funeral, which took place at Rheinhartsbrünn by the wish of Ludwig himself. Nobles and citizens alike forgot their wicked and cruel treatment of the dead man's wife and children, and for the sake of appearances, Henry and Conrad did not dare to behave differently from the rest. Sophia was there by the side of Elizabeth, who wept tears of thankfulness that the desire of her heart was fulfilled and that Ludwig rested in the place he had chosen.

∞

But the knights who had returned from the crusade were determined that justice should be done to the son of their master, and with Walter von Varila as their spokesman, they told the usurper sternly what they thought of him and his conduct. It is hardly to be supposed that Henry was really ashamed of himself, or that the knights' words could have thrown a new light upon his behavior. He was only ashamed, as many people are, of being publicly blamed, and, when he found he could not help himself, he agreed to be regent for his nephew until the boy grew up, and to reconcile himself to Elizabeth. She, we may be sure, went more than halfway to meet his repentance and joyfully consented to return to Wartburg with her children. But she soon found that the stir of a castle, with its continued feastings and hunting parties, had become impossible to her and begged that she might be allowed to go and live at Marburg on the banks of the river Lahn.

Now, Elizabeth might have led a long and peaceful life had it not been for a very foolish action of her own in days gone by. Two years before the death of her husband, she had, with his full consent, taken an oath to obey in small things as well as great, the priest Conrad of Marburg, a man who was the trusted friend of many popes. While Ludwig lived, things went on much as they had done in the time of her other confessor; but as soon as she became a widow, Conrad grew more and more tyrannical and set himself to deprive her of every pleasure and to force her into acts of untold humiliation. He would not allow her to remain in the house Henry had given her, but worked on her mind until she left it for a tumbledown hut, where she cooked her own food. In this place she stayed alone, while a little wooden cottage was built for her, and when all was ready for the move, she sent for her children and her two maids.

But still Conrad was not satisfied. It is true that he would not allow her to adopt all the rules of the Franciscan sisterhoods — she had long ago taken the lighter vows — and to beg from door to door like some of the sisters; but as Elizabeth would not have minded that at all, he required of her something that cut her to the heart: the dismissal of Ysentrude and separation from her children. This done, it was easy for her to give up all the possessions she had left and swear to observe the rules and wear a nun's dress to the end of her life, to fasten a cord around her waist, and to go barefoot. Guta, her maid, joyfully took the same vows and remained for a time with her mistress. Together they spun wool, which they sold for food, and the single garment, which each wore, was of the stuff used by the peasants. At last Guta was taken from her also, and two rough women placed with her by Conrad. She submitted to all, and soon the servants understood her patience and gentleness, and grew to love her.

But this life of constant work and constant privation could not go on forever. On first coming to Marburg, she had built a small hospital and here she spent much of her time, tending the sick as of old, and especially the lepers.

At the end of two years, she was attacked by a violent fever and, much against her will, was forced to take to her bed. For ten or twelve days she lingered, cheerful and happy, but always in prayer. One evening toward sunset, she fell asleep, when her maid, who was sitting with her, was startled by hearing a beautiful song proceeding from the pillow.

"Oh, madam, what lovely music!" cried the girl.

"Did you hear it too?" asked Elizabeth. "A charming little bird came and sat between me and the wall, and he sung so sweetly that he filled my soul with joy, and I could not help singing also! He told me besides," she added, after a pause, "that I shall die in three days."

∞

And in three days she was dead, as she had foretold, and was buried, as she wished, in the chapel of the hospital.

She was only twenty-four, but her whole life had been passed in the thought and service of others.

Saint and King

The man whose story I am now going to tell you stands, in some ways, alone among saints. Not because he was a king, for many kings have borne the title; not because he was a wise ruler, for wise rulers could not always claim to be considered saints; not even because he was good and charitable to his people; but because, not only in his own day but in ours, he was held by all men to be wiser and better and more fitted for his place than any king before or since; and in the words of Voltaire, the philosopher, who hated kings and did not set much store on goodness, "It was hardly possible for any man to reach greater excellence."

And who was this king whose memory still lived in the France of the eighteenth century, which had almost forgotten how to look up to anything higher than its own cleverness?

It was a king of France itself: Louis IX, St. Louis.

∞

He was only twelve years old when his father died, in 1226, within a few months of the death of St. Francis of Assisi. Louis VIII was ill only a few days. He had left Paris six months before, to fight against some of his vassals in the south, the heretics called Albigenses, and on his way home, he caught fever. It was quite clear to the king that he could never reach Paris, so he summoned to his presence the nobles and bishops to be found in his camp, and one by one they knelt at his bedside and swore that they would be faithful to his eldest son, and give help and support to the queen, Blanche of Castile, who would govern France until Prince Louis came of age. Afterward, those who could not write — and they were many — set their marks to a deed, and then the king's mind was at rest, and he died peacefully.

The queen's grief was great when the bishop of Senlis begged for a special audience with her and told her the terrible news. She was the granddaughter of Henry II of England and had married the French prince when she was only twelve. But girls, and especially princesses, grew up quickly in those days, and Blanche was soon allowed to be present at the state councils, and even sometimes to give her opinion.

She loved her husband dearly and, as often as possible, followed him in his various wars and shared his hardships. Yet she was a good mother to her children and is said to have taught her eldest boy herself until he was twelve years old.

Although, like most of the race of Plantagenets, from whom she sprang on her mother's side, Blanche had a hot temper, she had also plenty of tact, and much wisdom. She had done her best to help her husband, and the experience of state affairs, which she had gained since her marriage, enabled her to help her son. She had sensible advisers too, whom she could trust and was wise enough to make use of them. But clearly her first duty was to have the young king crowned, so that he might at once receive the homage of his nobles.

King Louis VIII had died on November 8, and the barons of the kingdom were ordered to appear at Rheims on the 29th. This step took by surprise — as the regent intended it should — some of the discontented nobles, who would have formed themselves into a strong party, had time been given them to do so. But Blanche was too quick for them; and twenty-one days after the death of his father, Louis IX was crowned by the bishop of Soissons, after receiving knighthood the day before, and watching alone in the cathedral until the dawn broke.

It is wonderful how in those days and in that short space, the queen-regent managed to make such splendid preparations; but although her heart was aching with sorrow for her husband, she put aside her grief and thought only of the danger of delay for her son. And she had her reward, for, according to the chronicler Joinville, who was with the king in his crusade, "It would be difficult to express how great was the effect of the coronation on the mind of the people, who beheld a child, fair of face and dignified of manner, called to a throne threatened by intriguing men, with no support but his mother." Blanche was right. The discontented nobles dared not stay away, and, during the ceremony itself, the countess of Champagne broke into a violent quarrel with the countess of Flanders as to who should carry the sword of state before the king on returning from the ceremony. Queen Blanche, however, wisely decided to give the honor to neither, and the sword was borne by the Count de Boulogne, Louis's uncle, one of the sharpest thorns in the side of the crown.

∞

Although Louis was carefully trained by his mother in the business of governing the kingdom and in learning all he could about the state of the people, and the country — the crops that were grown in certain parts; the horses, which were the pride of some provinces; the trade that supported the inhabitants of other towns — he still had friends of his own age besides his brothers, with whom he could wrestle and play in his spare time. As was the custom in those days, the nobles and even foreign princes sent their sons to court as pages to be taught good manners and knightly accomplishments. The queen was known all over Europe as the sovereign who was most strict in these matters, and she was never lacking in boys of all ages to attend on her. Indeed, if she had listened to the requests that poured in upon her, the court would have been overrun with them. She was sitting one day in the great hall, when, amid the corps of pages, her eyes fell on a fresh face, fair and golden-haired as the king's own.

"Who is that?' she asked of an officer standing near her, and he answered that the tall boy was Hermann, the son of Elizabeth of Hungary and Duke Ludwig of Thuringia. On hearing his name, Blanche rose and went to the spot where he stood.

"Good youth," she said, "you had a blessed mother. Where did she last kiss you?"

Blushing to the roots of his hair at the notice taken of him, Hermann pointed to a spot between his eyes. "I would kiss you there too," saind the queen, and stooped and kissed him. The rest of the pages looked on in wonder. They had never seen their mistress in this mood before; they were rather afraid of her, for she seldom spoke to them and had more than once ordered them a whipping, when they had been disobedient or unruly. Louis shared the whippings if he was idle and, instead of translating his Latin books to his tutor, gazed out of the narrow openings in the walls, which were the windows of those times, and longed for a good gallop over the plain. But after all, the whippings bore fruit, and almost alone among the sovereigns of his day, he could understand Latin nearly as well as if he had been a priest.

Of her seven children, Louis was his mother's favorite, but she did not think that was any reason for giving him his own way. She taught him to make rules for his own conduct, and to keep them, and to turn a deaf ear to the voice of flatterers who came about him speaking smooth things, and trying to make him think himself greater and better than other men, while they would accuse him behind his back of all sorts of wickedness. His enemies were, of course, not slow to spread the reports and to take advantage of them. Religious and honest people were grieved at what they heard of the king, and at last a monk made his way into the queen's

The queen kissed Hermann.

presence and reproached her for the manner in which she was bringing up her son.

Blanche listened quietly until he had finished, and then she said, "You did right to come, and I thank you for your courage; but know that although the king, my son, is the dearest thing I have on earth, yet if, to save his life, it was necessary that he should commit sin, far rather would I see him fall dead before me."

The monk bowed his head and answered nothing. It was true, of that he felt sure; and Louis, who was present also, laid his mother's words to heart and in after days repeated them to his children.

The years between his coronation and coming of age were spent by the king and his mother in trying to keep the powerful barons in order and in putting down a rebellion in the south, where the Albigenses were still fighting under Raymond, count of Toulouse. The war on both sides was carried on with what we should now consider great cruelty. But peace was at last made, and Queen Blanche was able to turn her attention to a more pleasant subject: the marriage of the king.

The first bride she thought of for him was Jeanne, the daughter of that very count of Toulouse with whom she had just been fighting. The child could be brought up under her own eye, and she would be able to train her as she ought to be trained; but after all, would the marriage be happy for Louis? He was only fifteen himself, of course, but Jeanne was such a baby; it would be years before she could be a companion to him such as she herself had been to her husband, for, unlike most of the women of her time, Blanche held marriage to be more than a matter of business. No. Jeanne should marry one of the younger ones — Alphonse, for instance, when he grew older, and so she did; and, in her right, Alphonse became count of Toulouse as well as of Poitiers.

One after another the great heiresses of France passed before her mind, and one by one they were rejected. The inquiry occupied some years, but the matter was very important, and the queen did not hurry. At length she decided on one against whom nothing could be said: Marguerite, the eldest daughter of the count of Provence, pretty, gentle, and well brought up, fourteen years old, but showing already a promise of the good sense and firmness, which Blanche knew to be necessary to the queen of France. Last, but not the least, Marguerite had, like herself, Spanish blood in her veins.

The queen-regent, as we have seen, never wasted time. No sooner had she talked the matter over with Louis, and he had accepted the bride proposed for him, than she sent ambassadors to the court of Provence, which was always filled with minstrels and wandering troubadours, to ask for the hand of Marguerite. The count was only too delighted at the brilliant marriage offered for his daughter and made no difficulties. "Their orders," said the ambassadors, "were to bring the young countess back with them," and in a very few weeks Marguerite bade her parents and sisters farewell and traveled northward along the Rhone. Louis met her at the gates of the town of Sens, and next day she was married by the archbishop in the great cathedral and crowned immediately afterward.

It had been the wise policy of the regent to show her son to his subjects by taking him with her in her journeys through the kingdom, when she was trying to make peace between the nobles or listening to the grievances of humbler people. At every place where they halted, the poor were sought out, and money given to them where they needed it, with a gentle politeness to which they were quite unused. Yet they soon felt that it was vain to deceive the king with long pitiful stories. A few grave questions speedily got to the truth of the matter, and the false beggar was sent away with some stern words that he did not easily forget.

The sight of their king on his way to church on the feast days induced several of his courtiers and citizens to go likewise, and a few of them might even have been seen helping the king to mix mortar and carry stones to build the famous Abbey of Royaumont, which was at that time rising from the ground.

Still, anxious though he was about doing his duty, Louis was a boy in many ways and was ready to amuse himself, as is shown by the bills for horses, hounds, falcons, and, strange to say, for lions and porcupines, found among his accounts, as well as those for the payment of minstrels and for fine clothes for himself and his brothers.

The first act of Louis, after coming of age and taking the government into his own hands, is very remarkable, when we remember what a religious man he was and how his mother had brought him up to be a true son of the Church and a hater of heresy. It was to protest against the manner in which the clergy had grown to disregard the laws of the kingdom and declined to obey the verdict of the law courts.

This way of thinking was brought to his notice by the behavior of the archbishop of Rheims, who had a quarrel with the citizens and cut them off from the services of the church. The king refused to support the archbishop without first examining the affair and seeing who was in the right. He even refused to be guided by the pope, and the archbishop had to submit, like any other man, to a fair trial, which was decided in his favor.

This showed the French nation, if they had not known it before, of what stuff their king was made, and that he had the two qualities necessary to every great sovereign: a sense of justice and the courage to carry out what was right. And the world outside watched the struggle also, and later, when the rulers of other lands disputed with their vassals or with each other, it was to the king of France that they turned as judge. Even the Jews, so hated and persecuted through all the Middle Ages, were safe in France from torture and death, although severe laws were passed forbidding them to lend money at high interest or usury.

∞

In 1244, at the close of a war with Henry III of England, the king fell ill of fever, and the fear of his death brought out all the love that his subjects felt for him. At the news of his danger, prayers were offered for his recovery, and every church in Paris was filled to overflowing. The Crown of Thorns — said to be the one worn by our Lord, and bought by Louis from the Venetians — was brought by his mother from the beautiful Sainte Chapelle, built to receive it, and laid upon his unconscious body; while Queen Blanche made a vow on his behalf that if her son's life was saved, he should take the cross and go to the rescue of the Holy Sepulcher at Jerusalem. But all her tears and prayers and vows seemed useless, and at length, the bishops who were present, convinced that he had ceased to breathe, gently forced both queens to leave the room. Two ladies remained, and one of them brought a cloth with which to cover his face, as was the custom. But the other snatched the cloth from her.

"No, no," she cried, "it is impossible! I will not believe it! He is alive still!" and as she spoke, the king opened his eyes and looked at her.

"By the grace of the Lord, the light from the East has shone upon me and has called me from the dead," he whispered. The cry of joy uttered by the ladies brought his wife and mother back to his bedside, but they stopped in surprise on the threshold, on hearing him bid the bishop of Paris to be fetched from the antechamber.

"Give me the cross," he said faintly, when the bishop entered.

"Oh, not yet! Wait until you are cured," exclaimed Queen Blanche, throwing herself on her knees before him.

"I will take no food until the cross is on my breast," he repeated, and the bishop gave it to him.

The state of the Christians in Palestine at that time was worse than ever. The sultan of Egypt, eager to get possession of the country, summoned a great host of wandering, half-savage Asiatic tribes to besiege Jerusalem from the north, and at the first rumors of their approach, the Christians, who had been allowed by the sultan of Damascus to occupy the city, fled to the fortified towns on the coast. Here, at least, the sea was before them, and they could escape if necessary.

But it seemed that it was not Jerusalem alone that the invaders wanted, but Christian blood, and when they found an empty town, they invented a plan to entice the fugitives back to their ruin. To this end, they hung over the walls all the Christian banners that had been left behind in the hurry of flight, in the hope that they might be seen by some stragglers. Unfortunately this wicked project succeeded. Some of the Christians who had taken refuge in the hills saw the flags, and, knowing that a few of their brethren had declared their intention of dying in defense of the Holy Sepulcher, imagined, very foolishly, that they had driven back the invading army. Without pausing to consider that this was nearly impossible for a handful of men to do, they sent messengers to the flying multitude, telling them they could return in safety. The news was received with shouts of joy, and the people seemed almost mad with delight.

In vain a few of the wiser tried to show them how unlikely it was that the besiegers had retreated: their excited countrymen refused to listen and would not lose a moment in retracing their steps. As soon as they were within the walls, the enemy who had hidden themselves in the surrounding hills entered the city and killed every creature. Not content with this, they tore down the altars of the churches, and heaped all the insults they could imagine on the places that the Christians held sacred and that even the Saracens had left untouched.

All this had happened during the king's illness, and when the pope heard of it, he lost no time in calling a council and bidding the princes of Europe take the cross and fly to avenge Jerusalem.

His quarrel with the Emperor Frederick II — the Wonder of the World — delayed matters for a while, but in France, at any rate, all were eager for the crusade. Only a few young nobles, lazy and pleasure-loving, hung back, and for these a trap was laid by Louis.

It had long been the practice in France that every Christmas the king would give his courtiers rich mantles or tunics beautifully embroidered, and in this particular year, it was arranged that the ceremony should take place in the great hall, after the midnight Mass of Christmas Eve. The flickering torches, fixed along the walls, gave but little light, and only the glitter of the golden trimmings could be seen. However, the mantles seemed more splendid than usual, and the young men wrapped themselves proudly in them before they went to the little dark rooms in which they slept. Being, like most Frenchmen, fond of dress, the first thing they did in the morning was to carry the mantles to the windows and see how they looked in daylight.

On the shoulder of each was embroidered a cross — the mark of a Crusader. "The king has been too much for us," they said with a laugh, and no better fighters were found among the Crusaders than these idle young nobles.

∽

But a king could not go off to the wars at once as if he were a common knight, and it took Louis nearly two years to make his preparations. He had to see that his kingdom would be properly governed in his absence, and once more Blanche was appointed regent, with a council to help her. Then money had to be collected, which was a very difficult matter, and the well-being of the army to be provided for, as, like Hannibal, Louis was very careful for the comfort of his men. But at length everything was ready, and on June 12, 1248, the king, accompanied by his brothers, rode to the Abbey of Saint-Denis, where the pope's legate, or envoy, delivered to him the staff and wallet of a pilgrim, and the standard of France.

Queen Margaret had refused to be left behind, and the king's two brothers — Robert, count of Artois, and Charles, count of Anjou, both unlucky, violent, and reckless — had taken the cross with the king. Near Corbeil he bade farewell to his mother, who knew full well she would see him no more, and started on the road south.

Two months later, he entered the little town of Aigues-Mortes, hardly bigger today than when the army of seven thousand men marched through its narrow streets and down the narrow spit of land jutting out into the sea, known as the Grau Louis, where the fleet awaited them. They sailed first to Cyprus, where they were forced to spend nine months, for, as always happened in the crusades, quarrels broke out between the different princes, and it required all Louis's tact and firmness to reconcile them. They were also disagreed as to the best point of attack on the enemy, but at length Louis decided that as the assault on Jerusalem had been made by the Turcoman tribes, under the orders of the sultan of Egypt, and that he was the real master of the city, it would be wiser to begin by subduing Egypt, and with this purpose, the army crossed the sea and landed at Damietta.

After one victory, everything seemed to go against the Crusaders. They had forgotten that Egypt was a country quite unlike every other, and that the rise of the Nile would interfere with the movement of troops. When they understood this, they determined to pass the summer in Damietta, a resolve that, perhaps more than anything else, led to the failure of the expedition. The troops, overcome by the heat, grew lazy and declined to obey orders or submit to discipline. They robbed the peasants, extorted money from them, and, encouraged by the example of their leaders, spent their days in eating and drinking. They neglected, too, their military duties, and many a sentry was killed by the enemy as he slept at his post. Louis did all he could to stop the state of things and at first punished the wrongdoers severely, especially his own countrymen. But very soon he saw that he was powerless to restore discipline; the offenders were too numerous, and, under the feudal system, were only responsible each to his own leader.

Then the king's brothers gave him bad advice and caused serious mischief. At the battle of Mansourah, forced on by the rashness of the count of Artois, the young man himself was killed, as well as the flower of the nobility. Louis himself was in the thickest of the melee and fought desperately, and by the end of the day, the Crusaders had beaten back the Saracens and had the victory — a barren one — in their hands. But instead of returning at once to Damietta, where all their provisions were stored, the king, most imprudently, stayed where he was and suffered the enemy to lie between him and the town. Their supplies were cut off and soon famine broke out, while plague followed. In every place where lay the sick and the dying, the king might be seen, tending them himself and praying with them.

"I cannot die until I have beheld my holy master," said his valet, and when Louis heard of it, he ran to the man's bedside and took him in his arms.

As the weeks went on, things grew worse and food more scarce. Crowds of soldiers, rendered desperate by hunger, went over to the Saracen camp, and those of them who were ready to give up their religion and become Mohammedans were sure for the future to lead an easy life. At last, just when the king had issued orders for a retreat to Damietta, he was himself struck down with the plague.

"Leave the king as a hostage, and we will exchange Jerusalem for Damietta": so ran a message the Saracens sent into the Christian camp. The French barons rejected the terms with horror, but there was a large part of the army who would have thankfully agreed to the proposal, had they been consulted. Murmurs were heard in the tents, and the men went sullenly about their work. The generals saw that the move to Damietta must be made at once or there would be a revolt and wished to send Louis with the rest of the sick by boat down the Nile. But the king would not listen to them.

"My soldiers have risked their lives for the service of God and for me," he said, "and I will lead them back to France or die a prisoner with them."

That night, the army, hardly more than skin and bone, began the retreat — the king, as weak as any of them, riding in the rear, in the most dangerous place of all. At daybreak, the Saracens fell on them, and feeble as they were, the Crusaders were instantly put to the rout. The royal standard of France, the *Oriflamme*, and many other famous banners, were taken, and Louis and his brothers, the counts of Poitiers and Anjou, were obliged to surrender.

Whether from pity, or from dread lest death should deprive him of the king's ransom, the sultan gave orders that the skillful Saracen doctors should nurse the king carefully, and slowly he began to mend. He bore the harsh treatment that he suffered without one complaint and devoted his thoughts to arranging a truce that would include the ransoming of the entire army. "The poor should be set free, as well as the rich," he said, "and I will never leave my prison until the money needed is obtained."

Thanks to Queen Margaret at Damietta, brave and energetic as Louis himself, the ransom was found. The news of her husband's captivity was a terrible blow to her and to his mother in France. But Margaret kept her sorrows to herself and went about the streets of Damietta with a calm face, seeing that the fortifications were in good order and managing to enlist for the defense a number of Genoese and Pisan soldiers, who were excellent fighters.

"If the Saracens should take the town, I command you to kill me. I will never fall into their hands," she said to the knight eighty years old, who was her only bodyguard. However, Damietta was not taken, but surrendered, and Queen Margaret set sail for Acre, carrying with her the little son who had been born a few days before and was called Tristan, or "sorrow."

There are many stories that show that Louis's truth and justice, and still more his patience, made a deep impression on his captors and gradually led them to treat him with more kindness than in the beginning. He did not care whether he lived or died himself; it was entirely, as they saw, of his people that he was thinking.

"The *Frankish* king," they said to each other, "discusses the terms of peace as if we were in his power and not he in ours." And they looked on him as a creature they could not understand, when he refused to take advantage of a mistake of the Saracens in counting out the ransom, and paid the ten thousand pounds needed to complete the sum agreed upon. Surely a man must be mad to act thus!

Nor was he less indifferent when an ignoble death at the hands of a common soldier threatened him.

"Dub me a knight, or I will kill you," a mameluke, or Turkish guard, said to him one day.

"Become a Christian, and I will knight you, but not until then," answered Louis, and the man held his peace and let him go.

∞

The king and his army did not go back to France after the truce was made, but set sail for the Holy Land, accompanied very reluctantly by the nobles who broke out into open rebellion when they reached Acre. Only Joinville, the seneschal and chronicler, who was one of Louis's closest friends for twenty-two years, urged him not to leave Palestine, for the various Mohammedan states both in Egypt and Syria were divided among themselves, and there was a chance that Jerusalem might yet fall into the hands of the Crusaders. At any rate, the presence of an army would be a help to their own people.

This was the king's opinion also, but he could not prevail on the barons to stay, and in August they departed to France, the king's brothers sailing with them.

"Dub me a knight, or I will kill you," a Turkish guard said.

For four years, Louis maintained his position in the Holy Land, in spite of a lack of both men and money, for all the European sovereigns and powerful cities, such as Venice and Genoa, were too busy with their own affairs to give him help. His mother alone was faithful and sent him all the supplies she could raise. Patiently he went from place to place, building walls and towers for defense, many of which may still be seen. As in the days of his boyhood at Royaumont, he mixed mortar and fixed stones. He also encouraged other workers by his example, tended those who fell ill, visiting them constantly and ransoming as far as he could the Christian slaves in Egypt and Syria. He even succeeded, so strong was the force of his goodness, in converting some of the Saracens whom he had taken captive, and he always protected the women and children. More surprising still, he never suffered the Mohammedans who later returned to their own faith to be mocked or ill-treated.

In the midst of these labors, a new sorrow fell upon him in the death of his mother, and there was no one to take her place in France or to keep down the turbulent nobles. Louis felt that his country needed him and the Christians in Palestine did not, for he had done the work he had set himself, and for the present they were in safety.

So amid the tears and blessings of the people, he started from Acre at Easter 1254 and made straight for Cyprus.

Once again he was pursued by misfortune, for during a fog, the ship struck on a sand bank and was in danger of sinking. The sailors and passengers gave way to panic, but the king quietly went to the bridge of the vessel and knelt in prayer until the captain ordered a sounding to be taken and found that, although they could not move, they were in deep water and for the present were safe. The next day, divers went down and discovered that the keel was broken, and it was very doubtful if the ship could weather a heavy sea.

"You must leave the ship, sire," said they, "for she will never stand the waves."

"And suppose that the ship belonged to you and was full of cargo. Would you abandon her?" asked the king.

"No, indeed," they all cried at once. "We would stick by her."

"Then why do you advise me to go?"

"Ah, sire, it is very different for you! And besides, there are the queen and your three children to think of."

But Louis shook his head. "If I go," said he, "every man who is on board — and there are five hundred of them — will land in Cyprus and perhaps be afraid to enter a ship again, and so be lost to France. I would rather put myself and the queen and my children in peril than have that upon my conscience."

In this way it was decided: the ship was patched up and spread its sails once more, only to encounter a heavy gale, which, as the divers had foretold, nearly wrecked them. And when that subsided, they came face-to-face with a yet more terrible death, for one of the queen's maids left her mistress's veil hanging in the cabin near a taper, and it caught fire, fragments of it being blown onto the sheets. Margaret, who had been asleep at the time, was awakened by the smell of burning. With the presence of mind that never failed her, she leapt out of bed and flung the veil into the sea, crushing the sheets in her hands.

For the rest of the voyage, the king himself went around every night to see that all the fires were put out.

Altogether it took them between two and three months to reach French soil, and from the town of Hyères, they traveled slowly to Paris. But, however joyful was the welcome given to him, Louis himself was very sad. Not only had he failed in the work he had undertaken, but he had lost many men and brought pain and suffering upon more. As to all he had suffered himself, and his patience and courage in trying to repair his mistakes, he never gave that a thought. Happily, there was much business waiting for him in Paris, and not having any time to brood upon his troubles, he soon became as sensible and cheerful as usual.

Louis's first act was to put an end to the war with Flanders, and then he turned his attention to the struggle with England for the possession of the southern part of France, which had come into the hands of Henry II, as the inheritance of his wife, Eleanor of Aquitaine. Now Eleanor's grandson, Henry III, was on the throne, and he had married another Eleanor, daughter of the count of Provence, and sister of Queen Margaret. In this year (1254), Henry had been obliged to visit his French dominions to quell a revolt, and he took the queen with him. When all was quiet again, he wrote to his brother-in-law, King Louis, saying that he greatly wished to see Paris and the wonders of the Sainte-Chapelle, of whose beauty he had heard from travelers, and he entreated permission to pass a short time at the court. He would bring with him, he added, Queen Eleanor, her mother, the old countess of Provence, and her two sisters: Sanchia, wife of his brother Richard of Cornwall, and Beatrice, countess of Anjou. This proposal pleased everybody.

It was rare, indeed, in those times for a whole family to meet once they had married and left their early home, and Queen Margaret rejoiced to see them all again and to show them her children. The citizens of Paris, who had so long lived in gloom and anxiety, were delighted at the chance of being glad once more and gave the visitors a splendid welcome. Garlands of flowers wreathed the houses, and multitudes of torches lit up the streets at night — not the long, wide streets that we know, of course, but narrow, crooked ones, with towers and pointed roofs and arched doorways. And while the princesses were sitting in their bower, chattering fast over all that had happened since, one by one, they had left the castle in Provence, the two kings were riding through Paris, and Henry saw, as he wished, the Sainte-Chapelle and the glorious windows that we also may see, and beheld the Crown of Thorns that many years before, the king had carried barefoot from the town of Sens, to lay it for a while in the Cathedral of Notre-Dame.

Then they all, ladies as well as gentlemen, dined at a banquet in the Temple, and the king of England made presents to the French nobles, and everyone was merry and happy. Yet, if they could have looked forward down the centuries, they would have seen a sight to bring tears to the eyes of the most hardened. From the prison, built on the very spot where they were then sitting, the King of France, Louis XVI, was led to his execution. At the foot of the guillotine, mingling with the hooting mob, stood the abbé Edgworth, and his eyes met the king's.

"Son of Saint-Louis, ascend to Heaven," said the abbé, as the knife fell.

But that scene was five hundred fifty years distant.

∞

The result of the king of England's visit was a peace, granting favorable terms to France, with the cession of Normandy and some other provinces, in exchange for territories north of the river Garonne, not half so valuable. Besides which, Henry swore to do homage for the whole of his possessions, and Louis was quite satisfied, although his barons were not, thinking he might have gotten more.

The remaining years of Louis's reign were occupied in establishing law and order throughout France and in constantly acting as peacemaker in foreign quarrels. He, as many other kings have done, forbade duels, although not with much success, and was at all times ready to listen to his people. Anyone had liberty to come to him as he sat under an oak in the wood of Vincennes or in his own garden, and either he would judge the case or listen to his counselors doing so, as Joinville, himself one of those chosen, describes to us. The king's dress on these occasions was very simple, consisting of a loose cloth coat without sleeves, a tunic or sort of waistcoat, and a cap with a white peacock's feather. Unlike most judges of that day, he was more merciful to the poor than to the rich and noble, and with his own brother, Charles of Anjou, he was most severe of all. Charles gave him much trouble all through his life, owing to his violence and rashness. It seems strange that Queen Blanche, who had brought up Louis so well and was so strict with him, should have suffered the younger ones to grow up so unruly. But she was a great deal away from Paris and might have been obliged to leave them to other people who, from laziness or a desire to make themselves liked, allowed them to do as they pleased.

After Louis's return from the crusade, men noticed that he was even more spare in his way of living than before. Except on great occasions, he was seen no more in the scarlet gowns and furs in which, as a young man, he had taken pride, and his food was of the plainest. He fed the poor with his own hands during Lent and often went the round of the hospitals in Paris, bathing the wounds of the patients and not shrinking even from the lepers. Yet he could still laugh and enjoy a good story, and he encouraged his friends to talk as freely before him as when he was not present. As for swearing, he never practiced it himself and, when he could, punished it severely in others. Hunting he had long given up; "dicing" — Charles of Anjou's favorite game — he disliked; but he watched with the deepest interest the progress of the magnificent cathedrals of Amiens, Rheims, and others, which were then rising throughout France. He collected books and welcomed scholars to his palace. In addition, he was very particular about his children's education and had them with him whenever it was possible. He insisted that his sons should go to Mass with him and keep the fasts and feasts of the Church; and although he left his daughters chiefly to their mother's direction, he wrote to them after their marriages as often as he could, begging them not to forget their duty both to God and to their people.

It was a sad day for France when the king publicly took the cross, an example that was followed by his three elder sons and a few of the great nobles. The citizens and most of the barons strongly disapproved, but during the three years of preparation, many were won over. At length, in 1270, all was ready. Two of the king's most trusted counselors were appointed regents, and a second time he received the *Oriflamme* at Saint-Denis, and the pilgrim's wallet and staff from the legate. Now it was his wife and not his mother who was to be left behind, and bitter was the parting, for he was worn out with a life's hard work, and well she knew that she would see his face no more.

It was the middle of July when the army, which had sailed from Aigues-Mortes, landed near Tunis and at once formed camp on the ruins of Carthage. But what had occurred at Damietta was repeated here. The enemy would not give a pitched battle, but cut off their supplies until illness broke out, Prince John being one of the first victims. The grief at his son's death gave the final blow to the king, and he had no strength to resist when the disease laid hold of him also. He knew the end was at hand, and for himself he welcomed it. His affairs he had set in order before he left France, but he managed to write down a few directions for his eldest son, Philip, who was to succeed him. Then he begged that the last sacraments might be given him, and said aloud the seven Penitential Psalms, after which he was laid on a bed of ashes, with his hands crossed on his breast, and remained speechless until the hour of three, when he gave up his soul. Nine months later, his bones were carried to France and buried in the Abbey of Saint-Denis.

"A piteous thing and worthy of tears is the death of this holy prince," said one who loved him.

Preacher to the Birds

There is not surer proof of the greatness of any man or woman than the eagerness with which we fly to read all that is written about them. "Oh, there can't be anything more to be said about him, people cry again and again. "I'm tired to death of his name." But, although that is an exclamation often made about certain heroes and heroines of history, it is never uttered about such men as Napoleon or Francis of Assisi. It is as impossible to write a book of saints and leave Francis out as it would be to write a book of great captains and omit Caesar.

In the part of Italy known as Umbria, there stands the little town of Assisi, built on the slopes of Monte Subasio. Assisi is a very old city — some say it dates as far back as 400 or 500 BC — and underneath its streets are long passages that come out far away in the hills, as if the citizens had used them in time of siege as a means of escape. If you studied its ruins of temples, theaters, and circuses, you would learn a great deal of history, not only of Assisi itself, but of Rome also. Totila, the Goth, halted there for a short space on his way to besiege the Eternal City. Charlemagne passed through it two hundred fifty years later; while in the struggle for power between the pope and the emperor during the Middle Ages, the town sided first with one and then with the other. But against one enemy, the people of Assisi never ceased fighting, and that was with the citizens of Perugia, which lay across the hills and could be seen plainly from the castle on the top.

∞

Among all the merchants of Assisi, none was so rich or well thought of as Bernadone, who carried on with France a large trade in silks and embroidered stuffs. He had an only son, Giovanni, or John, born in 1182, and as soon as the child was four or five years old, he had been taught French, so that by and by his father might send him to sell his goods to the noble ladies of the French court; and as no one in Assisi ever thought of learning any language but Italian, the boy was nicknamed "Il Francesco," or "the French-man." Such, at any rate, is the story, whether it is true or not.

Francis was a lively boy, quick to notice and to remember. He must have heard, from his earliest years, tales of the martyrs who had been put to death by the pagan lords of the town and could listen for hours to stories of "battles long ago." He was himself fond of fighting, as became a good citizen, and dressed in fine clothes (which he loved), would frequently ride out through the gates with a company of friends to attack Perugia.

But he went along that road once too often, for at last he was taken prisoner and shut up for a year in the castle. When peace was made between the two cities and Francis was set free, he was so weakened by all the hardships he had undergone that he grew very ill. For some weeks, they thought he would die, but he slowly got better and at length was nearly as strong as he had been before his illness and could ride and walk once more through the streets of Assisi. Yet now and then his companions would look at him with a puzzled expression. He seemed different, somehow, from the friend they had known, although they could not have told you why.

One day, Francis, now twenty-one, and as tall as he ever was likely to be, was walking down the road leading from the castle of

Assisi, when a ragged man rose from a doorstep where he had been basking in the sun and stood before the young man, holding out his hand for money. Francis stopped and looked at him.

"Surely I know you," he said. "I am certain I have seen you before, but I cannot remember your name."

"Well may you know me," answered the beggar, "but when you last saw me, I wore clothes as fine as yours, for I too was once noble and rich, and commanded a troop of soldiers who went out to fight against Perugia. But yesterday is not today, as most of us find sooner or later."

"Poor man! Poor man!" murmured Francis to himself. Then he added aloud, "Here, take my clothes; they are warmer than yours," and unfastening his tunic of grey velvet, he put it on the beggar and wrapped his mantle of scarlet cloth about him.

"Now I shall pretend to be you," he cried gaily, picking up the torn and dirty cloak that lay on the ground. "Fare you well. I will not forget you," and he went away smiling.

That night a strange dream came to Francis. He thought he was in a large room, filled to overflowing with jewels and silks, and beautifully inlaid swords and daggers, and on every weapon was the sign of the Cross. In the midst of the pile stood Christ, and as Francis looked, he seemed to hear the words: "These are the riches that are the reward of my servants, and the swords are for those who fight for me." But, even as he gazed, the dream vanished, and Francis lay awake wondering if it had any special meaning. Long he pondered over it, and at last he seemed to understand.

"I am to be a soldier and not a merchant, I suppose," he said to himself. "Perhaps someday I shall be sent on a crusade. Oh, I hope so! But I must wait and see."

∞

Not long after his meeting with the beggar, Francis was praying in the church of St. Damiano, which had suffered so severely in

A strange dream came to Francis.

many sieges that it was more than half in ruins. He was kneeling before the altar when a voice again struck on his ears: "Francis, thou shalt repair my Church," and he looked about him, waiting to hear more. But as all was silent, he at once resolved to lose no time in obeying the Lord's command; and he hastened to buy some bricks, which he carried away on his back and set down near the church, ready to begin his work the next day. On his way back with the bricks, he met some friends, who stopped and laughed at him for turning mason. Francis laughed too and said they had better come and help him, so they parted merrily.

As soon as he had put the bricks in a convenient place, he went home and, taking a roll of cloth from his father's warehouse, sold it in the market, giving the money to the priest of St. Damiano to spend as he thought fit for the benefit of the church. When old Bernadone returned and discovered the cloth missing, and that his son had stolen it, he was so angry that Francis fled from his fury, and hid in a cave in the hills, where he stayed for many days without food. At last, driven by hunger, he crept back to his father's house, so changed in the short time that even his friends hardly knew him. His mother wept over him, thinking he was going to die, but his father declared he was mad, and locked him in his room until he could be taken before the bishop. As soon as he found himself in the old man's presence, Francis did not wait to be asked questions, but flung off his clothes and, throwing himself at the bishop's feet, exclaimed, "Henceforth, I have no father but the one in Heaven," which caused the bishop so much joy that he almost wept. Then, covering Francis with a tattered cloak that lay on a chair, he gave him his blessing.

It was in this manner that Francis Bernadone, at twenty-four, yielded himself to the service of God.

His first act was to go for some time to a small hospital, which was set apart for lepers, and help to tend the poor creatures who were objects of terror and loathing to all. His friends were horrified when they heard what he had done, for they felt sure he would catch the disease and die a dreadful death. Francis, however, had no fears for himself and, while he was nursing the lepers, was as glad and cheerful as usual.

But, by and by, he felt new duties were required of him. He set out on a sort of pilgrimage over the Umbrian mountains, singing hymns in the joy of his heart and praising God for the birds in the woods and the fishes in the rivers, and all the beauty he saw around him. At night, he slept in a little cell at the foot of the mountain on which Assisi was built; and by day, he went from door to door, asking for food or money or clothes or anything else he needed, and when he got it, he would hurry off gladly to seek out some sick or miserable being and give away all that was not absolutely necessary to keep himself alive.

∽

"Take nothing for your journey, neither gold, nor silver, neither two coats, neither shoes nor yet staves": this was the text of a sermon Francis heard one Sunday at Mass, and he thought it was meant especially for him, and to be a sign that such was to be the rule of his life. He had long parted with all his rich garments, and now his dress consisted of a loose grey tunic, with a little cape and hood, a leathern girdle around the waist and wooden sandals on his feet, unless, as often happened, he went barefoot. It is thus we see him in the early pictures, but two centuries after his death, his followers exchanged the grey habit for a brown one.

Was there, he wondered, any part of his dress that he could manage to do without? At first he thought not; then an idea occurred to him. Yes, of course! He wanted only something to fasten his robe, and a rope would do as well as anything else, in fact better. And then he would have his girdle to give away! So from that day forward, instead of the girdle, he wore the rope, which gained both for him and his followers the name of "Cordeliers."

By this time, his untiring humility and charity had drawn many to him. It was a period of restlessness and excitement; men — and women too — were dissatisfied with the lives they were leading and wanted something different, although *what*, they did not exactly know. But Francis knew, and so they followed his teaching and did his bidding; and the rich gave to the poor, and even the laborers in the fields stopped sowing and ploughing and preached peace to each other. Soon the women formed themselves into a society, a large number taking no vows and remaining as before in their homes, only giving up balls and tournaments and the parties of which the Italians were so fond. Later, some of them entered convents, living near big towns and working to support themselves. These were known as the Order of the Poor Clares, from the name of their foundress.

∞

Like Mère Angélique, in France, four hundred years after, Francis would not allow his friars — the friars minor, or lesser, he called them in his humility — either to own any property or to decorate their churches. At a period when in northern Europe the most beautiful of all cathedrals were slowly being raised, the churches of the Franciscans were small and low and made of the cheapest materials that would last. Many of the brothers found this very hard to bear, and entreated, when joining, to be permitted to spend their wealth on more splendid buildings. But Francis was firm.

That was not their business. The money they collected was for the poor, and to the poor it must go.

Ever since he had heard the sermon that had caused him to part with his leathern girdle, Francis had longed to be a missionary and had even set sail for Syria. They had not lost sight of Italy when a violent storm forced the ship to put back disabled into port. Most likely he took this to be a sign that he must give up his plan, for he relinquished the project of going to the Holy Land and made up his mind to embark for Spain, and to cross from there to Morocco. This was in the year 1214, when Francis was thirty-two years old.

After landing in Spain, he went from one place to another, preaching and founding many convents; but he was never very strong, and after some months the fatigue of the life proved too much for him. He became very ill, and for a while it was feared that he would not recover.

However, at last he got better, and as soon as he was well enough to bear the journey he traveled down to the coast and was put on board a ship just starting for Italy.

∞

It was in 1216 that the two great founders of orders in the Middle Ages — Dominic and Francis — met in Rome; and it was there that Pope Innocent III delivered to them their charters of confirmation. That is, he permitted the orders formed by the two saints to exist and gave his seal to the rules they had drawn up. The Franciscans mixed with the people, who felt them to be their friends, and talked to them freely of their difficulties and of the hard lives led by many of them. In their turn, the friars or brothers used, as we have seen, the gifts of rich or kind persons to help those who were in need, and tried by gentle words to make them repent of their sins and to soothe their troubles, while in their leisure hours they practiced the trade that Francis insisted every man should learn.

By and by, Pope Nicholas III revoked this excellent rule, and all sorts of lazy men who would not work became friars and passed their time in begging — and begging, too, not for others but for themselves — so that they became pests to the country. But in the beginning, the spirit of St. Francis was still with them, and they served as a link between the rich and poor and were always welcomed by both.

The order had been in existence for ten years when Francis called a gathering of all the members, in the plain at the foot of Assisi. Five thousand friars met there, each bringing a little tent of his own, with a mat on top of it, so the assembly is known as the "Chapter of Mats." Some of them, besides the founder, had been born in the small walled town on the hill above them and, like him, had ridden forth as young men to make war on Perugia. Now their warfare was of a different kind and needed far more courage and endurance, and often their grief for the sins they were continually committing led them to do very foolish things.

For instance, in his rounds among the tents where he could speak unheard to each man, Francis noticed that some of the brothers looked very ill, with an expression as of bodily pain on their faces. He guessed what was the matter, and at length brought them to confess that little iron hearts were bound closely on their bosoms and ate into their flesh, so that day and night they were in torture. Others again had tied strips of linen round their arms and thighs so tightly that the blood could not flow properly in their veins. To all, Francis pointed out that if they deliberately chose to make themselves weak and unable to move, they were putting aside the work set apart for them to do and hindering the cause of Christ instead of helping it. Then he bade them take off both crosses and bandages, and gather them into a heap. The bandages he burned, and the crosses he threw into the river.

As for the friars, he washed their wounds and rubbed healing ointment into them; and when they were cured, he sent the brothers forth as missionaries to distant countries.

∞

It was never the way of Francis to demand sacrifices from others that he was not ready to make himself, and for the third time, he sailed from Italy in the hope of turning the followers of the Crescent of Mohammed into soldiers of the Cross of Christ.

Strong in his faith, he set sail for Damietta on one of the mouths of the Nile, where so many years later St. Louis of France was to land his crusading army — and entered the Moslem camp. At his own request, he was at once led into the presence of the sultan, whom, he says himself, he had great hopes of making a Christian.

The sultan received him kindly — in reality he thought his guest a bit mad — and listened politely while Francis first preached to him and then offered to prove his faith in his religion.

He was ready, said the missionary, to pass through a fire if only one of the Moslem priests, or imams, would pass through with him. The sultan gazed at him wonderingly but declined to put him to the test, nor was he more encouraging when Francis next proposed to cast himself into the fire and be burned, provided the sultan and the whole nation would become Christians. A guard was summoned to take charge of him and put him on board a ship bound for Italy, with special orders from the sultan himself to treat him with all care and kindness. Never do we hear of anyone — except his father long ago — being rough and rude to him, he was so gentle and good to all.

Thus ended St. Francis's last attempt at crusading. The next few years he spent in wandering over Italy, and many stories are told of his adventures both at that time and earlier. He had one or two friends who went with him everywhere, when he would allow them to do so; and some of his most faithful companions had been, in the beginning, the greatest hinderers of his work. One of these, Silvester by name, formerly owner of a quarry near Assisi, was filled with envy at seeing Francis divide a large sum of money, given him by a rich noble, among the people of a poor village who sorely needed it. Silvester cast about in his mind for some excuse by which he could obtain part of it, and at length he found one he thought would do.

"Francis," he said, "never have you paid me the debt you owe me for the stones you bought of me long ago to rebuild your church. Now, therefore, that gold is in your possession, give me what is mine."

Francis did not answer at once. He knew that Silvester was not speaking the truth, and that Silvester himself knew it. But he also knew that his friend Bernard, who was standing by, had in his wallet the prices of all his goods he had sold to give to the poor, and that what was Bernard's was likewise his. So turning, he took from the wallet two handfuls of money and held it out to Silvester, saying, "If you will have more, I will give it you."

No reproaches could have shamed the thief and the liar as bitterly as those few words. For three nights, he dreamed that St. Francis stood before him with a cross of gold stretching up from his mouth to Heaven. His eyes were opened, and he beheld the gulf between their two souls, and he repented, and gave away all that he had and straightway became a member of the order.

But in spite of all the cares on his shoulders, and the thousands of people who looked to him for guidance, Francis still kept something of the old gaiety that had made him such a favorite in his youth at Assisi. On a journey with Brother Masseo through Tuscany, preaching and visiting as they went, they reached a spot where three great roads met, one leading to Florence, another to Arezzo, and a third to Siena. Here Francis halted and looked about him.

"Which road shall we take, Father?" asked Masseo.

"That which God wills, my son," answered the saint.

"And how can we tell which He wills?" inquired Masseo.

"He has given me a sign," replied Francis, "and it is this: I command you — and see that you break not your vow of obedience — I command you, in the road where you now stand, to turn around and around as the children do, until I tell you to stop."

So poor Masseo twirled and twirled, until he fell down from giddiness. Then he got up and looked beseechingly at the saint; but the saint said nothing, and Masseo, remembering his vow of obedience, began again to twirl his best. He continued to twirl and to fall for some time, until he seemed to have spent all his life in twirling, when, at last, he heard the welcome words: "Stop, and tell me whither your face is turned."

"To Siena," gasped Masseo, who felt the earth rock around him.

"Then to Siena we must go," said Francis.

∞

He was passing with two or three friends through the little city of Agobio, when he perceived that the people were all in mortal terror of a great wolf that lay in hiding near the walls and slew every creature, man or beast, which ventured outside. Nobody dared walk about alone, said the inhabitants, and when they were forced to travel to some distant place, they were obliged to form companies of six or seven men, armed with bows and spears, lest the wolf should attack them.

Such was their tale; and, after it was ended, Francis answered them, "Fear nothing. I and my friends will speak to that wolf," and he stepped toward the gate.

"Oh, Father! Father, no!" they cried. "It is bad enough that he should slay us and our children, but we cannot spare you."

"Fear nothing," repeated Francis. "The wolf has no power over me," and he went through the gate and out into the country, followed boldly by his friends.

And the people stood on the walls, watching.

At a little distance from the town was a small wood, and as Francis drew near, a curious snarl was heard coming from it. At the sound, his companions turned and fled wildly to the gates, which swung open to receive them. But Francis did not seem to know that they had forsaken him at the moment of danger, and he continued his path without even looking back.

And the people on the walls stood watching. As they watched, a large grey body flew through the air, and those who had good eyes saw a gleam of white teeth and a long red tongue. They held their breath, and their hearts seemed to stop beating, for they thought that the next instant would find the wolf and his victim rolling together in the dust. But, instead, they beheld Francis make the Sign of the Cross, as he said — although they were too far off to hear the words — "Come hither, brother wolf. I command you, in the name of Christ, that you hurt not me, nor do harm anymore to man or beast."

In the middle of his spring, the wolf checked himself and, instead of landing on the saint's shoulder, dropped at his feet.

"Do you know," said Francis, speaking gravely, "all the mischief you have done? You have slain not only men but the beasts on whom they depended, and many have gone nigh to starvation in consequence. Richly you deserve hanging" — here the wolf stretched himself out and buried his nose in the dust, beating his tail in shame as he listened — "but I will give you yet another chance, for I believe that you did not know how evil were your deeds, and if you will come with me, I will make peace between you, for I think that it is hunger and not wickedness, which has driven you to these ways. Therefore, if I obtain a promise from the people that nevermore shall you be hungry, will you undertake, on your part, henceforth to spare both man and beast?"

And Francis, as he spoke, held out his hand, and the wolf sat up and put his paw into it.

Much did those on the walls marvel as they beheld these things, and still more when Francis turned toward the gates of the city, with the wolf following after him. They flocked eagerly into the marketplace, and there, with the beast beside him, Francis told them of the compact he had made to feed the wolf and asked if they would keep it.

"We will," they cried. "We will, and gladly."

"And will you," he said to the wolf, "on your part, abstain from ill-doings, and not put to shame my trust in you?"

And the wolf again held up his paw, and he and the saint shook hands.

The next day Francis, with his friends who were greatly humbled at their own conduct, continued their journey; but, if you wish to know what became of the wolf, I can tell you. He lived on for two years in Agobio, respected by all, and then died — perhaps of too little exercise and too much food — regretted by all, and especially by the children.

∞

As we know, St. Francis loved dearly "the world and all that therein is," but best he loved the birds and the fishes; and this he had in common with his friend St. Anthony of Padua, who was much in his company. Often they walked long distances while their roads lay together, and then they would part and each go his own way.

On one occasion, Anthony had gone alone to preach to the people of Rimini, on the coast of the Adriatic, but they would not hear him, and shut themselves up in their houses. This Anthony saw and straightway went down to the seashore and called to the fishes, bidding them come and listen to his words, seeing that the inhabitants of the city turned a deaf ear to him.

And the fishes came up in multitudes out of the sea and stood on their tails in the water, the little ones in front, the middle-size ones in the middle, and the big ones behind, and bowed their heads before him. So great was their number that the whole sea seemed covered with fishes; and the people, seeing this sight, felt shame that the fishes were wiser than they. Then they unlocked the gates and ran down to the shore and, giving heed to the words of the saint, were converted.

But when we think of St. Francis, it is not surrounded with fishes or wolves that we picture him, but in the midst of the birds, and it is so that he is most often painted.

Francis turned toward the gates of the city,
with the wolf following after him.

"Wait here, and I will preach to my little sisters, the birds," he said to his companions, Masseo and Agnolo, when on one of their journeys they passed a thicket so full of birds that every leaf seemed singing. Alone he walked into the field, and birds of every kind flew about him, and stood on his shoulders and his feet, and covered the ground in front of him, and bent down from the bushes. Not a wing fluttered as he talked, and even after he had given them his blessing, they remained quite still, until he said, "Go, little sisters." Then they bowed their heads and rose upward, filling the air with their songs. And singing, they took their way to the ends of the earth.

∾

Four years after his return to Italy, Francis resigned the headship of the order he had founded, feeling, although he did not let anybody know it, too weak and ill to perform the duties of his office. He bade his friends farewell, and set out for Monte Alvernia, where he knew of a little cave in which he wished to end his life. The way to it was rough and led uphill, and often the saint was forced to lean upon his staff and gasp for breath.

He had felt bitterly the parting with his friends whom he loved so much, some of whom had grown up with him. It was one of the moments that come to all of us as we get older, when we seem to be alone in the world; and he paused where he stood and bowed his head, his heart sinking within him. Then a sudden rush of wings was heard, and a chorus of joy wrapped him round, as his little sisters, the birds, flew out of the cave and came to meet him, circling around him and alighting on him, and giving him greeting. So he was comforted; and he entered the cave that was soon to be his deathbed. And the birds slept in the trees outside, and every day a falcon came into the cave and beat her wings around the head of the saint, singing in her own language, "Wake up! Wake up, O holy man! Arise and pray and give thanks, for the hour of Matins is here." Yet sometimes when Francis looked pale and tired and more ill than usual, she would gaze at him sorrowfully and let him sleep on, while she flew noiselessly away.

One night, when Francis had suffered all day from pain and had felt that the blindness he so greatly dreaded was coming fast upon him, he had fallen sound asleep, worn out with weariness and exhaustion and a long fast. As he slept, a vision appeared to him, and he beheld hovering over him a seraph with six wings, and on the seraph was a man crucified. At the sight, all his pain and terrors fell away and, instead, a feeling of peace and glory seemed to enfold him. How long the vision lasted he could not tell, but when it vanished, he found on his hands, his feet, and his side the marks of the five wounds of Christ, which are known as the stigmata. Of this and of some other visions he never spoke, but the marks were there for all to see who visited him. Henceforth, for the time he remained on earth, he possessed a joy that nothing could take away, and illness and blindness were almost forgotten.

"Bury me with the robbers and evildoers in the place of execution," he said, when he knew that the hour of his death was at hand — for no man was ever more humble than he. But his followers would not have it so; and in four years' time, a magnificent cathedral had been built in Assisi in his honor, and there his bones were laid to rest by his friends.

St. Richard of Chichester

Bishop Without a Diocese

In the early thirteenth century, when King John was on the throne, two little boys and their sister were living in a neglected manor house on the borders of a Worcestershire forest. Their parents were dead, and their guardians were too busy with their own affairs to fulfill the trust committed to them by Richard de Wyche the elder, so the lands were allowed to go to rack and ruin. After heavy rains, the water was left to settle in the hollows on the wastelands until the low-lying meadows became a marsh, and the woods were never thinned out or the brushwood cut down, and at last it was almost impossible to force your way through them.

Little, however, did the children care for all this. The old servants saw that the fires in the great hall were large and that they had plenty to eat and drink, and as far as we can tell, there was no one else to look after them. But they were free to do as they liked all the day long, and what more does any child want?

Still, their ideas of amusement were different. The elder boy and girl roamed about when the sun was shining and played at being knights and robbers. When they could persuade Richard to play too, they had "a lady in distress" as well, but in general they were obliged to leave him perched up on the seat of the tiny window with his eyes glued to a book taken out of his father's library. For Richard had managed to learn to read. Most likely the priest had taught him.

"A dull boy," his guardians declared, on the few occasions that they happened to see him. "He will make a rare parish priest someday, when his brother is gaining his spurs in the wars. It is lucky that *he* is the eldest." But his brother knew very well that it was Richard who faced the wild bull that *he* was afraid of and had borne the brunt of the farmer's wrath when Henry's dogs had trampled down his field of young wheat; and whatever plans Henry formed, it was Richard of whom he asked counsel, although it never occurred to him to wonder what Richard was thinking of when he wandered about their mother's garden of tangled roses or stared with unseeing eyes at the waterlilies in the marsh pools.

∞

Yet Richard had his dreams as well as his brother, and they were just as dear to his heart. He longed to go to the University of Oxford, of which he had heard marvelous tales from the sons of the knights and gentlemen who were his neighbors. There he could sit on the banks of the Cherwell or the Isis and read the books whose very names were now barely known to him, and talk with scholars who had traveled into distant lands, perhaps into Italy itself. Ah, what would he not give to go there too!

But then his brother would come up and ask whether Richard thought that such a field should be plowed and sown with corn, or such a piece of marshy ground would, if drained, bring forth a good crop, for by this time, the boys had grown up and the elder was not to be a soldier for some years yet. Still, after all, the true farmer was not Henry but Richard, for it was he who read in the old Latin authors, such as Virgil and Colomella, descriptions of how lands should be properly farmed, and it was Richard who learned which trees should be cut down and what prices to ask for the wood from the owners of the salt works round about; the word *wych* meaning "salt." And for a while Richard put the thought of Oxford steadily out of his mind and helped his brother so well and cleverly that at last, Henry, grateful for the flourishing condition of his lands, offered to make them all over to Richard. At the same time, a bride was proposed for him, the daughter of a nobleman who had heard how good and honorable the young man was.

But neither of these proposals tempted Richard. He had worked hard for years, not only to bring the estates into a condition of prosperity, but also to teach his brother how to keep them so. Now he might follow his own wish, which was to prepare himself to enter the priesthood.

By this time, to the relief of all men, John was dead and his son Henry III had succeeded him. The English barons had not forgotten the struggle with the king that had ended with their obtaining Magna Carta, nor their invitation to Prince Louis of France to invade England. There was plenty of trouble still in store for everyone, yet things were better than they had been. Louis had gone back to his own country, and the barons hoped that the young king would be easily bent to their will.

Richard was about twenty-three when he rode up to Oxford to attend the lectures of the famous Robert Grosstête, afterward bishop of Lincoln and the first English cardinal. But the town the young man had dreamed of was very different from the beautiful city that we know. It was surrounded with walls and fortified with towers; the houses in which the undergraduates lived — for there were as yet no colleges — were mostly built of wood and thatched. The river Isis spread itself wide over the plain, breaking up into numerous channels, and its islands were covered with buildings, while on the hills around were dense forests. But there was the great Abbey of St. Frideswide, where Wolsey was afterward to build the College of Christ Church, and the clang of the bells in St. Mary's tower told the students that there was a chance of fighting in the narrow streets, which no one, of course, would desire to miss; and seeming to rise straight out of the water was the Abbey of Oseney, in a year or two to be rivaled by schools belonging to the order of St. Dominic, while Franciscan brothers crowded the streets. If Oxford can be noisy now when undergraduates are excited, it was a thousand times worse then when there were few, if any, rules they were bound to obey, and the town was swarming with a crowd of lively young men, eager to seize an excuse for brawling. And if now and then a life was lost in a scuffle, well, it did not much signify and there were plenty of people to shelter the murderer!

∞

When Richard first went up to Oxford, he supposed himself to be a rich man, but very soon he learned that the bag of money which was his share of the family estates had been made away with by the priest to whom he had entrusted it for safekeeping. During the years in which he was studying, Richard was naturally prevented from earning his living, and he was obliged to accept a small sum from his brother to keep him from starving. Lodgings were dear in Oxford, and the room Richard dwelt in was shared with two very poor students. Indeed the whole three owned only one gown, so they had to take it in turns to wear it for lectures.

In spite of all this, they never lost heart. Each morning, as soon as it was light enough to see to read, they sprang out of bed and forgot that they were cold and hungry in the delight of study or striving to understand some obscure philosophy before the lucky one who had the gown that day went off to his lectures. They ate as seldom as they could and as little — just a little bread and soup and wine, to which meat or fish was added on feast days. Richard, at any rate, was cheerful and happy during the six or seven years he remained there and would never ask for pensions or places, as was the way of most of his friends.

After he had taken his degree, he went over to Paris, like most young men of his day, and when he had qualified there as a teacher, he came back to Oxford to seek for some pupils, for in those times every student was allowed to choose his own master. He was one morning at a dinner given by a youth to celebrate his success in his examination, when a servant who was waiting told Richard that someone desired to speak with him at the door.

"Let us have him in and give him a cup of wine," cried the host, jumping up and leaving the room as he spoke; but the man, who was on horseback, refused, saying that his message was for Richard alone. Fearing ill news of his brother or sister, Richard hastened out, but found no one at the door and the street was empty. Much astonished, he returned to the banqueting-room, exclaiming, "There is nobody there; it must be —" when he stopped, surprised at the look on the faces of all present.

"What is the matter?" he asked, and the host answered, "Look, Richard! Scarcely had you left us when this stone fell from the roof, and had you been here, you would of a surety been crushed."

Then Richard knew it was an angel who had brought him the message and that his life had been preserved for him to do God's work.

Soon after this, Richard's dream was fulfilled, and he set out for Italy to study the canon law, or law of the church, at Bologna. To a man who had only beheld the plains of Northern France and the woods and fields of the Midlands of England, the sight of the Alps must have been almost terrifying. In those days, and indeed nearly as late as the nineteenth century, mountains and waterfalls were considered ugly and ungainly objects, and no one would have thought of going to visit them for pleasure. No doubt Richard was no different from the rest of the world, and most likely he breathed a sigh of relief when he found himself past those awful precipices and safe among the walled cities of Lombardy. At any rate, it would be long before he need cross those fearful passes again, he thought, for he had been told that the course of study at the University of Bologna lasted for seven years.

Large as Oxford had seemed to the country-bred Richard, Bologna was about three times the size and counted ten thousand students alone; and if Oxford had appeared noisy with its perpetual fights between the students and the townspeople — "Town and Gown" they were called then, as now — Bologna was a hundred times worse, for the city was the headquarters of the league that supported the power of the pope against the emperor. When Richard arrived there, the town was in an unusual state of excitement, as if it were preparing itself for a war with the Emperor Frederick II. Some of the high brick towers, from which you can see miles over the country, were rising fast, and the streets were full of chattering people who never seemed to go to bed, but asked each other the news all night under the arcades. It was in vain that John of Vicenza, the Dominican friar, bore the cross through the streets and summoned the citizens to follow him and to make peace with their enemies. The peace, indeed, was made, and solemn vows taken, but they were broken again almost as soon as sworn.

Yet through all the noise and the tumult and party cries, Richard and his fellow students continued to read, and the Englishman soon forgot the din of men and the clash of arms in the interest of his books. Probably he was older than the others; certainly he studied harder than most, for when his master became too ill to teach, he handed over his pupils to Richard, now a doctor in law, and offered him besides his daughter in marriage. Then Richard had to tell him that, grateful as he was for his kindness, he hoped to become a priest and was intending shortly to return home and take orders in the English Church.

∽

Richard must have been about thirty-eight when he returned to Oxford and was made chancellor of the university, with the power of conferring degrees on the undergraduates. He had a great deal of work to do, from looking after each student as far as he could, to advising about every deed and contract that affected the university. Luckily for him, the bishop who ruled over Oxford at the time was his old friend Robert Grosstête, bishop of Lincoln, and when they met, it was easier for Richard to talk over anything that puzzled or worried him than it would have been with a stranger. These conversations caused the bishop to think so highly of his old pupil that when the chancellor of Lincoln died, he wrote at once to beg Richard to accept the vacant place. But it was too late, for Richard had just been appointed chancellor of Canterbury by the archbishop.

If pope and emperor were fighting with each other in Italy, Church and state were disputing with each other at home, and neither side could depend upon King Henry, who was swayed first by this person and then by that. At length Archbishop Edmund decided that he must go to Rome to ask counsel of the pope, and in his absence, the whole of his work was done by Richard. When the papal legate informed the archbishop after his return that his journey had been in vain and that he could not receive the help on which he had counted, the poor man's health gave way, and he retired with Richard to the French Abbey of Pontigny, where he shortly afterward died.

Notwithstanding the loss of his friend, Richard appears to have been happy enough at Pontigny. It was a Cistercian monastery, and the Cistercians were always great farmers, so once again Richard spent his time going from field to field, watching the progress of the crops and making sure that the corn and hay were dry before they were placed in the barns. Then some of the farms were situated beyond a walk and the monks were forced to ride to visit them, and how pleasant it was to feel a horse beneath you after so many years!

Too pleasant, perhaps, for we next find Richard in a Dominican convent at Orléans, teaching and preaching and studying the holy books. Here he was at peace, and unless he was sent on some special mission, he never had to go beyond the beautiful garden, with its masses of red and white roses kept for the altar of the church. And here, after his years of preparation, he was ordained a priest at last by William de Bussi, bishop of Orléans.

∞

The work of a parish priest must have seemed strange to him, but he had the gift of making friends with his people, who, on their side, talked to him freely of their troubles. He enjoyed the quiet life and hoped he might end his days in the little place, but in this he was mistaken, for in 1244 he was appointed to the bishopric of Chichester.

Now, at that time, the struggle in the church that had driven Archbishop Edmund from his see still continued. The king declared that it was *his* right to make the bishops, whereas the chapters (consisting of the deans and canons of the cathedral) declared that the right of election rested with them. The fight was long and hard, and the existence of every bishop was nothing but weariness and anxiety. Richard fared no better than the rest; the king's officers seized all his fees, and he was obliged to go to Lyons, where a council of bishops was then sitting, and ask Pope Innocent IV what he was to do. Should he resign his see, as personally he would have wished, or should he hold on to it and take the consequences?

The pope's answer was to consecrate Richard himself and to inform King Henry that he had done so.

Then, armed with the letter of appointment bearing the pope's seal, Richard returned to England, visiting on the way the grave of Archbishop Edmund at Pontigny.

∞

"The king has taken possession of all your lands and of all your revenues": this was the news that greeted him when once more he was on English soil. In vain he hastened to the palace and showed the parchment, sealed with the seal of the pope, to the king. Henry would listen to nothing and, after pouring forth a torrent of angry words, bade Richard begone.

So he went out from the palace gates, a bishop without a see and without money, and was glad to accept a home with Simon the priest, in a little village on the Sussex coast. Here he passed his time in a manner after his own heart, for greatness had no charms for him. The hours that were not spent in visiting the poor or in prayer were taken up in gardening, and he was pleased to find that his old skill in budding roses or in grafting young trees had not been forgotten.

But after waiting a few months to see if the king would change his mind and allow him to enter Chichester, and finding that things remained as before, Richard determined to fulfill the duties of his office in another manner. Like Cuthbert of old, he might have been met on the wild downs, going to preach in some lonely cottage or scrambling over the rocks by the sea to a tiny village, hidden in a cove.

When he was going far, he borrowed a horse, and glad enough were the farmers to lend them to him. At other times he walked, but in one way or another, every corner of his diocese became known to him — every corner, that is, except Chichester and the houses of great men. Yet he was always happy and pleasant, and if his face looked sad, it was only when he had returned from one of the fruitless visits to the court, which he thought himself bound to make.

∽

It seems strange that the pope allowed the bishop, whom he himself had consecrated, to be treated in such a manner; but he was greatly absorbed in his struggle with the emperor, and England was very far away. At length, however, he had leisure to consider the reports that were sent to him, which were confirmed by travelers, as to the mode in which Richard was served, and his anger was roused. He sent strict orders to two of the bishops that they were to present themselves instantly before the king and to inform him that, unless he immediately gave up all the lands and moneys belonging to Chichester and allowed Richard to take his rightful place, the whole of England would at once be laid under an interdict, as it had been in the days of John, his father, and that meant that no priest was permitted to baptize or to bury or to perform the ceremony of marriage. Under this threat, Henry gave way, and after two years of exile, Richard sat on his cathedral throne, and from a penniless missionary now became a great lord.

Unlike some men who know how to be poor, but do not know how to be rich, Richard filled the duties of his new position as well as he had done those of his old one. He was hospitable to all comers and gave dinners to the nobles and high-born travelers passing through Chichester on their way to court, for he felt that it was not only the poor who had claims on him. But at his own table, his food was hardly different from what it had been in the house of Simon the priest, and his dress was the white tunic worn by his chaplains, with a cape over his shoulders.

He was eager to question any newcomer as to what was happening in the world outside, and the condition of farming — for he never forgot his own experiences — and his eyes would twinkle with pleasure at a lively story or a merry retort, while if anything was said that seemed worth remembering, he wrote it down himself in a book; and when his guests had gone to bed in their cold, draughty rooms, where the wind whistled even through the silk hangings, he would spend hours on his knees, praying for himself and his people also.

But gentle though Richard was, he always found courage enough to reprove evildoers and to insist that, as far as possible, wrong should be set right. Injuries to himself personally he not only forgave but apparently forgot, and never lost a chance of repaying

Richard might have been met on the wild downs.

them with kindness. But injuries to others he dealt with in a wholly different way. Once, in the town of Lewes, a thief who had stolen some goods belonging to the shopkeepers took refuge in the church, where, by all the laws of the time, he should have been safe until he could have a fair trial. The shopkeepers, however, were too angry to think or care for the law and, dragging him out, hung him on the nearest tree. The news speedily reached the ears of the bishop, who at once rode to Lewes in wrath to punish the offenders, and this was his sentence:

> You have torn that man from the steps of the altar, where he had sought sanctuary, as was his right; you have hanged him without a trial, thus breaking the law yourselves a second time; and you have buried him in unconsecrated ground, thus taking for granted that he was guilty without giving him a chance of defending himself. Therefore, you, who have done these things with your own hands, will dig up the body and carry it between you to the church whence you took him, living. And you who stood by and never lifted a voice or a hand to prevent this wickedness, you will walk in your shirts with ropes around your necks through the streets of Lewes. Ah! I know what you would say [he added quickly, as one of the richest of the citizens stepped forward as if to speak]. You would offer me a large bribe to let the matter rest and be forgotten, but learn that I am not one of those whose conscience is in the market.

And he turned away indignantly, leaving orders with his steward to see that his judgment was carried out.

There was no part of the country under Richard's charge that he did not visit and inquire into. In this manner he found out many things that he was able to remedy. As bishop, he was responsible for the state of the prisons in his diocese, for the carrying out of the law, and for showing mercy where mercy could be shown.

For the threats of those in power he cared nothing at all, and here is an example.

A priest who had for kinsfolk some of the greatest nobles in the kingdom had committed a grievous sin, and Richard sternly told him he was unfit to perform the duties of his holy office and bade him resign his benefice. An outcry was raised through the land, and Richard was beset with petitions from the king and queen, the man's relations, and even the bishops to pardon the priest and to allow them to pay a fine to absolve him. But their prayers were useless. "The sin was the same whoever the sinner might be," said Richard, "and the penalty was the same also, whether the priest's birth were high or low." Then at last came a bishop who earnestly entreated, with tears and prayers, that the man might be pardoned. To him Richard made answer: "You ask me, to whom power has been given to judge evildoers, to forgive the sin of this priest. Well, the power that has been given to me I now give to you. Pardon him, if you will, but remember that if you do, your soul will answer for it in the Day of Judgment. Are you ready to accept the responsibility?"

The pleader was silent, and his soul answered for him.

∞

The last work of Richard's life was to go through his diocese, preaching a crusade at the command of the pope. It does not seem as if the bishop approved of the undertaking, but he thought it his duty to obey commands of Innocent IV, and after a sermon, preached in Chichester Cathedral on the necessity of taking the cross, went about among the fishing-villages of the coast, trying to stir the hearts of men. Here he had some success, but he found a very different state of matters when he was summoned to London to attend a Parliament and preach before the citizens in the abbey. His words fell on stony ground indeed. English churchmen as well as London merchants and powerful nobles were all irritated at the interference of the pope with the affairs of England, his demands for money, and his giving away of English bishoprics to foreigners. The barons, besides, were always at war with the king about some question or other and did not mean to quit the kingdom and leave him to do as he pleased. So all the bishop's efforts were a failure, and the following year it was still worse, for it fell to him to read from the pulpit a letter from the pope granting the king certain taxes on church property. This produced an outburst of anger from the listening audience, and Robert Grosstête, bishop of Lincoln, was the first to declare that whatever the pope might write, the consent of the English Church should never be given.

Richard was hardly surprised. He voted in Parliament according to his conscience and then returned to his labors among his people.

He was at Dover, consecrating a small church to the memory of his friend Archbishop Edmund when his final illness came upon him. It was a labor of love amid all his disappointments, and he felt it was the last office he should perform. The following day, he suddenly fainted and was carried to his bed, from which, as soon as he became conscious again, he gave directions about his funeral and made his will, which is still to be seen. His books he left to various monasteries; little gifts to his servants and old friends, a small dowry to his niece, and money for the building fund of Chichester Cathedral.

According to his wish, he was buried near St. Edmund's altar, but about ten years later, his body was removed into the south transept, where it now rests.

Reformer of the Poor Clares

In the year 1381, when Richard II was King of England, although always boasting that he was a Frenchman born, a carpenter called Robert Boellet dwelt with his wife in the little town of Corbie, in Picardy. Ever since they had been married, the Boellets had longed for a baby, and now to their great joy a plump little girl lay in the little wooden cradle.

"There is only one name we can give her, of course," said the proud mother, and the father answered, "Yes, she must have the name of St. Nicholas, the patron saint of all children," so the baby was christened Nicolette.

Although Nicolette's father was only a carpenter, he made plenty of money by his trade. He bought several houses in Corbie and gave one of them to be a home for friendless people who had gotten into bad ways, where they stayed until they had learned to do better and their neighbors would employ them again.

Robert Boellet was held in great respect by the townspeople; many was the quarrel that was brought to him to decide, and seldom was his decision disputed. The abbot, too, of the big Benedictine monastery that towered above the town, set much store by him, and not a stroke of work was done in the abbey without the knowledge and superintendence of Master Boellet. As for his wife, she kept the house clean and cooked the food and did not even think of having a servant to help her. But she never missed going to church early every morning, and very soon she took Colette with her.

From the first, the child was a solitary little creature; she never cared to play with other children, but would sit for hours at a time by her mother's spinning wheel listening to stories from the Gospels, or kneeling by her side in church. As she grew older, her parents sent her to some kind of a school where she was perhaps taught to read and write as well as to spin; but books were very scarce in those days, before printing was invented, and had all to be copied by hand.

Everyone liked her; she was so kind and had such a pleasant voice, and she was always ready to do anything harmless that her schoolfellows wanted, even if it was to play games she hated. After a while, she used to slip away and hide from them, often under her own bed at home, but probably they soon guessed how unwilling she was and let her alone, for nothing is so dull as to play a game with a person who does not care for it.

∞

Now, it was the custom in the monastery of Corbie to sing the office of matins in the middle of the night, and very often some of the townspeople were present. When Colette was about eleven, she was seized with a longing to go with them, and night after night she left her room to join the company on their way to the monastery. We do not know whether she told her parents where she was going, but, as they had always allowed her to attend what services she pleased, she would probably never have thought she was doing any wrong, nor, it seems, would they have thought of it either, if some busybodies had not begun to find fault.

"How strange of Monsieur and Madame Boellet," they whispered, "to let a child of that age be going to church at an hour when she ought to be asleep. No good would come of it, of that they might be quite sure. But, after all, it was well known that since Colette was born, neither father nor mother had ever said her nay, so what could you expect?" And the gossip grew louder and louder, until at length it reached the ears of Colette's parents. Madame Boellet, who thought that her little girl was as much under the direct guidance of God as was the infant Samuel, wished to take no notice and to let her daughter attend matins as before, but the carpenter held a different view of the matter.

"There was a great deal of truth in what the neighbors said," he told his wife, and if Colette wanted to go to church, she could do so by day. As to matins in the monastery, he would have no more of it, and he ordered Colette to sleep in a little room, almost a closet, which could be reached only by passing through the chamber in which her parents slept.

Thus the matter would have ended had it not been for the interference of a friend of the family, one Adam Monnier, who openly disagreed with Boellet and told him that Colette was not to be treated like other children; and that he would himself take her every night to the monastery. But Boellet naturally thought that it was he, and not Monnier, who was responsible for the safety of his own child, and answered that he had made up his mind as to what was best and expected to be obeyed. So far, Colette seems to have made no resistance, but one night when her father and mother were asleep, the little girl was awakened by a voice calling softly to her from the window: "Colette! Colette! It is I, Adam Monnier. I have a ladder here and have come to take you to matins. It will be all right. I will arrange it with your father."

Of course, Adam Monnier must have known perfectly well that it was extremely wrong of him to tempt Colette to disobey her father's express orders, or he would not have come in this secret way. And Colette, who was always thought to be so much better and holier than other children, and who spent half her life in church and on her knees, was equally wrong to listen. However, she did not stop to consider what was right or wrong, but at once got up, and after dressing herself quickly, scrambled out of the window and was carried by Monnier down to the ground. And off the two culprits went to the monastery.

We do not know what Boellet said the next day to the friend who had interfered in what did not concern him, or to his disobedient daughter, but he took the best measures he could to keep her at home, by fitting up an oratory for her, where she could pray when she was not in church. This delighted Colette; she felt as if she owed it to Adam Monnier, and preferred consulting him to anyone else. He was always ready to encourage her, and by his advice, she not only persuaded her mother to give her nothing but common or ugly garments, but wore rough cords round her body and secretly left the bed, on which she now slept in a corner of her parents' room, to lie on some knotted twigs on the floor. Still, in spite of her care for her own soul, Colette had thought left for others, and used to save part of her food, and whatever clothes she was allowed to give away, for the sick and the poor about her.

∞

So the years went on, and Colette was nearly grown up, but at sixteen she was no taller than she had been at ten or eleven.

"You are so small that you will never be able to keep the house clean when your mother dies," remarked her father one day, seeing Colette in vain trying to lift something from a shelf that was out of her reach, and although the words hurt her, the girl knew that they were true. What would become of them when her mother died? And she was nearly sixty now. Night and day the thought troubled her, and at length she resolved to go on a pilgrimage to the shrine of a saint not very far from Corbie to ask for help, as many of her friends had done before her.

"Let me become tall and strong," she prayed, and tall and strong she became, to her great joy, so that when her mother died, she was able to take her place and do all that was required of her.

"What a good daughter old Robert Boellet has," said the neighbors, when their own girls wished to leave their work and dance in the meadows by the river; and the children, instead of disliking her because she was held up to them as an example, would go and talk to her and ask her questions about her faith, until the numbers who flocked to her teaching were so large that no room in her father's house was big enough to hold them.

For the most part, the people saw nothing but good come of the talks and were grateful to Colette for the difference it made to their children's lives. But some persons were discontented and complained to the bishop of Amiens that it was not fitting that a young girl should take on herself the office of a preacher. The bishop listened to all they had to say and sent a priest to hear her secretly; and the priest was so touched and interested in her words that at the end he stood up and thanked her, and returning to the bishop, told him he was quite content.

But if the bishop and the priest were satisfied, the others were not. Once more complaints were made, and this time Colette was summoned to Amiens.

"Keep silence for a little while, my daughter," said the bishop, "and let men's minds grow calm again. Then, when peace has been restored, you may continue your work."

So Colette went back to her home and kept the house clean and tended her father, now in his last illness. Very soon he died, leaving his property to his daughter, and herself to the care of Raoul, abbot of the monastery.

Left alone, Colette thought she might at last indulge in what she had always longed for: a life of entire solitude, devoted wholly to prayer. Great as was her love and respect for her guardian, Raoul the abbot, she feared he might think it his duty to find her a husband, and in this she was perfectly right. So without giving him or anyone else notice of her intention, she set out for Amiens to consult a famous priest, Father Bassadan, on what she ought to do.

The bishop sent a priest to hear Colette secretly.

The priest bade her do nothing hurriedly. "He that believeth shall not make haste." She must think over it all calmly and quietly and come to him again. Colette obeyed, and when he perceived that she was in a fit state to decide, he bade her make her own choice as to what convent or order she would enter. It was not very easy to satisfy her, and she tried several communities, both at Corbie and elsewhere, but all of them fell short of the strictness she desired. Finally, her life was determined by a meeting with a great Franciscan monk traveling through Picardy. To him she told the tale of her disappointments in the past and her doubts for the future.

"Be a recluse, my daughter, and thus will you find the peace you seek," he said; and by the joy that filled her, Colette knew that that was what she wanted.

A recluse! Can you guess what that means? Not a hermit dwelling apart in a cell, where at any time a traveler riding by may seek shelter, and the "solitary" can hear again news of the world he has left, or, at any rate, listen to human speech. Not a monk or a nun in a convent, where, although the gates are shut, there is left human companionship, and common duties and interests that every life, however simple, which is lived with others must hold.

But to Colette a recluse meant to be alone always, and in one place, with one small window in her cell looking into the church; and that she might speak only through a grating to the two girls who brought her daily the vegetables and bread for her one meal. And this to last, perhaps, for fifty years, for at this time she was only twenty-two!

No wonder Raoul the abbot tried his hardest to dissuade her. It was quite useless, so he could but obey her wishes, and, selling the houses her father had given her, she placed the money in the hands of the parish priest to be divided among the poor.

The angles between the walls of the church of St. Etienne and the Benedictine cloister were built up, and a short staircase ending in a grating led up to the two tiny cells in which the recluse was to live. When all was ready, a solemn service was held, and amid the grief and tears of her old friends, Colette, with Father Pinet beside her, walked behind the procession of the clergy to the chamber on the walls. Steadily, and without lifting her eyes, she entered, and the door, which she hoped never to pass again, was shut on her by the abbot.

∞

It is a comfort to think that even Colette understood that it was not possible to fill her life entirely with prayers and holy thoughts, however much she might wish to do so; or rather, that her hands must be employed for part of the day, whatever her mind might be fixed on. She kept in order the beautiful linen of the church, and not a day passed that the girls who brought her food did not also bring some garments belonging to the poor people, to be patched or darned.

Soon there arose a longing in the breasts of those who had watched her from a child, or even in strangers who had heard of the "Saint of Corbie," to take counsel with her as to their troubles and difficulties. Day by day they pressed up the narrow staircase as far as the grille or grating, pouring out their trials to Colette, who sat on the other side. Hour by hour they came, and in such numbers that at last her friend Father Pinet interfered and fixed certain hours at which she could be seen. For a while she listened with sympathy and gave carefully considered answers to all who asked her advice; and whatever she said, they implicitly believed and faithfully acted on. But at length she grew weary of her task. She wanted, it would seem, to serve God in her own way, not in His. She wished to be free to pray all day, not to help her neighbors in the only way in which she could now help them. "These people," she said, "rob me of my time and interfere with my devotions"; and at last she obtained leave to shut out everything that reminded her of the world. Only her two friends might bring her food as before, and *they* were to be silent.

A great cry of disappointment arose in Corbie, in which the clergy joined. But, although Colette might have guessed at their feelings, no echo of their murmurs reached her ears. Perhaps she would not have cared, even had she known how much unhappiness and disturbance she was causing. "There was very little left of the human in Colette," says one of her biographers and fondest admirers; forgetting that there was so vast a humanity left up to the end, in the Lord whom she wished to serve.

Little though she knew it, only one more year remained of her present mode of existence, but the four years she passed in the cell of a recluse were laden, according to her own account, with strange experiences. Not very long after she had entered, whispers began to be heard among the townspeople of temptations by the Evil One himself; of visions of specters, meant to terrify her into calling for man's aid to dispel them; of awful shrieks and screams, coming from none could tell where; of loathsome animals, of shapes known and unknown, playing around her cell. Any tale of horror that had ever been told was now told of Colette, and weakened as she was with fasting and want of air, all seemed real to her, and no doubt she suffered as much as if she had indeed seen outward things of the kind she described. But the end of each trial was always the same: Satan was overcome, and exhausted by the struggle Colette was left for a while in peace.

It was in the last year of her life as a recluse that, when praying in her oratory, she had a vision of St. Francis and learned that she was set aside for the reformation of the great orders he had founded, into which abuses had already crept. Not desiring to leave her cell, she put the vision from her, or rather, tried to do so, for it would not go. In despair she sent for Father Pinet, but he could only bid her pray. The struggle with her own will and the path she had chosen lasted many days. At length she gave in and agreed to return to the world, which she had hoped she had quitted forever.

It was through a Franciscan friar, Henri de Baume by name, that Colette obtained from the pope the necessary dispensation from the vows she had taken of perpetual seclusion. At that time, there were two popes supported by different nations, and the papal palace at Avignon, where one of them lived through most of the fourteenth century, was, and still is, one of the glories of France. Party hate between their followers was as fierce as it had been in Italy a century before, in the strife of emperor and pope, of Guelf and Ghibelline. The pope had left Avignon, and loud was the clamor that the people should leave Avignon and return to Rome. But there were still two or three popes instead of one, and it was this scandal that Colette and Father Henri de Baume meant to fight.

Under his protection, and that of a noble lady, the Baroness de Brissay, Colette left Corbie so early one morning that scarcely anyone was up to bid her farewell. It almost broke her heart to quit her cell, which she called paradise, and she could hardly tear herself away from it. Passing through Paris, the little company traveled to Dijon, the capital of the great duchy of Burgundy, and then turned sharp to the south, where the count of Savoy awaited her, and down to Nice where the anti-pope, Benedict XIII, was at that time living. To him she presented a petition, beseeching him to allow her to enter the order of the Poor Clares — an order for women closely associated with the order of St. Francis — and to follow strictly the rule laid down by the foundress. The pope not only granted this, but made Colette, who was not yet even a nun, abbess-general over the whole three orders, with power to open fresh houses if they were needed; and Father Henri was created superior-general over all the houses that should submit to being reformed. Then she was consecrated a nun and allowed to enter on her duties as abbess without going through the months of training known as "the period of novitiate." At first she shrank from the responsibility; she longed to be simply "Sister Colette," but Father Henri pointed out that she could not take her hand from the plow and must pray for courage to do her work.

And here we must leave her. Henceforth, her path was clear, and, in spite of opposition where she often expected help, and abuse where she thought to have found love, her work prospered. As, nearly three hundred years later in the case of Mère Angélique, whole families of well-born novices with everything to hold them to the world enlisted under her banner. Far and near she went, attracting all by her preaching and holy life. At Baume, the house placed at her disposal soon grew too small for the numbers who flocked into it, and they moved to a large convent at Besançon, empty of all its community except two nuns. The archbishop and a vast multitude received her, and daily the people thronged for advice to the gate of the convent as they had once done to the cell at Corbie.

Other houses were shortly needed, and Colette was forced to take many journeys to found them. They were mostly situated in the east of France, for the duchess of Burgundy was her friend and helper. Again, like Mère Angélique in after years, she kept herself informed of the state of every convent and dealt with every difficulty herself. She was still believed to perform miracles, and certainly she had complete faith in her own power to accomplish them, but the visions of wild beasts that had so terrified her in her cell never came back. Instead, birds flew about her, and a lark drank from her cup, while a lamb trotted after her and stood quietly in her oratory while she prayed. In her last years, a convent was opened at Amiens and the inhabitants of Corbie offered land for a religious house, but the Benedictine monks would not allow her to build it. This was a bitter sorrow to the abbess, and it is very likely that it preyed on her mind on a cold winter journey to Ghent. At any rate, a change was noticed in her soon after her arrival there, and she laid herself down for the last time, covering her head with a black veil. In three days she died, at the time that Nicholas V was elected pope, and received the submission of the Duke of Savoy. Truly she might be accounted happy in her death. The scandal of the anti-pope, which had so grieved her, was ended, and but a few years before France had been delivered from the English by the sword of a girl.

Apostle of the Japanese

It is difficult in these days when no one is ever still, and our friends on their travels can send us news nearly as often as they choose, for us to understand how strange it must have felt to our forefathers when they deliberately set sail for countries that were almost unknown and became practically dead to their families. Yet, of course, it was just this very fact that the countries *were* unknown which made their charm in the eyes of many and induced bands of navigators to leave their homes and "cast their bread" upon very troubled waters. Portugal was always first and foremost in these expeditions, and nine years before Francis Xavier was born, Vasco da Gama set sail from Lisbon and, after planting a golden cross on the Cape of Good Hope, landed some months later at Goa, a town on the west, or Malabar, coast of India.

During the forty years and more that elapsed before the arrival of the famous missionary, Goa grew into a beautiful city. It was situated on a peninsula, and the soil was kept rich and green by the heavy rains attracted by the range of mountains called the Ghauts, which run along that part of the coast. In some places of the range, they get as much as three hundred inches of rain in the year. Think of that, when we, in London, consider that it has been terribly wet with only twenty-five inches!

Well, under the rule of the Portuguese, Goa became larger and wealthier. Factories were built, and barracks for the soldiers who

263

were needed to keep order among the mixed population of Mohammedans, Indians, and Catholics; and by and by, priests came out to work among the people of Goa and other towns further south, which were gradually conquered by the Portuguese.

∞

The Xaviers were a noble Spanish family whose castle was built near the city of Pamplona, in Navarre. Francis was the youngest of many sons and was looked upon by the other boys as a creature hardly human, because from his earliest days he preferred books to their rough games, although they allowed that he could, if he liked, run races and jump with the best of them. His father, however, had the same tastes; therefore, when Francis, at seventeen, declared his wish to study in the famous University of Paris, he instantly gave his consent. His son was, he knew, a good scholar already, and, although he was young, he could be trusted to take care of himself and not get into any foolish scrapes, the echoes of which sometimes reached distant Navarre.

Those were pleasant, peaceful years that Francis passed in Paris, first as a student, then as a teacher or lecturer. On fine days, he and his friends, Pierre Lefèvre and Ignatius Loyola, a countryman of his own much older than he, took long walks by the river Seine, or, when their work was done, climbed the hill to Montmartre to visit the men who spent the time from dawn to dark hewing blocks of stone in the quarries. Had he preferred an easy life to the one he ultimately chose, he could have had it, for in the course of these years, a canonry in the cathedral at Pamplona was offered him, and this might have led in time to a bishopric and perhaps — who could tell? — to the triple crown of the pope. But Ignatius Loyola was stronger even than the ambitious dreams of a young man, and on a moonlight night in August 1534, six friends, of whom Francis was one, met secretly in the crypt of a church and vowed to obey rules laid down by the former soldier of Charles V.

Thus was founded the order of the Jesuits, which was recognized six years after by the pope, Paul III.

∽

Francis's first experience of travel was very rough, even for a poor scholar of those times. Fired by Ignatius Loyola's description of Jerusalem and the holy places he had visited there, the new members all desired to devote their lives to preaching to the Turks settled in Palestine. It was agreed, in 1536, that Ignatius should go to Spain and arrange his own affairs as well as those of Francis, who dared not trust himself to undergo the tears and reproaches of his family, and that the others should meet him at Venice, where, if you only waited long enough, ships could always be found sailing for the East.

But how to get there? That was the difficulty, for a war was raging between the Emperor Charles V and Francis I, king of France, so the natural way from Marseilles to Genoa and through the Lombard plains was closed to them. The only route open was by Lorraine, Switzerland, and the Tyrol, and snow lay on the ground; they had scarcely any money and knew no German. Undaunted, however, by these or any other obstacles, they tucked up the long garment worn by University of Paris students, put Bibles and service books or breviaries into their knapsacks, and taking stout sticks that would serve many purposes, started on their journey.

Considering the length and roughness of the walk, it seems wonderful that they accomplished it so quickly, for it was in January 1537, two months after their departure from Paris, that they found themselves in Venice, where Ignatius had just arrived. Thankful the travelers were to rest a little, and to have boats to carry them when they went to comfort the sick and dying in the hospitals; but after two months, they were bidden by Ignatius to proceed to Rome, as it was necessary to obtain the pope's leave before going as missionaries to Jerusalem.

Although it was now Lent, and March, this journey was scarcely less severe than the last. The pilgrims at once made up their minds to fast — which perhaps was as well, as food was often not to be had — and to live by begging. The incessant rains flooded the rivers and washed the roads; the people could not understand who they were, but supposed they had formed part of the Spanish army that had sacked Rome in 1527. This was an insult that still burned deep, even among the peasants, and the Jesuits were made to feel it at every turn. The beds given to them in the hospitals where they sheltered were often so dirty that even for the sake of penance they could hardly force themselves to get into them; cottage doors were shut in their faces if they asked to be allowed to rest; ferrymen declined to take them over rivers unless the Jesuits gave them a shirt or something in exchange.

At length, with sighs of relief, they reached Ravenna, and, without stopping to look at its wonders, they embarked immediately for Ancona. But here, again, they experienced the fact that he who trusts to the charity of his neighbors in his travels, and neglects to supply himself with money, does a very foolish thing. The captain of the vessel refused to let them land at Ancona because they could not pay their fares, and of course, this was quite natural, but at last he consented that Francis should go into the town with Simon Rodriguez and obtain the passage money by pawning his breviary. This done, Francis entered the marketplace and threw himself upon the charity of the stall-keepers, begging for an apple or a radish or something no one would buy. But the kindhearted peasant women, full of pity for his pale face and weak voice, gave him so much more than he asked that there was enough for himself and his friends to dine off, and the rest he sold for a sum that was sufficient to pay their passage.

The Apennines were at last crossed, and Rome lay before them. Here, the pope received them most kindly, and arranged that a discussion on some points of church discipline and doctrine should be held during his dinner, between the Jesuits and some Roman priests, in order that he might see what manner of men they were. The strangers bore themselves so much to his satisfaction that he not only granted permission to go to Jerusalem (well knowing that a war was shortly to break out between Venice and the Turks, which would prevent their starting), but also bestowed on them money to pay their passage to the Holy Land. It was a pity he did not likewise give them enough to carry them back to Venice, for they were frequently in great straits and had nothing to eat but pinecones, which are neither agreeable nor nourishing.

As the pope had foreseen, war was speedily declared, and it was impossible for them to sail to Jerusalem, but it is pleasant to be able to state that they honestly returned all the money that had been given them for the purpose.

∞

For the next three years, Francis remained in Italy, going wherever he was sent by Ignatius and in spite of frequent illnesses brought on by too much fasting and many hardships, visiting hospitals, preaching, teaching children, and gaining many disciples to the order, which was shortly confirmed by the pope. But six months before this happened, Francis was told by his superior that he must now go further afield, and as Jerusalem was closed to Christians for the present, he must carry on his missionary labors in India.

The summons was sudden, for he was bidden to set out for Lisbon the following morning in company with Simon Rodriguez, as the father whose place he was to fill had suddenly been seized with illness. Francis obeyed without a word; in his heart he felt that he was saying an eternal farewell to Europe, and although in his journey across Spain he passed within a few miles of his father's house, he pressed on steadily, resolved to give neither himself nor his family the pain of parting. In Lisbon, he was luckily far too busy to have time to think of his feelings. He had a hundred things to do and people to see; the royal family were deeply interested in all his plans and were ready to help him to the utmost, but the only gift he would accept was some warm clothes for the voyage.

It was on his thirty-fifth birthday, April 7, 1541, that the governor's vessel, with Francis Xavier on board, weighed anchor. It was a terrible voyage and always full of anxieties of various kinds: they might be becalmed and unable to proceed until their provisions were exhausted; they might be wrecked or be captured by pirates; or the crowded state of the vessels and the bad food might cause illness. At that period, the dread of the rocky coast off the Cape of Good Hope was so great that nervous passengers were in the habit of taking winding sheets, so that if the ship struck and they died, they might be buried decently at sea, although it does not appear who was to have leisure at such a time to attend to their corpses.

It was the custom for five or six vessels to sail together so as to help each other in case of danger, and if the governor's own ship was crowded with nine hundred people, the rest are likely to have been yet more full. Except for crossing from Italy to Spain, it was Xavier's first voyage, and at the beginning he was very seasick; however, as soon as he could stand up, he made friends with the crew and passengers, all of them apt to be lawless and undisciplined. When scurvy broke out as they crossed the equator, so many were struck down that it was left to Francis and the two companions who had sailed with him to nurse the poor plague-stricken creatures, and even to wash their clothes as well as their bodies. The Cape of Good Hope with its golden cross, was at length reached and passed, but the voyage had taken so much longer than usual that the governor determined to spend the winter in the Portuguese settlement of Mozambique, opposite the island of Madagascar. Here Francis, worn out with all he had undergone, fell ill of a bad fever, and by his own desire was taken to the hospital.

When, in March 1542, orders were given for the fleet to put to sea, Xavier was well enough to go on board, but he left his companions, Father Paul of Camerino, and Mancias, who was as yet unordained, to tend the sick until they also had recovered.

In two months, Goa appeared on the horizon, the golden cross of Vasco da Gama glittering in the sun. Xavier lost no time in visiting the bishop and in expressing his readiness to do whatever was required of him, although, as the pope had appointed him apostolical legate, he really owed obedience to nobody. He then went to the boys' college, which had been founded a few years earlier and was in a very flourishing state. It was hoped that, by and by, the boys, when well educated — for as to this the Jesuits were very particular — might in their turn become missionaries and go out and teach others. Xavier stirred up the governor to inspect the prisons and hospitals constantly, in order that he might at once perceive and check abuses, and he spent hours each day seeing the poor in their homes. Sometimes he would stand in public places preaching, and after he had been in Goa a little while and had taught the children the catechism and the creed, they would all walk through the streets singing them, with Xavier marching at the head.

∞

A long way to the south of Goa, the Indian peninsula ends in Cape Comorin, with the island of Ceylon lying opposite. On the eastern side of the cape is situated the most famous pearl fishing in the world, and here dwelt the tribe of Paravas, a poor and weak people who some years earlier had been drawn into a quarrel with the much stronger Mohammedans and had appealed to the Portuguese for help. The Portuguese instantly offered their protection if the Paravas would become subjects of their king, which the natives, perceiving no other way of peace, willingly accepted. The Portuguese fulfilled their part of the bargain; the enemies of the

Paravas were put to flight, the pearl fisheries became again the property of the tribe, and they themselves were baptized wholesale.

It reminds us of the baptism of the Russians in the time of the Grand Prince Vladimir, five hundred years before, when one group was sent into the river and all christened "John," to be followed by another called "Peter," and so on.

Having baptized the Paravas and made them nominal Christians, the Portuguese left them to themselves, and when Francis arrived among them, they were as ignorant of Christianity as babies. He began, as usual, by instructing the children, whom he represents as being very eager to learn. "It often happens to me," he says, "to be hardly able to use my hands from the fatigue of baptizing them, and their hatred for idolatry is marvelous. They run at the idols, dash them down, and trample on them." Francis must have forgotten his own childhood and that of his brothers, if he thinks these actions were entirely due to holy zeal; or that their "fearlessly witnessing against their parents in case of their quarreling and using bad language and getting drunk," was wholly "a sign of grace."

∞

Having provided for the future teaching of the Christians along the fishing coast, and after having preached in many of the towns in that part of the country, Xavier found other work awaiting him on the opposite side of the Indian Ocean.

Trade with Portugal had caused the kings of Celebes, and of several of the neighboring islands, to make inquiries about Christianity, and many even to adopt it. At Malacca, on the Malay Peninsula, the great market for the goods of China and India, Arabia and Persia, there was already a Christian station, and when Francis heard that priests had been sent for from thence to preach to the various islanders, he made up his mind to join them without delay.

In September 1545, he reached Malacca, and although he obtained many converts during the four months he stayed there, and was always treated politely and kindly, he felt himself that he had made no real impression on the people, and that most likely those he had baptized would fall back as soon as he left them. Some months were passed among the other islands, and it was at Amboyna that he met with the Spaniard Cosmo Torres, who became his friend and the sharer of his labors, to the end of his life in Japan.

It was on the occasion of a second voyage to Malacca after a visit to India that he heard of the existence, in the seas north of China, of a group of islands called Japan, where "the whole nation surpassed all others in its desire for knowledge." A few Portuguese merchants, always on the lookout to extend their trade, had already touched at their ports, but it was from a young Japanese, who had fled from the Buddhist monastery where he had taken refuge to escape the punishment of murder, and had been brought by a friend of Xavier to Malacca in search of peace, that Francis learned more about this strange people. Anger, for that was his name, or at any rate, it was as near as Xavier could get to it, had frequent talks at Malacca with "the Apostle of the Indies," for he had managed to pick up a little Portuguese during his voyage. It is curious to notice that, in the main, the impression made by the young man on the missionary hardly differs from the accounts given by modern travelers. Anger asked endless questions as to the doctrines of Christianity and never needed to be told anything twice. And when, in his turn, Xavier inquired if he thought that there was any chance of the Japanese adopting the Christian Faith, he answered that they would listen, and question and weigh the words of the preacher, but they would likewise require that his life should be good and kind.

"If the rest of the Japanese have the same zeal for gaining knowledge that Anger has, they surpass in genius all nations anywhere to be found," cries Xavier and the exclamation rings in our ears today.

∞

After Francis had settled the business of the missions in India, he embarked in April 1549, at the town of Cochin, intending to go to Japan by way of Malacca. He had with him a little band of friends, among whom were Father Cosmo Torres; Anger, now called Father Paul of Santa Fe, or "the Holy Faith"; and two or three Japanese students who had somehow found their way to the college at Goa. It was, of course, an immense help to him to have these young men to talk to for so many weeks. First, they could teach him the Japanese language and the customs of the people, as well as their history and the two religions of the group of islands. Xavier was chiefly brought into contact with the one called Buddhism, taught five hundred years before Christ by a young Indian prince who lived near the Ganges, which had since spread over a large part of Asia. In the beginning, the founder, Gautama, or Buddha, had laid down strict rules of good living, but in the two thousand years that had passed since his death, his disciples had sadly fallen away from his teaching.

The governor of Malacca was a son of Vasco da Gama, the discoverer of the Cape of Good Hope, and he gave the missionaries everything that could be needed in their voyage, as well as handsome presents to the *real* ruler of Japan. For ever since the twelfth century, the power that for about 1,800 years had been exercised by the dynasty of Jimmu, still represented by the present emperor or Mikado, had fallen into the hands of his minister and commander-in-chief, the shogun. Until 1868, when the reigning Mikado suddenly broke his bonds and adopted, to a great extent, European ways, he was merely a shadow; spoken of with awe and respect, it is true, and surrounded with luxury, but with no more power than the youngest of his subjects.

Before starting on the second part of his travels, Xavier was much cheered by letters from some of the Portuguese merchants in Japan, saying that they had spoken of the doctrines of Christianity to several people in the country who were well inclined to the Faith, while a powerful noble (or daimio, as the nobles are called) had sent an envoy to Goa to ask for teachers. The letter goes on to say that when, on landing, the merchants had requested the daimio of that district to appoint them a house where they might stay while they were doing their business, he had put a group of empty buildings at their disposal.

The houses looked large and good, and the merchants rejoiced at getting such comfortable quarters — much better than anything they had expected. But in the night they were awakened by the cold — for it was still winter — and found that the warm blankets and quilts they had piled over them had slipped onto the floor. Pulling them up again, and tucking them in more securely, they went to sleep, but soon the same thing happened. Thus it was for many nights, until the poor, sleepy men began to think that someone was playing tricks on them, although they could find nobody anywhere near the place. A few nights later, they were all aroused by a frightful shriek, and seizing their swords, they rushed to the room from which the sound proceeded, then occupied by a servant. But the door was bolted from inside, and in answer to their shouts, a voice inquired what was the matter.

"That is for *you* to tell *us*," cried the merchants; and when the man pulled aside the bolt, they found him safe and the room empty.

"We thought you were being murdered," they grumbled, and the servant replied, "No, but I woke feeling that someone was there, and on opening my eyes there was the most terrible specter that ever I saw in my life. But in my fright I made the Sign of the Cross, and it vanished."

The next day, as the servant was nailing up crosses on all the doors, the neighbors who had heard the noise — for the houses were mostly of paper, on account of the great earthquakes — came running to know what it was the foreigners had seen.

"Why should we have seen anything?" answered one of the merchants who did not like being made game of, as he thought was the case. Then the Japanese told him that the house was haunted by an evil spirit — "a kind of plague common in these parts" — and that they wondered that the Christians had been able to bear its tricks for so long. Had they a charm that prevented them from being frightened? And if so, would the honorable gentlemen tell their servants what it was?

"It was by this sign the specter was conquered," replied the merchant, holding up a cross, and forthwith the Japanese set about making crosses of paper or wood and fixing them on to their houses. "And from henceforth," ends the writer, "the town was delivered from such ill-doings."

∞

A voyage was always a terror to Francis, and he seems to have expected the one from Malacca to Japan to be more than usually full of danger. However, his fears did not prevent his holding long conversations with his Japanese pupils, and again expressing his surprise at "their eagerness for knowledge." On his side, Xavier sends home accounts of the Japanese people and of his reception at the city of Kagoshima, and his first impressions were very favorable. "Of all nations I have ever seen, I cannot remember ever to have found any, Christian or heathen, so averse to theft," he writes. "They are wonderfully inclined to all that is good and honest." "Among barbarous nations there can be none with more natural goodness than the Japanese."

Perhaps he set too high a value on the *interest* they showed in his preaching, for curiosity is a characteristic of every Japanese, but they listened to him eagerly, and for a while it seemed indeed as if Christianity would displace the two old religions.

As has been said, the Jesuits were the great educational order of the church, and it was seldom that they opened a mission church without opening a school also. Their cleverest masters were given to the youngest pupils because they were more difficult to teach. Therefore, it was natural that Xavier should be struck with the number of colleges and the large university at Kioto or Miako where the shogun lived, and the attention paid to the education of the boys who went to school at eight and stayed there until they were twenty, after which wives were found for them.

The love of children for which Xavier was always noted made him notice with pleasure the care taken of the funny little black-haired things, tumbling about in their loose dresses, and crowing with delight at the wonderful masses of flowers that springtime brought. He soon made friends with them and taught them their catechism, and his heart was full of high hopes for their future. Little did he think, when he left Japan to return to India, that some of his small playfellows would be called upon to lay down their lives for their Faith.

It was, as was natural, the bonzes, or Buddhist priests, who first stirred up strife and persuaded one of the daimios near Kagoshima to forbid any of his people to become Christian on pain of death. In spite of this edict, however, for some months they were left alone, and Francis and his followers went about from one island to another, teaching and preaching as usual. The very journeys were full of difficulties that would have been impossibilities to most men. A civil war had broken out, and bands of soldiers were to be met with all over the country. The peasants insulted the missionaries and often threw stones at them. Snow lay deep, and on one occasion, the missionaries lost their way in a forest. The sun was hidden in the clouds, and they had nothing to guide them, and it seemed as if they must spend the night where they were and would

Francis made friends with the children and taught them their catechism.

probably be found frozen to death the next morning. While they were in this plight, a horseman came up, burdened by a box that threatened every moment to slip to the ground. He stopped when he saw the little band and asked how they came there. They told him that they did not know in what direction they ought to go, on which he laughed roughly, and said, "Let this man carry my luggage and follow me, and you will find yourselves by and by at the end of the forest."

Thankfully Francis laid the box on his shoulders, and started off rapidly, as he dared not lose sight of the horse. So fast did he go that his companions were soon left behind, and when, many hours later, led by the tracks of both man and horse, they emerged into a plain with a small town on it, they found Xavier lying exhausted on a bank, his feet and legs so badly bruised and swollen that they were obliged to carry him to an inn and let him rest for many days before he could proceed on his journey.

∞

The history of the mission to Japan is a history of contrasts. The shogun, the daimios, and the people seem to have been eager to adopt Christianity, and nothing could have been more splendid than the reception given to Xavier at this time at Miako. Almost unexampled honors were showered upon him; he was seated at the shogun's table and went daily to see him and to talk to him about his religion. More than one bonze had been converted, which made the rest more bitter than ever; and all his experiences told Francis that everything was ripe for persecution. The lives of the Christians depended only on the good will of the various rulers, and especially of the shogun; and who could tell how long that might last?

It was, therefore, with very mixed feelings that he received letters bidding him return to India at once with the Portuguese trading fleet. He had never meant to do more than spend a couple of years in Japan, so as to organize the different missions, and the two years were now up. Yet the promising beginning had given place to dark fears for the future, and it was very hard to leave his converts when danger was so close at hand. But obedience was his first duty, and for the rest he must trust in God. So he went over to Bongo for the last time to rebuke the prince for his evil life, and, as usual, his words did not fail of their effect at the moment. Still he did not feel confident; the Japanese, he knew, were easily moved — in either direction.

In November 1551, Xavier sailed for India, having written beforehand to request that other missionaries might be sent to Japan, as the work and constant traveling was too much for the few fathers. In answer to his appeal, Father Balthazar Gago and some other priests embarked for Miako and, after a kind welcome from the shogun, went on to the port of Amanguchi, across the mountains, where Father Torres awaited them. The two priests were not long together: Balthazar departed to the district allotted to him, and a month later, on the outbreak of a civil war, Torres was literally forced by the converts to put himself out of danger by leaving for Bongo, which was at present at peace.

Things remained much in this state for the next five years. The missionaries never faltered in preaching and teaching, and thousands allowed themselves to be baptized. The fathers rejoiced greatly, but at the same time, they knew well that in this fact lay their peril. Was it likely that the bonzes would stand tamely by and watch their power slipping way? Twice or thrice they had already stirred up their followers to revolt, and it did not need a very wise head to tell that on the next occasion the struggle would be more serious.

The opportunity of the bonzes came at last in Firando, when the Portuguese priests were commanded by the prince to quit the town, and for the sake of their converts, they dared not disobey. Their departure was the signal for a general riot, when the churches were sacked and the altars were pulled down — no doubt with the assistance of the Buddhist children! But vain were the threats or persuasions of the bonzes; the converts stood firm, and even the execution of a slave-woman had no power to move the rest. Japanese, unlike many Europeans, are never afraid to die.

The persecution, once begun, spread rapidly. The fathers who had escaped from Firando were caught by some Japanese, stripped and turned loose, although their lives were spared. For days they remained hidden in a cave, without food or light, until, with the help of some friends, they managed to reach Bongo. Here they went about from city to city and even founded three hospitals in which they gathered the sick, the foundling babies, and the lepers. As before, the prince was on their side and offered them money, and when they refused this for themselves, he gave it, at their request, for the support of the hospitals.

∞

In accordance with the changes that were so strong a feature of the Japanese mission, affairs now began to take a turn for the better. The most powerful man in Japan took the Christians under his protection, and although he did not himself become one, a daimio was converted and was baptized by the name of Bartholomew. A cross was embroidered on his robes, which of itself was an act of courage, for death on the cross was reserved, as was the case in Rome, for the lowest felons. Thus proclaiming his faith, he rode at the head of his troops during the war and surrounded the city temple.

The soldiers occupied the position unsuspiciously, for it was their custom, before marching to battle, to pray for success to the war god, but it is strange to learn that they obeyed their prince without a word when he ordered them to break down the image of Buddha. After the peace was made, he destroyed the other temples in his dominions, and even, one is sorry to hear, interfered with the harmless custom of spreading out a feast once a year to the dead relatives of the people.

Now, reverence for their ancestors is one of the most cherished beliefs of the Japanese, and they arose as one man against this insult. It was to no purpose that Bartholomew gave the money that the feast would have cost to feed the poor. He had touched them in their tenderest place, and they would not forget it. The rebellion burst forth. Bartholomew, after escaping once, was besieged in his huge stone mountain fortress, but although he got the better of them on that occasion, his action had dealt a severe blow to the Christian religion.

∞

The year 1582 marks a stage in the history of Japan, for it was the date of the interesting embassy sent to the pope, Gregory XIII, by some of the most powerful princes to ask for more help in Christianizing the country. The ambassadors themselves were unusual also, for they were four young daimios, all under sixteen. They set out under the charge of two Jesuit fathers and, after spending some time in Goa, went on to Lisbon and Madrid. Everywhere they were received with the utmost kindness and were shown all that the capitals held of wonder and magnificence, and we may be sure that the sights were keenly appreciated by their young eyes and quick brains.

As soon as they entered Italy, crowds turned out to see them, curious to know what these strangers from the ends of the earth would look like and how they would behave. They saw only four slight, pale-faced, rather short boys, quiet, but not in the least shy, managing with perfect ease the horses sent for them. Their dress alone would have marked them out as different from Europeans. Their white silk, wide-sleeved robes were covered with birds and flowers, all beautifully worked in their natural colors, and kept in place by a folded sash, and their finely tempered swords had their sheaths and hilts covered with precious stones and enameled designs. In this guise they followed the carriages of the Spanish, French, and Venetian ambassadors, and surrounded by the Roman nobles, they rode through the city for their audience of the pope. When they left Rome, after witnessing the coronation of the new pope, Sixtus V, it was as Knights of the Order of the Golden Spur, and under the promise to maintain the Christian religion with the last drop of their blood.

∞

The persecution, which had for so long been smoldering, was destined to come to a head under the famous Hideyoshi the shogun, the conqueror — with the help of an army largely composed of Christians — of the kingdom of Corea.

Perhaps if the Jesuits had been left to manage by themselves, peace might have existed for some time longer, but a body of Franciscan missionaries came over from the Philippine Islands, and their zeal was greater than their discretion. By their tactless conduct in thrusting their religion openly in the face of the people of Nagasaki, the most prosperous missionary settlement in the country, they drew on themselves a sentence of banishment. The Jesuits, out of their long experience, implored them to be more careful and pointed out that the future of the Catholic Church was at stake; and the arrival of the new bishop appointed by the pope, a man of sense called Martinez, smoothed things over with the shogun for a short time. Then stories reached Hideyoshi's ears that the Franciscans were again transgressing the orders he had given, and he began to suspect a deep-laid plot to destroy his government. This idea was fostered when he learned that a Spanish captain had been heard to say that Philip II owed his wide possessions chiefly to the missionaries.

That silly and imprudent speech was the death-knell of the Christians in Japan.

The first thing to be done was to discover exactly who were Christians, and so papers were prepared and the Christians ordered to come and sign their names. One and all — even the children — obeyed, although they understood fully that the object of this census was to be able to find them at once in case the persecution was decided on. But at this moment, Hideyoshi intended only the Franciscans to die; the Jesuits, as a body, he liked and wished to spare as long as he had an excuse for doing so.

A huge multitude was gathered on the plain of Nagasaki to see the sentence carried out. The martyrs were led out all together, the Franciscan friars, two or three Jesuits who had attended their church, and several young children. The punishment was the same for them all: crucifixion, but in Japan, that death, although suffered only by those who are considered degraded, was more merciful perhaps than any other. The victims were only tied to the crosses and were killed by one thrust of a sword.

Thus died the martyrs, scorning alike the prayers of their relatives and the offers of pardon made by the governors if they would give up this new faith and apostatize.

Hideyoshi's death afforded Christians a short breathing space, but under his successor (who usurped the place of Hideyoshi's son), the many edicts that were in force against them, Jesuits as well as Franciscans, were carried out or not, just as it pleased the various princes.

In Higo large numbers were driven from their houses, and anyone who sheltered them incurred the penalty of death. At the end of six months, however, the few survivors were allowed to take refuge with their fellow Christians.

Thankful they were to be permitted to rest for a little with the kind Jesuits, although they were greatly saddened by the news that a fresh edict had been proclaimed in Higo summoning Christians, on pain of death, to be present at a ceremony that was to be performed on a certain day in the house of a bonze. The governor was ordered to see that the edict was carried out, and it was understood that those who obeyed should be considered to have returned to the Buddhist religion and be pardoned. The governor did his utmost to persuade two nobles, John and Simon — his own personal friends — to comply with the order, hoping that the others might follow their example, but it was in vain that he urged them to bribe the bonze to say they had apostatized, or to allow the ceremony to take place in private, so that none might know. Neither John nor Simon would listen to his proposals, and when, in pursuance of his duty, the governor was obliged to suffer John to be brought before the bonze, and the Buddhist book was placed by force upon his head, he proclaimed his faith so loudly that it was impossible to prevent the punishment being executed at once.

With Simon he fared no better. The young man was with his mother when the governor entered, and he entreated the poor lady to induce her son not to throw his life away. But the mother, herself a Christian, declared it was an honor that Simon should die for his Lord; and the governor, angry and sorrowful, left the house, sending, as was the custom, a friend of both himself and Simon to behead the condemned man. This friend, Jotivava, was joyfully received by Simon, who begged his mother to fetch warm water, as if it was a feast, that he might wash himself. This done, he walked between his wife and his mother to the great hall, followed by three Christian brothers and the noble sent to be his executioner. He died, praying to God for mercy, and twenty-four hours after, his wife and his mother died likewise.

From all parts of the country, news poured in of hundreds and thousands who had fallen victim to their religion, and among these many were children. A story is told of a whole Christian family who were condemned in the province of Arima. The father and uncle were put to death first, but there was a short delay in the execution of the grandmother and the two little boys. "Your father has died for Christ, and so must you," she said to them when she received the message. "Is there anything better that could happen to us?" answered they. "When is it to be?" "Now," she replied. "Go and bid farewell to your mother." The boys left her, and arranged with their nurses how their toys should be given away among their friends; and they put on the white garments their grandmother had prepared for this day that she knew would come. Then they went in to their mother.

"Farewell, dear mother," they said, kneeling. "We are going to be martyred."

"Oh! If I could only be with you," she cried, for she and her daughter had escaped condemnation, "but your father is holding out his arms to receive you. Kneel down, loosen your collars, bow your heads, and call, 'Jesus! Mercy!'" As she spoke, the soldiers entered and, taking the children from her, carried them to the palanquin where their grandmother awaited them.

∽

Happy were those who suffered death from the sword, for soon the martyrs passed through fire and other horrible tortures from this life to another. At length, in 1614, it was resolved to banish the Christians from the kingdom, but out of all the four orders at that time working in Japan — for the Dominicans and Augustinians now had missions there — the Jesuits alone were allowed to say a farewell Mass at Miako. Then they were sent to Nagasaki, whence they embarked for their different places of exile.

The massacres went on for many years longer, and at last there was hardly a Christian left in Japan. Then all the ports, except Nagasaki and Firando, were closed to foreigners, and the country remained a sealed book until the mikado, in 1868, resolved to make it as free as the Western World.

Servant of the Poor

San Juan de Dios — St. John of God: this was the name by which a baby, born in a Portuguese town in 1495, afterward became known throughout the whole of Christendom. His father and mother were so poor that they could not afford to send him to school, and although this was a great grief to them, it was a joy to little John, who thought how much better off he was than his companions in not having to learn all sorts of tiresome things. To be sure, he was now and then called away from his play to receive some simple teaching from his father, but it was little indeed that the good man knew, and the boy was soon free to roam into the country and watch the birds flying and the flowers growing.

Luckily, John was not a stupid child; he used his eyes and ears and picked up, one way and another, a surprising deal of knowledge, and his parents took care that he went regularly to church.

Things went on in this manner until John was nine, and then one day a knock was heard at the house door, and he was bidden by his mother to open it. A priest was standing there — well, there was nothing very unusual in that, and the boy little guessed that his whole future depended on whether his mother would grant the traveler's prayer for food and shelter, or whether she would bid him seek them elsewhere. But the moment she knew that it was a priest who was asking hospitality, John's mother left the soup she was stirring and hurried to give him welcome.

"Come in, come in," she said. "It is little enough we have, but gladly will we share it with you." And the priest entered the house and seemed in no hurry to leave it.

Now, the father was out all day at his work, and his wife had a thousand things to do at home — cooking and washing and cleaning and mending — and well-pleased they both felt when they saw their little son passing whole hours by the side of the priest, and caught sight of him lying in the sun on the slope of the hill, listening earnestly to the words of the holy man.

"Ah! In a few years he will be such another," they whispered, their hearts swelling with pride; but the talk between the two was very different from what they imagined.

There was nothing at all about heavenly things, or the church, or the privileges of being a priest, but a great deal concerning the wonderful adventures the holy man had met with during his travels; and the distant lands, with their strange customs, in which he had dwelt.

"Can't I go there too?" asked the boy. "Nothing ever happens down here, and, perhaps, if I went to those places, *I* might be able to save people from robbers, or wolves, or drowning, like you," for the priest had made himself out a great hero.

"Oh, yes, you can go. I will take you with me, for next month I shall have business elsewhere," replied the priest, who was getting very tired of the little town of Monte-Mayor. "But mind, not a word to your parents, or they are sure to forbid it and lock you up. We will steal away secretly, and when your father and mother know that you are seeing the world, they will soon forget all about you."

John made no answer to this. He was not quite sure that he wanted his mother to forget all about him, but he comforted himself by thinking that he would soon become rich and famous, and counted up all the beautiful jewels he would bring back to her. They should be finer even than those worn by the wife of the governor on a feast day.

Perhaps John would have understood that there was something his mother cared for more than jewels if he could have looked back one morning when he and the priest were several miles on the road to Madrid.

"John! John! Little John!" she cried, running distractedly from place to place, and bursting into the neighbors' houses to know if they had news of him. Many were the journeys she took, because someone had passed a boy whose description sounded like hers, only to return exhausted in body and sick at heart, when she found that she had been deceived once more. At last there came a day when she was too weak to leave the house, or even to do her work inside it. Her husband, who had scarcely spoken since the child had left them, watched her with eyes of despair, and his strength, too, was fast failing. Then the neighbors missed them and sought them out in their cottage; but it was too late. Only one thing could save them, and that was the return of the boy; and who could tell if he was not dead also?

∽

And where was John during these months? And had he met with the adventures he had been so anxious to find?

Well, if the truth is to be told, John had only had one adventure — and that one was not at all to his liking. His friend, the priest, had become weary of having to look after a little boy whose short legs could not keep up with his own long strides; and when John opened his eyes one fine morning in a little inn at Oropesa, he found that the priest had gone and had left him to shift for himself.

At first John felt desolate indeed, yet he never thought of going home again. He would manage somehow, and perhaps the landlady would help him. Fortunately she was a kindhearted woman and full of pity for the deserted child, who forced back his tears and declared that he was ready to do any work that was offered him. Thanks to the landlady, he heard that a boy was wanted to help a shepherd whose flocks were grazing on the meadows outside the town. He got the place, and for several years, he led a quiet life with his sheep, and, to all seeming, the love of adventure had died within him.

But after all it was not dead, only sleeping, while he grew daily taller and stronger, and at length it sprang into life at the tales of an old soldier who was going to join the army of the Emperor Charles V in his wars with the French king, Francis I. This, John knew at once, was the chance he had been waiting for. He, too, would go with the man and enlist under the banner of the king, Charles I, in Spain, although "emperor" to the rest of Europe. Very soon the shepherd-boy became a byword among his comrades for his reckless daring, and, if ever a man was needed for some special service of danger, John was the first to apply. In general, the wounds he received were few and slight, yet once he was left for dead on the battlefield; and on another occasion, he almost lost his life, in a less honorable way.

From a child, John had been subject to fits of dreaming, and then he became quite unconscious of what was going on around him. It happened that after a battle, where he had been placed as sentry over a great heap of spoils that had been taken from the enemy, he suddenly fell into one of these daydreams and neither heard nor saw a man creep stealthily up and load himself with as much of the booty as he could carry. Shortly after, the captain of the troop came by, and seeing the big heap of valuable things that had been piled up under his directions reduced to a few utterly useless articles, he fell into a violent rage and dragged the dreaming sentry to his feet.

"Hang him on the spot," he cried furiously to some soldiers who were with him, and in a few seconds a rope was being knotted around John's neck, when, luckily for the future saint, the colonel happened to pass on the way to his quarters.

"What is the matter? What has the man done to be hanged?" asked he.

"I placed him as sentry over the booty we had taken, and he went to sleep and suffered it to be stolen," answered the captain, stammering in his anger.

"It is a grave charge," replied the colonel, "but he is young, and — well, we will let him off this time. Only his majesty can have no soldiers in his army who sleep at their posts, so he must quit the camp."

∞

Downcast and ashamed, John retraced his steps along the road that it seemed only yesterday he had trodden with a glad heart, and returned to his old master, the shepherd of Oropesa. His pride and wounded feelings were quickly soothed by the warm welcome given him by everyone, and the quiet hours on the wide plains gave him a sense of rest. But after two or three years, he began to grow weary of the sameness of the days, and when at last the count of Oropesa came to his estates to raise levies for the war in Hungary, John bade farewell to his old master and marched away to the war. On this campaign we hear nothing of dreams, so perhaps he had outgrown them. At any rate he remained with the army until peace was made and the troops were disbanded, when he started on a pilgrimage to the shrine of Santiago of Compostella, in the province of Galicia. Then he took the road southward to Monte-Mayor, with prize money in his pockets to give to his parents.

Of course no one recognized the pale little boy of nine in the rough, bronzed soldier who walked quickly up the village street, looking eagerly into every face he passed. The people turned and watched him as he went along, curious to know where he was going. At length he stopped before a tiny house and gave a sharp knock at the door. It was opened by a woman who inquired what he wanted.

"My mother — my father. They lived here once. Where are they now?" he faltered, a strange feeling of terror coming over him as he spoke.

"Was it long ago? Many people have had this house. What were their names?" asked the woman, bending forward to catch his answer, which was given almost in a whisper.

"Ah, poor souls! They died of grief, so I have heard, when their little boy ran off with a priest, and *that* must have been the year before I was married. But it surely can't be *you?*" she continued, as his first words came back to her. "Ah! How time does fly, to be sure. Come in and rest. Your clothes are dusty as if you had traveled far, and perhaps a wound you have gotten in the wars troubles you?"

John looked at her with eyes that seemed to see nothing. Then, without speaking, he turned away and went slowly down the road.

Where he slept that night he never could tell, nor how he lived for the next few weeks. At length he knew how great had been their love and how deep must have been their suffering. He did not try to make excuses for himself — that he was only a child; that he was tempted by the priest, on whose shoulders the blame really lay. Remorse filled every part of him, and he vowed that he would wipe out his sin with his life.

Meanwhile he must find some work. There were only two trades he understood: fighting and keeping sheep, so he walked southward, asking if anyone wanted a shepherd, and took service with a rich widow who owned a large farm near Seville. Here, alone with his flock, he had time not only to pray, but also to think about things, which he never had done before. He saw that the peasants passed their lives in poverty so great that the horses in the stables of the rich nobles, or even his own sheep, were better cared for than they. Many among them had sons or husbands captive in Morocco, and they would pause sadly in their work and tell him how poorly the poor prisoners were treated, and how faint was the chance that they would ever return to their homes. And with each fresh story, the heart of John would grow more and more sore within him, until at last he went to his mistress and begged her to find a fresh shepherd, for he was going to Morocco to do what he could for the men who were imprisoned there.

∞

It is not a very long journey from Seville to Gibraltar, which was not to become English for another 170 or 180 years, and on his arrival, John went at once to the harbor to see what ships were about to sail for Africa. On the quay he fell in with a fellow countryman — a Portuguese noble — who, with his wife and four daughters, had been banished to Ceuta, on the opposite coast. All their possessions were taken from them, and they were in desperate poverty. John was filled with pity for their condition, and at once offered himself as their servant. The poor people brightened at the thought that there was one person at least who was ready to help them, but they refused his aid, as they had no money to pay him.

"I want none," answered John. "My only wish is to try to make things better for those who need it, and where shall I meet a family in greater distress than yours?"

At this they resisted no longer, and they all crossed over to their place of exile, the burning Ceuta.

No sooner had they reached Ceuta than a fresh misfortune befell them. The journey through Portugal in the heat, their agony at parting with the home where so many of their forefathers had dwelt, and the hunger and thirst they had endured on the way proved too much for them. One after another, they fell ill, and the girls were forced to sell their clothes to save them from starvation. Even so, they would have died had not John nursed them day and night until they were able to get up again. Then he got work as a day laborer and gave all the money he earned to support them.

At last things improved. Either the king allowed some part of the rent of their estates to be paid to them, or their friends collected enough money to keep them in comfort. But, at any rate, they were richer and happier than they ever expected to be again, and John felt that this part of his task was done.

Bidding a sorrowful farewell to the Portuguese exiles for whose sakes he had struggled so long, John returned to Spain and went about the country selling religious books and little statues of the saints, finding all the while time to look after any sick and poor people whom he might hear of in distress.

One night he walked back very weary after a hard day's work to the rough shed where he was living, and no sooner did he lie down than he fell sound asleep. In his sleep, he had a vision of a child standing before him, holding a pomegranate and saying, "Thou shalt bear the cross in Granada!"

This John took to be the sign that he must go at once to the beautiful Moorish city, where he arrived on the feast day of the martyr San Sebastian, which was being celebrated with much splendor, great crowds having assembled to listen to some famous preacher. John pressed into the church and listened with the rest, until the preacher's words urging repentance for sin so moved him that he fled shrieking into the streets, crying, "Mercy! Mercy!" The people, thinking he was possessed by a devil, seized hold of him and scourged him, hoping by this means to set the evil spirit free. But John still flung himself on the stones and bewailed his sins, and prayed for mercy until the preacher, hearing of his sad state, took pity on him and visited him. His soothing words were more powerful against the evil spirit than railings or scourgings, and with a soul strengthened and comforted, John returned to his life-work among the poor.

We do not know exactly who gave the money necessary for his purpose, and, of course, he had not a penny of his own, but in those days, men and women were very generous in bestowing whatever was asked for by anyone whom they considered holy, although in many ways they were harsh and unkind to their laborers and servants. So when John came around to their castles to beg for food and clothes, or anything he could get, they were showered on him willingly, and he carried them back joyfully to the deserted shed that he called his home. Then he would go in search of some poor man whom he knew to be alone, naked and almost dying, and bear him on his back to the shed — a burden often far lighter than the one he had dragged from the rich man's house. After he had collected three or four such cases, the shed was full, and at night John lay outside on the ground, ready at any moment to jump up at the first moan from his charges.

Soon the fame of his little hospital began to spread abroad. Help was offered him of different kinds, and he accepted it all gladly. One would sit by a wounded man, bathing his sores and giving him now and then a little milk to drink; a woman would look over a bundle of garments sent by some rich noble and take them home to mend; a third would bring eggs or chickens for the patients' dinner, and if anyone ever went hungry, it was John and not his people; and at last, best of all, a large round house was given him, a great big hall, perhaps, more than a house, with a huge fire in the middle of it, and sometimes as many as two hundred travelers would bask contentedly in the light and warmth, until the dawn beckoned them to continue their journey.

∞

In this way began the first of the shelters for homeless people, which afterward spread over Europe. For ten years John labored at his work and was never too tired or too busy to give help when he was asked for it. But the best machine will not go on forever, and at length men whispered to each other that "The Father of the Poor" — for that was what they called him — seemed weak and ill. Very gradually he faded from them, and he was spared the pain that so many feel, that as far as could be seen, the task of his life would fall to pieces when his hand was removed. Most likely John would always have known that if it appeared to die, it would be carried on in some other way; but now he could rejoice from his heart that the seed he had sown was spreading under his eyes into a great tree, whose branches promised to cover the earth.

He was only fifty-five when he died in Granada, in 1550, and, in spite of his humility, pictures of him hung in every hospital that counted him as its founder. You may always know him from any other saint, for he is dressed in a dark-brown tunic with a hood and cape, holding a pomegranate (or "apple of Granada") with a cross on it. At his feet a beggar is generally kneeling, and in the distance is a hospital. In the church of the Caridad (or Charity) in Seville he is represented again, this time with a man on his back, whom he is bearing to the hospital, while an angel by his side is whispering to him strengthening words. That angel must often have been there, and John would have known it and worked all the harder, although "his eyes were holden" and he could only guess why his burdens seemed so light and easy to bear.

Founder of Hospitals

The man whose name has for three hundred years been bound up with the hospitals and nursing orders of France was born in 1576, in the little village of Poy, not far from the Pyrenees. He had three brothers and two sisters, and when they were big enough, they all went to work on their father's small farm. Vincent, who was the third son, was sent to keep the sheep. This was considered the easiest task to which a child could be put, and Vincent liked wandering after his flock through the green meadows or sitting under a tree while they were feeding, watching the shadows of the clouds on the distant mountains. When he grew older, a younger brother took his place, and Vincent helped to sow the corn, to toss the hay, and to chop the wood for the winter. His father, Guillaume de Paul, was a good man and saw that his children went regularly to church, and were not behindhand in doing anything they could for a poor or sick neighbor; but of the whole six, none was so often found on his knees or so ready to carry some of his own food to his suffering friends as was Vincent.

"You ought to send that boy to school," said the curé of the parish one day to the farmer. "Perhaps — who knows? — he may by and by become a priest."

"Yes, Father, I have been thinking of that," answered Guillaume. And before many weeks had passed, Vincent's life in the fields was a thing of the past, and he was being taught to read and write, to study Latin, and all that had to do with religion, at the monastery of the Cordeliers in the town of Acqs. He loved his lessons and worked harder than any boy in the school, but, happy though he was, he must sometimes have longed for his old home and a ramble with his brothers and sisters in the meadows of Poy.

In four years, his masters declared that he now knew enough to be able to earn his own living and obtained for him a place as tutor to the children of Monsieur de Commet, a lawyer in Acqs. His pupils were very young, and he had a good deal of time to himself, and this he spent in the study of religious books, for by this time he had resolved to be a priest. At twenty he bade farewell to Monsieur de Commet and set out for Toulouse, where after two years he was ordained a deacon and later entered the priesthood. But he did not give up his whole life to praying either in church or in his cell. As of old, he went about among the sick, hearing their troubles both of mind and body, and easing both when he was able. Thus he grew to know their needs in a way he could never have done had he always remained within the walls of a monastery.

∞

The young priest's life flowed on peacefully for the next five years, and then a startling adventure befell him. An old friend of his died at Marseilles, and Vincent received news that he had been left in the will a sum of fifteen hundred livres, which in those days was a considerable deal of money. Vincent's heart was full of gratitude. What could he not do now to help his poor people? And he began to plan all the things the legacy would buy until it struck him with a laugh that ten times the amount could hardly get him all he wanted. Besides, it was not yet in his possession, and with that reflection he set about his preparations for his journey to Marseilles.

He probably went the greater part of the way on foot, and it must have taken him about as long as it would take us to go to

India. But he was a man who had his eyes about him, and the country he passed through was alive with the history he had read. Greeks, Romans, Crusaders, and the scandal, now two hundred years old, of the two popes would be brought to his mind by the very names of the towns where he rested and the rivers he crossed, but at length they were all left behind, and Marseilles was reached.

His business was soon done, and with the money in his pocket, he was ready to begin his long walk back to Toulouse, when he received an invitation from a friend of the lawyer to go in his vessel by sea to Narbonne, which would cut off a large corner. He gladly accepted and went on board at once; but the ship was hardly out of sight of Marseilles when three African vessels, such as then haunted the Mediterranean, bore down upon them and opened fire. The French were powerless to resist, and one and all refused to surrender, which so increased the fury of the Mohammedans that they killed three of the crew and wounded the rest. Vincent himself had an arm pierced by an arrow, and although it was not poisoned, it was many years before the pain it caused ceased to trouble him. The "Infidels" boarded the ship and, chaining their prisoners together, coasted about for another week, attacking wherever they thought they had a chance of success, and it was not until they had collected as much booty as the vessel could carry that they returned to Africa.

Vincent and his fellow captors had all this while been cherishing the hope that, once landed on the coast of Tunis, the French authorities would hear of their misfortunes and come to their aid. But the Mohammedan captain had foreseen the possibility of this and took measures to prevent it by declaring that the prisoners had been taken on a Spanish ship. Heavy were their hearts when they learned what had befallen them, and Vincent needed all his faith and patience to keep the rest from despair. The following day they were dressed as slaves and marched through the principal streets of Tunis five or six times in case anyone should wish to purchase them. Suffering from wounds though they were, they all felt that it was worth any pain to get out of the hold of the ship and to see life moving around them once more. But after a while it became clear that the strength of many was failing, and the captain, not wishing to damage his goods, ordered them back to the ship, where they were given food and wine, so that any possible buyers who might appear the next day should not expect them to die on their hands.

∞

Early the next morning several small boats could be seen putting out from the shore, and one by one, the intending purchasers scrambled up the side of the vessel. They passed down the row of captives drawn up to receive them, pinched their sides to find if they had any flesh on their bones, felt their muscles, looked at their teeth, and finally made them run up and down to see if they were strong enough to work. If the blood of the poor wretches stirred under this treatment, they dared not show it, and Vincent had so trained his thoughts that he hardly knew the humiliation to which he was subjected.

A master was soon found for him in a fisherman, who wanted a man to help him with his boat. The fisherman, as far as we know, treated his slave quite kindly; but when he discovered that as soon as the wind rose, the young man became hopelessly ill, he repented of his bargain, and sold him as soon as he could to an old chemist, one of the many who had wasted his life in seeking the Philosopher's Stone.

The chemist took a great fancy to the French priest and offered to leave him all his money and teach him the secrets of his science if he would abandon Christianity and become a follower of Mohammed, terms that, needless to say, Vincent refused with horror. Most people would speedily have seen the hopelessness of this undertaking, but the old chemist was very obstinate and died at the end of a year without being able to flatter himself that he had made a convert of his Christian slave.

The chemist's possessions passed to his nephew, and with them, of course, Father Vincent. The priest bore his captivity cheerfully and did not vex his soul as to his future lot. The life of a slave had been sent him to bear, and he must bear it contentedly whatever happened; and so he did, and his patience and ready obedience gained him the favor of his masters.

Very soon he had a new one to serve, for not long after the chemist's death, he was sold to a man who had been born a Christian and a native of Savoy, but had adopted the religion of Mohammed for worldly advantages. There were many of these renegades in the Turkish service during the sixteenth and seventeenth centuries, and nearly all of them were men of talent and rose high. Vincent de Paul's master had, after the Turkish manner, married three wives, and one of them, a Turk by birth and religion, hated the life of the town, where she was shut up most of the day in the women's apartments, and went, whenever she could, to her husband's farm in the country, where Vincent was working. It was a barren place on a mountainside, where the sun beat even more fiercely than in Tunis; but at least she was able to wander in the early mornings and cool evenings about the garden, which had been made with much care and toil.

Here she met the slave, always busy — watering plants, trimming shrubs, sowing seeds, and generally singing to himself in an unknown tongue. He looked so different from the sad or sullen men she was used to seeing that she began to wonder who he was and where he came from, and one day she stopped to ask him how he happened to be there. By this time, Vincent had learned enough Arabic to be able to talk, and in answer to her questions, told her of his boyhood in Gascony and how he had come to be a priest.

"A priest! What is that?" she said.

And he explained, and little by little he taught her the doctrines and the customs of the Christian Faith.

"Is that what you sing about?" she asked again. "I should like to hear some of your songs," and Vincent chanted to her "By the Waters of Babylon," feeling, indeed, that he was "singing the Lord's songs in a strange land." And day by day the Turkish woman went away, and thought over all she had heard, until one evening her husband rode over to see her, and she made up her mind to speak to him about something that puzzled her greatly.

"I have been talking to your white slave who works in the garden about his religion — the religion that was once yours. It seems full of good things, and so is he. You need never watch him as you do the other men, and the overseer has not had to beat him once. Why, then, did you give up that religion for another? In that, my lord, you did not well."

The renegade was silent, but in his heart he wondered if, indeed, he had "done well" to sell his soul for that which had given him no peace. He too would talk to that Christian slave and hear if he still might retrace his steps, although he knew that if he was discovered, death awaited the Mohammedan who changed his faith. But his eyes having been opened, he could rest no more, and arranged that he and Vincent should disguise themselves and make for the coast and sail in a small boat to France. As the boat was so tiny that the slightest gale of wind would capsize it, it seems strange that they did not steer to Sicily, and thence journey to Rome; but instead they directed their course toward France, and on June 28, 1607, they stepped on shore on one of those long, narrow spits of land that run out into the sea from the little walled town of Aigues-Mortes.

Vincent drew a long breath as, after two years' captivity, he trod on French soil again. But he knew how eager his companion was to feel himself once more a Christian, so they waited only one day to rest and started early the next morning through the flowery fields to the old city of Avignon. Here he made confession of his faults to the pope's legate himself and was admitted back into the Christian religion. The following year he went with Father Vincent to Rome and entered a monastery of nursing brothers, who went about to the different hospitals attending the sick and poor.

It is very likely that it was Father Vincent's influence that led him to take up this special work, to which we must now leave him, for on the priest's return to Paris, he found a lodging in the Faubourg Saint-Germain, close to the Hôpital de la Charité — the constant object of his care for some months.

From Paris he turned south again toward his own country, but when near Bordeaux, he was accused by a judge, who was living in the same house, of a theft of four hundred crowns. The robbery was due to the judge's own carelessness in going out with so large a sum upon him, but this did not strike him; and although, of course, he could prove nothing, he lost no opportunity of repeating the falsehood to everyone he met. After denying the story, Vincent let the matter drop and went quietly about his own work, and, at the end of six years, his innocence was established. A man of the town was arrested on some charge and thrown into prison. Here, filled with remorse, the thief sent for this very judge and confessed that it was he who had robbed him as he was passing along the street. Bitterly ashamed of his conduct, the judge, on his part, proclaimed the facts, and thus Vincent was justified in the belief that, as he had said from the beginning, "God would proclaim the truth when He thought good."

Humble and unobtrusive as the priest was, his fame had reached far, and he was pressed by one of the most powerful of French churchmen to accept the care of a village on the outskirts of Paris. While there he worked hard for the bodies and souls of his people, until the parish, which seems to have been somewhat neglected, was completely changed. Then a post of another kind was offered him, and although he would much rather have remained where he was, he would not disobey his superiors.

Sadly he bade his people farewell and went to educate the children of the Comte de Joigny, general of the French galleys. But he was only there a few months, during which his time was as much occupied in preaching to the peasants, by the desire of Madame de Joigny, as in teaching her children. Great was the good lady's sorrow when Vincent was snatched away on a mission to the inhabitants of a wild and ignorant part of France, although she gave him a considerable amount of money for their benefit. Later she made him head of a mission-house, founded and endowed by herself and her husband for the benefit of their own people, so that their poor tenants and peasants might never be in the state in which they had been discovered by the priest when he first visited and came to Joigny.

After a while Vincent returned to the house of the Joignys, where he chiefly lived when he was not absent on special missions.

∞

The earliest of all the miserable and helpless classes of beings to attract the attention of Father Vincent were the galley-slaves, heretics sometimes, and generally the lowest sort of criminals, whose lives were spent in every kind of iniquity. However wicked they might have been before they were chained together in the darkness of the galleys, or thrown together in the horrible prisons (which must have killed many of the weaker ones), they were for the most part far worse when they came out, from what they had learned from each other.

"Once criminals, they must always be criminals," said the world, and turned its back on them, but Vincent de Paul thought otherwise. The first thing he did on returning to the house of their "general," the Comte de Joigny, was to visit these rough men scattered about in the prisons of Paris. They were not easy to make friends with, these galley-slaves, and were suspicious of kind words and deeds, because they had never known them; and the priest soon understood that if he wished to make an impression on them, he must collect them all under one roof where he could see them daily and begin by caring for their bodily comforts. So, after obtaining leave from Monsieur de Gondi, the archbishop of Paris, and brother of the Comte de Joigny, he collected subscriptions, found a house, and soon, for the first time in their lives, the galley-slaves knew what it was to feel clean and to have *real* beds to sleep in, instead of damp and dirty straw, if not stone floors.

Little by little they were won over; the few rules made by the priest were broken more and more seldom, and when he felt he had gained their confidence, he told them a few simple things about their souls.

The archbishop looked on with amazement. Obedience from the worst and most lawless of men — he would never have believed it! But there it was, an undoubted fact, and the archbishop craved an audience of the king, Louis XIII, in order to tell him the marvelous tale and to ask his permission to establish similar houses all over the country. The king, who was not easy to interest, listened eagerly to Gondi's words, and in February 1619 he issued an edict, nominating Father Vincent de Paul royal almoner of the galleys of France.

His new post compelled Vincent to travel constantly, and in 1622 he set out for Marseilles to examine into the condition of the large number of convicts of all sorts in the city. The better to learn the truth, he avoided giving his real name, but he went into all the prisons and even, it is said, took the place of one of the most wretched among the criminals and was loaded with chains in his stead. That might not be true, but at any rate the story shows what was felt about him, and he did everything possible to inspire their jailers with pity and to ensure the prisoners being kindly treated. When they were ill besides, their state was more dreadful still, and it was then that he formed the plan of having a hospital for the galley-slaves, although he was not able to carry it out for many years.

∞

The Comtesse de Joigny died in June 1625, two months after her mission-house was opened. Father Vincent then went to live with his priests, the "Lazarists," as they came to be called, where, besides teaching and preaching both in the country and at home, they formed a society for looking after the sick and poor in every parish. Girls were educated by the Association of the Dames de la Croix — the Ladies of the Cross — and the older women served in the hospitals in Paris, notably in the largest of all, the Hôtel Dieu.

In addition to those already in existence, through Vincent's influence and under his direction, were founded the hospitals of Pity, of Bicêtre, of the Salpêtrière, and the world-famous Foundling Hospital or Enfants-Trouvés. Deserted babies, usually put hastily down at the door of a church or of some public place, died by hundreds. Some charitable ladies did what they could by adopting a few, but this only caused them to feel still more terribly the dreadful fate of the rest. Vincent appealed for help to the queen, Anne of Austria, and she persuaded the king to add 12,000 livres to the amount privately subscribed by the friends of the priest, and in the end he made over to them some buildings near the forest of Bicêtre. But the air was too keen for the poor little creatures, or at any rate it was thought so — for in those days, fresh air was considered deadly poison — and they were brought to the Faubourg, St. Lazare in Paris, and entrusted to the care of twelve ladies until two houses could be gotten ready for them.

Once set on foot, the hospital of the Enfants-Trouvés was never allowed to drop and always reckoned the kings of France among its supporters.

∞

It was enough for a man to be poor and needy for him to excite the sympathy of Vincent de Paul, and when he happened to be old also, the priest felt that he had a double claim. Almshouses, as we should call them, soon followed the hospitals; while the women were placed under the protection of Mademoiselle le Gras, foundress of the Order of Les Filles de la Charité — the Daughters of Charity — a society that also undertook the education of the foundlings.

When we read of all the work done by Father Vincent, we feel as if each of his days had a hundred hours instead of twenty-four. The various institutions he established, many of which flourished vigorously until a few years ago, when they were put down by the state, were always under his eye and in his thoughts. Nothing was beyond his help in any direction. While, on the one hand, he was collecting immense sums of money in Paris — it is said to amount to £80,000 — for the people of Lorraine who had been ruined by the wars, and were in the most miserable state, on the other, he was trying to revive in the clergy the love of their religion. This was perhaps the harder task of the two, for ambition and desire for wealth filled the hearts of many of the greater ecclesiastics and shut out everything else. But the king and the queen stood by him, and after Louis XIII's death, in 1642, when Anne of Austria became regent, she made him a member of the Council of Conscience and never gave away a bishopric or an important benefice without first consulting him.

But strong though he was by nature, the life of constant activity of mind and body, which Vincent de Paul had led for sixty years, wore him out at last. At the age of eighty-four, a sort of low fever seized him, and he had no longer power to fight against it, although he still rose at four every morning to say Mass and spent the rest of the day in prayer and in teaching those who gathered around him. He knew he was dying fast — perhaps he was glad to know it — and in September 1660, the end came. His work was done. The fire of time has tried it, "of what sort it is," and we may feel sure that it abides, as St. Paul says, "on its foundation," and that when the day comes, "he shall receive a reward."

Patron Saint of England

Now today, when I am writing, is St. George's Day, April 23, 1911, and this year will see the coronation of His Majesty King George V, so I think I ought to end this book with a little sketch of St. George, who was adopted long ago as the patron saint of England.

There are a great many stories about him, of the horrible things he suffered, and the wonderful and quite impossible things he did, and he is often mixed up with (a wholly different) George of Cappadocia, who was a bishop and a heretic. But although our George's sufferings for the Christian Faith were exaggerated, and his marvelous deeds a fairytale, there really *did* live once upon a time a man who grew famous as one of the Seven Champions of Christendom, and when you have heard the stories about him, you can choose which of them you would like to believe.

Of course you know that he is always spoken of as "St. George and the Dragon," almost as if he and the dragon made up one body, as the centaurs of old Greece were composed of a man and horse. But the first tales told of him from very early times make no mention of a dragon at all. George was, they said, born in Asia Minor, and his father, who was a Christian, was put to death for his religion in one of the Roman persecutions. His mother, in terror for the child's life, fled with him to Palestine, and when he was about fifteen or sixteen, he, like many other Christian boys, entered the

Roman Army and might have marched under the eagles eastward to the Euphrates and the Tigris, and might have made part of the force that besieged the splendid cities of Ctesiphon and Seleucia. At any rate, he speedily became known to his generals as a soldier who could be trusted, not only to attack but to defend, which often needs very different qualities; and there was no trained veteran among the legions who could bear cold or heat, hunger or thirst, better than young George. Then came the news that his mother was dead, leaving him a large fortune.

∞

George was now alone in the world, and feeling suddenly tired of the life he was leading, he bade his comrades farewell and took a ship for the West and the court of the emperor Diocletian. Here, he thought, he could soon rise to fame, and perhaps someday he would become the governor of a small province or the prefect of a large one. But his hopes were dashed by the breaking out of the persecution against the Christians. The estates of many rich people were seized, and the owners, if not condemned to death, were left to starve. So George divided his money between those who needed it most, and after that, he went straight to Diocletian and declared himself a Christian.

Up to this point, there is nothing in the story that might not have happened — which indeed *did* happen — to hundreds of young men, but the chroniclers of St. George were not content to stop here, and began to invent the marvels that they loved. As St. George refused to sacrifice to the Roman gods, he was sentenced to death, after first being tortured. Soldiers, so said the monkish historians, came to his prison to thrust him through with spears, but the moment the spear touched him it snapped in two. He was bound to a wheel that was set about with swords and knives, but an angel came and delivered him, and no wounds were found on his body. A pit of quicklime was powerless to injure his flesh, and, after running about in red-hot iron shoes, the following morning he walked up to the palace unhurt and did homage to Diocletian. The emperor, enraged at the failure of his plans, ordered him to be scourged and then given poisoned water to drink; but as neither whip nor poison could injure him, his persecutor, in despair, bade an officer cut off his head with a sword, and so St. George obtained his crown of martyrdom.

∞

Such was the tale that was told with eagerness among the Christians of the East, but quite another set of stories was accepted in the West and written down in the holy books, until in the sixteenth century the pope Clement VII commanded them to be left out and ordered St. George to be set down in the calendar of saints, merely as a holy martyr.

According to this western version, George early left his birthplace in Asia Minor and went to Africa, where he settled in a town called Silene. Near Silene was a large pond in which lived a dragon, with fierce eyes that seemed starting out of his head, and a long, thick, scaly tail that could curl itself up in rings and look quite small, when it was not being used to knock over men or houses or something of that sort; and more to be dreaded than its tail was the breath of the monster's nostrils, which poisoned everyone that approached it.

This horrible dragon was equally at home on land or in water, and great was the terror of the people of Silene when they beheld the tall reeds that fringed the pond beginning to wave and rustle, for they knew that their enemy was preparing to leave its lair and seek its dinner in the streets of the town. Hastily they swept their children inside their houses and shut their doors tight, but woe to any man or woman who did not get quickly enough under shelter! It was in vain that the soldiers marched out to destroy the dragon; its breath, or its tail, or its long, iron claws slew those who were foremost, and the others fled madly back to the protection of the town.

At length the king of Silene summoned a council of the wise men, and after much talk it was decided that two sheep should every day be sacrificed to the monster, on condition that it should allow the citizens to go free. Unluckily, the sheep were few and the citizens many, and by and by, there came a day when the sheep were all gone and the reeds on the pond waved and rustled more wildly than ever. Then another council was held by men with white faces and shaking voices, and it was agreed that every eve-ning, the names of all the young people belonging to the city should be placed in a bowl, and a child with a bandage over his eyes should pick one. The boy or girl thus chosen was to be the victim of the dragon.

A month passed and thirty children had vanished from the town, when one day the slip of paper drawn from the bowl bore the name of the princess. The king had known all along, of course, that it was likely to happen, and the princess knew it too, but she refused to be sent away to some other country as her father wished, declaring she would stay and take her chance with the rest. So the morning after the fatal lot had been drawn, she dressed herself in her royal robes and, with her head held high, went forth in the sunshine alone to her doom.

But as soon as she drew near to the horrible shaking reeds and there was no one to see, her courage gave way, and she flung her-self down on a stone and wept.

For a long while, the princess remained thus, when suddenly she sat up and looked about her. What was that noise she heard? Surely it was a horse's tread. And certainly that could be nothing but armor that glistened so brightly in the sun! Had a deliverer in-deed come? And as the thought passed through her mind, the reeds shook more violently than ever, and something large and heavy began to move among them.

But if the princess saw and shuddered, St. George had seen likewise, and rejoiced. The story of the dragon had reached to the far countries through which he had been traveling, and he instantly understood what lay before him. Yet, would he be in time? For the pond lay near to the weeping girl, and he must manage to get behind the dragon before he could strike, close enough for the tail to have no power over him and not so close as to be slain by the poisonous breath.

It was not easy — dragon-slaying never is — and if it *had* been, the name of the dragon would never have been bound up with that of St. George. So he rapidly unwound a scarf that lay about his helmet to keep off the sun, and tied it over his nose and mouth. Then, holding his spear in rest, he galloped up to the monster, which, with a roar of anger and triumph, advanced to meet him. But swiftly the knight sprang to one side, thrusting the spear as he did so right down the throat of the dragon. With a bellow that was heard far beyond Silene, the creature rolled over and, although not actually dead, was plainly dying.

"Take off your girdle," said St. George quickly, "and pass it from behind over the head of the beast. He cannot harm you now."

With trembling fingers the princess untied the long, silken cord from her dress and did as the knight bade her, and so they all three crossed the meadows to Silene, where St. George cut off the head of the dragon in the presence of the people, and at his urgent request, the king and the whole of his subjects consented to become Christians.

∞

But what, you will ask, has all this to do with England? And why should St. George be its patron saint? Well, that is another story.

According to this tale, it was the old city of Coventry that gave birth to our national hero, who was born with the mark of a dragon on his breast. As a baby he was stolen away by a witch and hidden in the woods until he was fourteen, when he besought his captor to tell him who he was and how he came there. For some time she resisted all his pleadings; she loved him dearly and feared that if the youth discovered that he was the son of a great noble, he would never be content to stay with her in the forest, but would ride away in search of adventures and perhaps lose his life. However, after working some spells, she found that she had no power to keep him, and very unwillingly she answered his questions and then took him to a castle of brass, where the Six Champions of Christendom were held captive.

Can you tell me their names? If not, *I* must tell *you*.

The Six Champions St. George found in the brazen castle, of whom he was to make the seventh, were St. Denis of France, St. James (or St. Iago) of Spain, St. Anthony of Italy, St. Andrew of Scotland, St. Patrick of Ireland, and St. David of Wales. In the stables stood seven horses — the strongest and cleverest in the world — and seven suits of armor against which every weapon would fall harmless. The heart of St. George beat high as he looked at these things; then he buckled on the armor and mounted the steed pointed out by the witch and, with his six companions, rode away from the castle.

The Seven Champions soon parted company and went in search of their different adventures. This story also tells how St. George slew the Egyptian dragon and delivered the princess, and goes on to say what happened afterward. A black king, named Almidor, so runs the tale, had fallen in love with the princess Sabra, who refused even to look at him. Mad with jealousy at hearing that St. George had slain the dragon — for he dreaded lest the king should give his daughter in marriage to her deliverer — he first tried to kill the young man by force and, failing, resolved to compass his death by poison. Fiercely his rage burned within him as he stood by and beheld the rewards and gifts heaped on the youth by the grateful father, although the honor most prized by the victor was the spurs of knighthood, but he did not see the princess bestow a magic diamond on St. George as soon as the ceremony was over and they were alone. Scarcely had the ring been placed on his finger when Almidor entered, bearing a wine cup, which he offered with fair words to the newly made knight. St. George was thirsty and tired with the day's excitement and eagerly stretched out his hand for the cup, when the princess observed all the light fade out of the diamond and a cloud come over it. At once she knew the meaning of these signs, for her nurse had taught her magic, and how to detect poison. Her shriek of horror caused St. George to let fall the cup and reached the ears of her father, who came running to see what was the matter; but so much love did he bear Almidor that he would not believe he had been guilty of so black a deed and told his daughter she had been dreaming.

Although this attempt also had failed, the black king did not give up hope; and the more clearly did he perceive that the princess's heart was given to St. George, the more determined was he to obtain her for himself. So he visited the king, her father, in his private rooms and told him, with tears, that he had discovered a plot concocted by the princess and the foreign knight to fly together to England, where Sabra would forsake the Faith of her country and be baptized. And once again Almidor gained his ends. The king listened to his words and was further persuaded to play the old trick and to send George to the Persian court with a letter containing a request to the king of Persia instantly to put the bearer to death. He further persuaded the young man to leave behind his invincible sword Ascalon, and his trusty horse, and to ride instead a palfrey from the king's stables.

After all, the Egyptian monarch need not have troubled himself to commit a crime, for St. George had scarcely passed through the city gates when he beheld a procession in honor of the prophet Mohammed. This was a sight no Christian knight could endure, and, dashing into the midst of the worshipers, he tore down the banners they carried and trampled on them.

In the uproar that followed, many of the Persians fell beneath the sword of St. George, but alas, it was not Ascalon that he carried, and his enemies were too much for him. Overpowered at last, he was dragged before the king of Persia, who heaped reproaches on his head and then ordered him to be tortured in all manner of dreadful ways. But St. George boldly answered that the royal blood of England flowed in his veins, and he claimed the right to challenge the king to single combat. Likewise, he said, he had come there as ambassador from the king of Egypt, and on that account, too, he demanded protection. Then, drawing from under his corselet the blood-stained letter, he held it out.

The eyes of the Persian king sparkled as he read it.

"So!" he cried, turning to the knight, standing tall and straight before him. "The game you thought to play here, you have played in Egypt already! Know you that the letter you have brought bids me put you to death without delay? And by the prophet, I will do it!"

As he spoke, he signed to his guards, who bore St. George away to a dungeon, the knight marveling all the while at the treachery that had befallen him and wondering when he should again see the face of the Princess Sabra.

∞

After letting loose two hungry lions into St. George's dungeon, which the knight instantly strangled, the king desired that his captive should be left alone and given barely enough food to keep him alive, for he had changed his mind about killing him. For seven years St. George lay there, and all that time the only pleasant thing he had to think about was the princess as she appeared to him during their stolen talks in the garden.

If he had but known what had happened to her, he would have slain himself from misery.

Day by day Princess Sabra grew thinner and weaker and could hardly be persuaded to eat and drink or to leave her rooms opening on the river Nile. At length her father, who, in spite of what he had done, loved his daughter dearly, resolved to rouse her at all costs and, putting on an air of sternness that he was far from feeling, told her that it was quite plain the English knight had forgotten her for some other maiden, and that by his orders preparations were even now being made for her marriage with Almidor, the black king of Morocco.

The poor girl did not attempt to oppose him. She was so ill and unhappy that she really did not care what became of her and only murmured in reply that although she might be the wife of Almidor, her heart would always belong to the Champion of England. Perhaps the king did not hear her words. At any rate, he pretended not to do so. The wedding festivities were hurried on, and in a few days the princess Sabra was the wife of Almidor.

Seven years were past, and St. George still lay in his Persian dungeon, when one night a frightful storm broke out, which caused the men in the city to quake with fear. Almost alone of the people, the unfortunate captive was indifferent to the noise of falling towers and the hissing of thunderbolts; if one fell into his dungeon and put an end to him, so much the better! At times the floor seemed to rock beneath him, and once he heard a rattle in the walls, but it was too dark to see anything except for the vivid lightning. When morning dawned, the tempest died away, and the knight sat up and looked about him. In one corner, some stones had fallen down, and among them lay a sort of iron pickaxe covered with rust. It must have been left in a niche on the other side by some workmen of former days, and forgotten.

At this sight, hope, which he had thought to be long dead, revived in his heart. Without losing a moment, he fell to work, and although from weakness he was often obliged to pause and rest, in the course of a few days he had, by aid of the pickaxe, hewn a hole in the loosened masonry big enough to pass through. Then he waited until night came.

When everything was quiet, St. George crept through his hole and found himself in a passage leading into a large court that formed part of the palace. Before venturing out of the shadow, he listened carefully, so as to make sure in which direction he had better turn, for having been cast into the dungeon the very evening of his arrival in the Persian city, he knew only the road by which he had come.

For a while all was silent, but at last he heard voices on the other side of the courtyard and stole cautiously in that direction. He soon gathered from the talk that in two or three hours the king of Persia would be setting out on a hunting expedition, and that the horses were being watered and gotten ready. Rushing in, he laid about him with the pickaxe so vigorously that the grooms, taken by surprise, one after another fell before him. As soon as all were dead, St. George put on a suit of armor and a sword that hung in the furnishing room, and, mounting the strongest horse he could find in the stable, rode boldly to the nearest gate.

"Open, porter, in the king's name," cried he. "Know you not that St. George of England has escaped from his dungeon and that the whole city is seeking him? It is thought he may have fled this way, and if you have let him pass, your head will answer for it."

"Not so! Not so, my lord!" answered the porter, fumbling at the lock with shaking fingers. "I swear by the prophet —" but St. George never knew what he swore, for he was galloping westward.

∞

Many were his adventures before he reached the country of Barbary, where few Christian knights had been before him. For this reason St. George went there, thinking thus to gain honor denied to other men. Near the borders of the kingdom, he paused to speak with a hermit, who, he thought, might be able to tell him somewhat of the customs of that strange land, and the name of the city whose distant towers he saw.

"Those towers and walls," answered the hermit, "surround the city of Tripoli, wherein is the palace of Almidor, the black king of Morocco."

"Ah! You know him?" he added, as St. George started and muttered something under his breath.

"Know him?" said the knight grimly. "I owe him a debt that I shall hasten to pay! It is thanks to him that I am here today, and that I have lost my bride, the princess Sabra."

"Princess Sabra! But she is queen of Barbary, and has been these seven years and more," replied the hermit. "Tell me, I pray you, how these things came to pass?" Then St. George sat down and told his tale and, in the end, besought the hermit to lend him his garments, and to take care of his horse and armor until he returned to claim them.

∞

It was in this guise that the knight approached the walls of Tripoli and found a hundred pilgrims kneeling before the palace gate. "What do you here, my friends?" he asked in surprise, and the pilgrims answered, "During seven years the queen of Barbary has given us alms every day for the sake of one St. George of England, long since dead, whom she loved above all the knights in the world."

"And when does she give them to you?" inquired St. George, whose voice so trembled with joy that he could hardly speak.

"At sunset, and until then we pray on our knees for the good fortune of the English knight."

"I will kneel with you," said he.

As the sun was sinking, the queen left the palace and moved slowly toward the gate. At the sight of her, St. George could have wept, so changed was she, yet still how beautiful. Black robes were wound about her; her hair had more in it of silver than of gold, and her eyelids were red as are the eyelids of those who have wept so much that they can weep no longer. Passing down the row of pilgrims, she held out her alms to each, but when she came to St. George, she stopped short and seemed as though she would have fallen. Then, with a mighty effort, she continued her way until she had come to the end of the row, after which she beckoned St. George aside and questioned him as to who he was and how he came there.

It did not take long for St. George to tell the story of the black king's treachery or to hear how Sabra had always feared and hated him.

"Take me away, I pray you," she entreated, "for he is now at the hunt, and before he returns, I shall be safe on the road to England. See, hidden in that stable is the horse you were forced to leave and your good sword, Ascalon. I will mount behind you and follow you wheresoever you go. For if he finds you here, he will slay you, and me also."

Therefore, within an hour St. George was riding through the city gates with Sabra the queen seated behind him. Many adventures were still in store for them before the shores of England came in sight. But not for long was he suffered to rest. As happened to the six other champions, his help was sought from the ends of the world, and the remainder of his life was spent in warring in Europe and in Asia. In this warfare he grew old and weary, until his heart drew him back to his native city, Coventry, set in the green of Warwickshire. Right glad were the people to behold him, and a doleful story they had to tell of a dragon that none could kill, which had laid waste their lands.

Old though he was in years, the heart of St. George burned as bravely as ever, as he rode forth to meet the dragon. Fierce was the fight and long, yet in the end the knight forced the monster on his back and thrust him through and through with his lance. But with his dying breath, the dragon cast his tail around the champion, and darted stings into every part of his body, so that he was wounded even unto death. As the tail unloosed again, he staggered, and for a moment it seemed as though he would have fallen; yet he rallied, and, gathering up all his strength, he cut off the dragon's head, and, mounting his horse with an effort, carried it back to Coventry, a trail of blood marking his track. As he reached the gate, a roar of welcome greeted him, but he scarcely heard it, and, swaying, would have fallen to the ground in his last agony, had it not been for the arms stretched out to catch him.

Thus he died, and on account of his mighty deeds, the king ordered that April 23, the day of his burial, should be named St. George's Day and that a royal procession should evermore be held upon it, in memory of the patron saint of England.

Biographical Note

Andrew and Lenora Lang

Journalist, poet, historian, literary critic, editor, and translator Andrew Lang (1844-1912), born in Selkirk, Scotland, studied at Edinburgh Academy, St. Andrews University, and Balliol College, Oxford. He spent most of his professional life in London, writing for the *Daily News* and for the *Morning Post* and was literary editor of *Longman's Magazine*.

He wrote scores of books, including several volumes of poetry; translations of the *Iliad* and the *Odyssey*; novels; books on culture and religion; a biography of novelist and biographer John Gibson Lockhart; and collections of fairy tales, on which his wife, Lenora, collaborated with him.

Sophia Institute Press®

Sophia Institute® is a nonprofit institution that seeks to restore man's knowledge of eternal truth, including man's knowledge of his own nature, his relation to other persons, and his relation to God.

Sophia Institute Press® serves this end in numerous ways. It publishes translations of foreign works to make them accessible to English-speaking readers, it brings back into print books that have been long out of print, and it publishes important new books that fulfill the ideals of Sophia Institute®. These books afford readers a rich source of the enduring wisdom of mankind. Sophia Institute Press® makes these high-quality books available to the public by using advanced technology and by soliciting donations to subsidize its publishing costs.

Your generosity can help provide the public with editions of works containing the enduring wisdom of the ages. Please send your tax-deductible contribution to the address below.

For your free catalog,
Call toll-free: 1-800-888-9344

Sophia Institute Press® • Box 5284 • Manchester, NH 03108
www.sophiainstitute.com

Sophia Institute® is a tax-exempt institution as defined by the Internal Revenue Code, Section 501(c)(3). Tax I.D. 22-2548708.